The Sustainable Aviation Flight Plan

By

Noel Cox

Contents

Introduction

Section 1

Sustainable Aviation Fuels (SAF)

Scaling Up Production for a Greener Future

SAF Production Pathways

Initiatives to achieve Net Zero Carbon Emissions by 2050

Clean Skies for Tomorrow Coalition

Costs of SAF

Synthetic Paraffinic Kerosene Produced from Hydroprocessed Esters and Fatty Acids (HEFA-SPK)

Alcohol-to-Jet Synthetic Paraffinic Kerosene (ATJ-SPK)

Synthesised Isoparaffins Produced from Hydroprocessed Fermented Sugars (HFS-SIP)

Fischer-Tropsch Synthetic Paraffinic Kerosene (FT-SPK)

Pyrolysis and Upgrading

Aqueous Phase Reforming

Hydrothermal Liquefaction

Power-to-Liquid with Fischer-Tropsch Synthesis

Electro-fuels

SAF Benefits

Deploying Sustainable Aviation Fuels (SAF)

Costs considerations and Investments in the future

The Energy Supply.

The Kerosene Project at Helmholtz-Zentrum Berlin. Developing Efficient Catalysts for Sustainable Aviation Fuel Production

Latin America and Sustainable Aviation Fuels. Addressing the Risk of Falling Behind

Major Petroleum Companies and Sustainable Aviation Fuel (SAF)

Feedstocks

Co-processing

Book and Claim System

Renewable Transport Fuel Obligation (RTFO) UK

Section 2

NEW TECHNOLOGY, ELECTRIC AND HYDROGEN

Technology

The challenges of design advancements

Hydrogen

Airframes

Propulsion

Electrification

Plugin Hybrid Electric Propulsion aircraft

Hybrid Electric Aircraft

Urban Air Mobility (UAM)

Promising Technologies

The Companies Working on Electric Flight Technologies

Full-Electric Aircraft

EVTOL

Hydrogen

Requirements

Hydrogen Turbofan

Hydrogen Fuel Cell Aircraft

Future Propulsion Fuels

Contrails

Section 3

INFRASTRUCTURE AND OPERATIONAL EFFICIENCIES

Improvements in Operations and Infrastructure

Infrastructure initiatives

Airlines

Environmental actions by airlines

Operational Efficiencies

Airports

Chicago O'Hare International Airport

ACI Europe

ATAG

Section 4

OFFSETS AND CARBON CAPTURE

Offsetting Carbon Reductions

Carbon Offsetting

CORSIA

Forestry Projects

ICAO Global Coalition for Sustainable Aviation

Paris Agreement and Aviation Net Zero Goals

Tradeoffs and compromise

IATA Aviation Strategy for Net Zero CO2 Emissions

Clean Skies of Tomorrow Coalition

FAA and NASA

Incentives in the USA

The European Union Aviation Safety Agency (EASA)

The European Green Deal

ReFuelEU Aviation

EU ETS

Section 5

HUMAN SUSTAINABILITY IN AVIATION

The human dimension of Aviation Sustainability.

Defining Human Sustainability. People at the Heart of Aviation

Fatigue Management

Mitigating Jetlag

Coping Mechanisms

Coping with Incidents and Accidents

Mental Health and Well-being. Supporting the Human Mind in Aviation

Technological Advancements and Human-Machine Interaction.

Training and Education.

Collaboration and Partnerships. Working Together for a Shared Goal

Regulatory Framework and Policy Initiatives.

Passenger Experience and Health

The Three Pillars of Wellbeing

How the Three Pillars of Wellbeing can be Applied to Flight Crews.

Relationship Management Skills Contribute to Wellbeing.

Zen

Zazen Exercise

Brain Performance and Enhancement.

Habits

Emotional Intelligence

How Crew and Team Members Develop Emotional Intelligence

The Spiral Training concept from Simple to Approaching Complex Tasks.

Precision can Beat Power, and Timing can Beat Speed.

Psychological Safety in Workplace and Its High Importance in Company and Cultures.

Professionalism and Airmanship

Autosuggestion

Visualization

Metacognition

Self-Regulated Learning (SRL)

Cognitive Restructuring

Exposure Therapy

Rest and Recovery

Qualities of Excellence

Developing Courage

Optimum Performance Focus.

The Discipline of Professional Excellence

Commitment

Values and Principles

Copyright 2024 by Noel Cox

All rights reserved. This book, or parts thereof, may not be reproduced in any form without permission.

avcox

Introduction

Global aviation is forecast to grow significantly between now and 2050. However, this growth trajectory is now being confronted by a pressing reality: escalating emissions pose an unacceptable risk amid the ongoing climate crisis. Societies and governments are becoming increasingly intolerant of industries that emit escalating levels of carbon without restraint. The imperative is clear - the aviation sector must proactively reduce its environmental impact or face stringent regulatory action. Recognizing this urgency, the industry is mobilizing to develop credible strategies to tackle emissions. In line with the scientific consensus, the global aviation sector is firmly committed to the transition to sustainability. With ambitious targets, including carbon neutrality by 2050, a holistic approach is essential for success. This book goes beyond technical solutions and recognizes the central role of human sustainability. As the industry grapples with the strains of growth, addressing human well-being becomes paramount. Within these pages lies an exploration of the aviation sector's flight plan for achieving sustainability goals. Offering a comprehensive analysis, this guide highlights the strategies and innovations that are driving aviation towards a more sustainable future.

Aviation is a fundamental pillar of the global economy, a facilitator of human connection, and a key driver of progress in our interconnected world. The aviation world has embarked on a flight plan towards efficiency and sustainability with the horizon set on 2050 and beyond. Airlines are investing in more efficient aircraft, while the aerospace sector pours billions into research and development aimed at cutting-edge efficiency. This concerted effort has led to significant reductions in CO_2 emissions per seat kilometer. Landmark agreements have been inked, including the world's first CO_2 standards for aircraft and pioneering carbon pricing mechanisms under the auspices of the International Civil Aviation Organization. Collaboration across the sector has also brought about advancements in air traffic management efficiency. To achieve the shared vision of sustainability, a monumental acceleration of efforts is imperative. Collaboration must deepen, encompassing not only within the aviation sector but also extending to governments and other key institutions.

Many nations and industries are setting ambitious net-zero emissions targets for 2050, yet progress varies across regions. Aviation finds itself among the 'hard to abate' sectors due to the scarcity of readily available solutions. There exists a myriad of measures to take aviation towards the technological, energy, and operational advancements needed to fulfill these aspirations. While daunting, they are all within reach with the right policy frameworks and dedicated allocation of resources. Projections suggest a sky by 2050 teeming with over 10 billion passengers annually. Absent further technological breakthroughs, fuel advancements, or operational enhancements, this surge in air traffic could result in nearly 2,000 megatons of CO_2 emissions if not mitigated in the meantime. The evolution of technology promises a steady 20% improvement in fuel efficiency with each new generation of aircraft. By 2050, the horizon gleams with the potential for electric, hybrid, and hydrogen-powered propulsion systems to serve regional, short-haul, and possibly some medium-haul routes. While traditional liquid uplift fuels will likely persist for long-haul flights and those short to medium haul journeys yet to embrace electric or hydrogen power, the trajectory points towards a transition to 100% sustainable and low carbon sources. Alongside technological advancements, operational enhancements, and infrastructure improvements present crucial avenues for early action. Airlines, airports, and air traffic management must collaborate tirelessly to implement a plethora of measures aimed at reducing CO_2 emissions from operations. Continuous refinement of operational efficiency is paramount, guarding against the encroaching specter of airspace congestion.

Perhaps the most significant opportunity lies in the widespread adoption of sustainable aviation fuel (SAF) and novel energy sources. Scaling up SAF production globally offers a formidable pathway to meet the industry's 2050 sustainability goals. Estimates suggest that aviation could require between 330-445 million tons of SAF annually by 2050—an ambitious target. The flight plan towards a sustainable aviation future hinge upon the synergistic interplay of technological innovation, operational efficiency measures, and the widespread adoption of sustainable aviation fuel.

In the ongoing flight plan towards sustainable aviation, a shift is underway—from traditional fuel sources to a diverse array of alternatives, ranging from crops to waste, and eventually, to power-to-liquid fuels derived from recycled or directly-captured CO_2 and low-carbon electricity. This transition poses a formidable challenge, necessitating an estimated investment of up to $1.45 trillion over the next three decades.

Policy intervention will play a central role in steering this transition, directing sustainable feedstocks towards aviation rather than other transport sectors already equipped with alternative energy sources.

While long-term, permanent reductions in CO_2 emissions are pursued through alternative energy and technology, carbon offsets provide a vital stopgap. However, it's crucial to recognize that these offsets should not serve as the primary means of meeting long-term goals. Even with advancements in sustainable aviation fuel and radical new technologies, residual CO_2 emissions may persist, necessitating the exploration of forestry, natural carbon sinks, and other carbon removal opportunities.

In the face of escalating concerns over climate change, the aviation industry finds itself at a critical juncture. The imperative to achieve carbon neutrality and prioritize sustainable practices has never been more pressing. As the effects of climate change intensify, stakeholders from governments to consumers are scrutinizing industries for their contributions to greenhouse gas emissions.

For aviation to retain its social license to operate and pursue future growth, it must confront the challenge of climate change head-on. The days of unabated expansion leading to soaring emissions are over. To avoid exacerbating the climate crisis, the industry must pivot towards sustainable practices, embracing innovation and efficiency at every turn.

A failure to address the environmental impact of aviation could have profound consequences, both environmentally and economically. With climate change increasingly disrupting ecosystems and economies worldwide, the aviation industry's role in contributing to greenhouse gas emissions cannot be overlooked.

Therefore, the aviation industry's path forward must prioritize sustainability as a core principle. From reducing emissions through fuel-efficient technologies to exploring alternative fuels and enhancing air traffic management, every effort counts. By aligning with the global imperative to combat climate change, the aviation industry can secure its relevance and legitimacy in a rapidly evolving world.

If the aviation industry hopes to continue its growth trajectory, it must do so responsibly. Regulators, policymakers, and the public are increasingly vocal about the need for sustainability in all sectors, including aviation. The industry simply cannot expect to double or triple in size while driving up emissions in the process. Sustainability is an absolute necessity for the aviation industry's future. Without a concerted effort to reduce carbon emissions, mitigate environmental impact, and embrace sustainable practices, the industry risks facing severe constraints on its growth and operations that regulators could potentially intervene in greater degrees. To maintain its social license to operate and secure approval for future expansion, the aviation industry must prioritize sustainability initiatives. This includes investing in fuel-efficient aircraft, adopting alternative fuels, improving air traffic management, and exploring innovative technologies to minimize environmental impact. It has to demonstrate a genuine commitment to sustainability in order to pave the way for responsible growth and ensure its long-term viability in a world increasingly concerned about climate change.

The aviation industry faces the prospect of significant revenue decline and job loss if regulations aimed at pricing carbon emissions, reducing short flights, and promoting sustainable transportation alternatives like electric trains are enacted. These measures could lead to reduced demand for air travel and a shift towards more environmentally friendly transportation options, impacting both the financial health of airlines and job opportunities within the industry.

Aviation, often seen as a sector that may decarbonize later due to perceived complexity and its relatively smaller contribution to global emissions compared to sectors like shipping, must nonetheless act urgently to combat climate change. The travelling public must be incentivized to choose airlines prioritizing lower emissions to in turn convince more airlines to invest in this as a differentiator. This can be achieved through recognition mechanisms and differentiated propositions. Airlines investing in emissions reduction technologies should receive acknowledgment and support from consumers, fostering a competitive environment where sustainability becomes a market advantage.

Policy incentives are crucial for accelerating the adoption of Sustainable Aviation Fuel (SAF) and promoting regulatory frameworks conducive to emissions reduction. Governments play a critical role in providing financial incentives and setting regulations that drive the aviation industry towards sustainability. By aligning policy incentives with supply and demand dynamics, nations can effectively stimulate investment in SAF production and utilization.

Offsets represent a pragmatic approach to funding the early stages of decarbonization. However, their effectiveness hinges on transparency and verifiability. For offsets to truly support emissions reduction efforts, they must undergo rigorous scrutiny to ensure their credibility. Moreover, enhancing the emotional appeal of offsets to passengers can foster greater acceptance and engagement. Communicating the tangible impact of offsets in mitigating environmental harm is crucial for garnering passenger support and participation.

Sustainable Aviation Fuels (SAF)

Scaling Up Production for a Greener Future

Sustainable aviation fuel (SAF) is a type of jet fuel produced from renewable sources, offering a significantly lower carbon footprint compared to conventional, fossil-based jet fuel. SAF plays a crucial role in the aviation industry's efforts to reduce greenhouse gas emissions and combat climate change. In 2022, only 300 million liters of SAF were produced globally, representing a mere 0.1% of total jet fuel uplift. To achieve net-zero emissions by 2050, the aviation sector will require an estimated 450 billion liters of SAF annually. This massive increase in production necessitates immediate and concerted action.

One of the key challenges hindering SAF adoption is its higher cost compared to conventional jet fuel. This price difference is primarily due to the limited production capacity and the nascent stage of SAF technologies. To overcome this hurdle, several actions are needed. Governments can play a crucial role by providing financial incentives for SAF production and use, such as tax breaks, subsidies, and loan guarantees. This would attract investment and encourage the development of new production facilities. Airlines and other aviation stakeholders should commit to purchasing larger volumes of SAF, even at a premium price. This guaranteed demand will incentivize producers to invest in scaling up production and drive down costs through economies of scale. Continued research and development in SAF production technologies are essential to improve efficiency and reduce costs. This includes exploring new feedstocks, optimizing production processes, and developing innovative technologies like synthetic fuels derived from captured carbon dioxide. Developing a functioning market for SAF is also critical. This involves establishing clear and consistent regulations, standardizing fuel specifications, and creating transparent pricing mechanisms. A well-functioning market will foster competition, attract new players, and ultimately lead to lower prices for SAF. While SAF has the potential to significantly reduce aviation's carbon footprint, scaling up production to meet future demand requires a collaborative effort from governments, the aviation industry, and fuel producers. SAF presents a promising avenue for reducing emissions. These fuels can be classified into two main categories: fully formulated and paraffinic SAF. Paraffinic SAF, although lacking certain hydrocarbon compounds found in conventional aviation fuel, poses challenges due to its incompatibility with existing aircraft systems. Notably, modifications are required to accommodate differences in fuel properties and composition. However, industry leaders have pledged to ensure compatibility with 100% paraffinic SAF by 2030, a pivotal milestone in the quest for achieving net-zero CO_2 emissions by 2050.

Conversely, fully formulated SAF mirrors the composition and properties of conventional aviation fuel, thereby obviating the need for aircraft modifications. Standards are currently being developed to facilitate the seamless integration of fully formulated SAF into existing aircraft systems, with anticipated completion before 2024. A gradual increase in SAF adoption from the present until around 2030 is expected. This initial phase will likely be driven by early adopters, government mandates, and increasing production capacity. Beyond that between 2030 and 2040, the adoption rate is expected to accelerate significantly. This acceleration can be attributed to factors like cost reductions due to economies of scale, technological advancements, and wider availability of SAF. Then by 2050, SAF is projected to become the dominant fuel source for aviation, replacing a significant portion of conventional jet fuel. This will be crucial for achieving the industry's net-zero emissions goals. While advancements in propulsion technologies and aerodynamics will undoubtedly contribute to reducing in-flight energy demand and associated emissions, they alone will not suffice to achieve net-zero CO_2 emissions by 2050. Consequently, there is a pressing need to scale up the production and integration of sustainable aviation fuels while concurrently exploring alternative energy solutions such as hydrogen and batteries. These zero-carbon energy solutions hold considerable promise in reshaping the aviation landscape and ushering in a sustainable future. In navigating the future of aviation fuels, it's clear that transitioning away from conventional options is essential for decoupling aviation growth from emissions. With batteries, hydrogen, and Sustainable Aviation Fuels (SAF) as primary contenders, the focus lies on compatibility and scalability. Paraffinic SAFs, while promising, necessitate aircraft modifications due to their chemical composition, prompting industry commitments to ensure compatibility by 2030. Conversely, fully formulated SAFs mirror conventional fuel, requiring no alterations. Yet, achieving net-zero CO_2 emissions by 2050 demands more than fuel advancements alone. Hydrogen and batteries emerge as vital zero-carbon energy solutions, supplementing sustainable fuels.

Despite its advancements, aviation has become a significant contributor to greenhouse gas emissions, with direct emissions accounting for 3% of the EU's total and over 2% globally. While the recent pandemic temporarily reduced emissions, a return to increasing air traffic necessitates intensified efforts to align with the Paris Agreement's goals of limiting global warming. The European Commission's December 2019 communication underscores the urgency of slashing transport emissions by 90% by 2050, with a focus on sustainable alternative fuels like those in the 'RefuelEU Aviation' initiative. Encouraging their adoption is pivotal in moving towards carbon neutrality, complemented by advancements in air traffic management and alternative propulsion technologies. While electric aircraft hold promise, sustainable aviation fuels offer the most immediate emissions reductions without infrastructure changes.

All airlines must actively explore opportunities for sustainable aviation fuel (SAF), regardless of their size. Governments and policymakers hold a crucial role in fostering a clean energy transition, with a specific focus on sustainable aviation fuel. Prioritizing aviation as a user of alternative fuel and exploring the potential for SAF development at a national or regional level is paramount. Governments must support the development of the SAF industry through various means, with robust incentives and loan guarantee programs to attract capital and direct research and development activities.

Traditional jet fuels, derived from crude oil, consist of various hydrocarbons like normal paraffins and aromatics. A promising alternative comes in the form of drop-in bio-based fuels, synthetic liquids with properties identical to conventional aviation fuels. The International Civil Aviation Organization (ICAO) distinguishes between aviation alternative fuels (AAF) sourced from non-petroleum origins, such as coal, natural gas, biomass, and hydrogenated fats, and sustainable aviation fuels (SAF), which are AAF meeting specific sustainability criteria. While there's no universally agreed-upon definition for SAF, sustainability criteria for AAF have been outlined under CORSIA and the Renewable Energy Directive (RED II) in the EU. CORSIA mandates SAF to achieve a minimum 10% reduction in life cycle emissions compared to a fossil fuel baseline. Similarly, RED II stipulates that biofuels must achieve a 65% greater reduction in emissions against a fossil fuel baseline to qualify as renewable energy sources. These standards underscore the importance of sustainability in aviation fuel development and align with our shared goal of mitigating greenhouse gas emissions.

The financial effects of Sustainable Aviation Fuel (SAF) adoption are subject to variability influenced by several key factors. Mandates established in certain regions necessitate airlines to blend a specific percentage of SAF into their fuel, impacting compliance costs and potentially affecting profitability. Additionally, government subsidies and incentives aimed at promoting SAF adoption vary across countries, providing an offset to costs but lacking consistency. Costs are contingent upon feedstock availability and production methods, highlighting the importance of sustainable sourcing practices. Airlines that voluntarily commit to integrating SAF into their operations may face higher initial costs but stand to gain long-term benefits, including reputational advantages and potential cost savings as technology advances. Also, the willingness of customers to pay a premium for sustainable travel influences airlines' decisions, shaping market demand and ultimately impacting financial outcomes.

SAF Production Pathways

Production pathways of bio-based drop-in fuels are crucial for our ongoing discussions on sustainable aviation. These fuels, certified under the specifications of the American Society for Testing and Materials (ASTM) standards, offer promising alternatives to conventional jet fuels. As of June 2020, eight production pathways have been certified for civil aviation, with several others undergoing approval processes. These pathways involve various methods, including blending synthetic fuels with conventional jet fuel and co-processing bio-based feedstock with fossil fuels in refineries. Blending is necessary to address compatibility issues with older engines, ensuring optimal performance. Among these pathways, two stand out in terms of commercial readiness: oil-to-fuel pathways, primarily utilizing vegetable oils and animal lipid feedstocks, and fuel production via Fischer-Tropsch (FT) synthesis, which utilizes biomass like forestry and agricultural residues. These pathways offer promising solutions towards achieving sustainable aviation fuel production. For further insights, a 2019 ICAO document provides detailed descriptions of these pathways and their life cycle emissions impacts compared to conventional jet fuel. These pathways offer diverse methods for producing SAF, each with unique characteristics and potential applications. HEFA-SPK (hydroprocessed fatty acid esters and free fatty acid) involves the conversion of lipid feedstocks, such as vegetable oils and used cooking oils, into green diesel through hydrogenation, which can then be further processed to obtain bio-based aviation fuel, with a maximum blending ratio of 50%. Secondly, FT-SPK (Fischer-Tropsch synthetic paraffinic kerosene) utilizes biomass to produce synthetic gas, which is then converted into bio-based aviation fuel, also with a maximum blending ratio of 50%. FT-SPK/A, a variation of FT-SPK, involves alkylation of light aromatics to create a hydrocarbon blend with aromatic compounds, also with a maximum blending ratio of 50%. HFS-SIP (hydroprocessing of fermented sugars – synthetic iso-paraffinic kerosene) employs modified yeasts to convert sugars into hydrocarbons, with a maximum blending ratio of 10%. ATJ-SPK (alcohol-to-jet synthetic paraffinic kerosene) utilizes dehydration, oligomerization, and hydroprocessing to convert alcohols like iso-butanol into hydrocarbons, with a maximum blending ratio of 50%. CHJ (catalytic hydrothermolysis jet fuel) utilizes triglycerides from various oils as feedstock, with a blending ratio of up to 50%. HC-HEFA-SPK involves synthesizing paraffinic kerosene from hydrocarbon-hydroprocessed esters and fatty acids, with algae as feedstock and a blending ratio of 10%. Lastly, co-processing allows for the incorporation of biocrude, up to 5% by volume of lipidic feedstock, in petroleum refinery processes.

Initiatives to achieve Net Zero Carbon Emissions by 2050

The 41st ICAO Assembly set a significant long-term goal (LTAG) for international aviation to achieve net zero carbon emissions by 2050 in line with the temperature goal of the UNFCCC Paris Agreement. The adopted resolution, known as Resolution A41-21, outlines the target. Importantly, the target does not impose specific emission reduction targets on individual countries. Instead, it recognizes that each country has unique circumstances and capabilities, such as its level of development and the maturity of its aviation market. Each country will therefore contribute to the goal in a way that reflects its national priorities, considering factors such as sustainable growth and just transition. The aim is for each country to work towards the goal in a socially, economically, and environmentally sustainable manner, considering its national circumstances.

The International Civil Aviation Organization (ICAO), the specialized UN body for civil aviation, has its roots in aviation safety and is renowned for its meticulous attention to detail and evidence-based technical standards. Currently, it is heavily involved in facilitating the adoption of sustainable aviation fuels (SAF) within the airline industry. This involves establishing a robust framework dictating how airlines can utilize and report their usage of SAF. The framework is designed to be comprehensive and rigorous, categorizing and measuring various aspects to ensure that SAF usage is genuinely sustainable.

ICAO mandates that member states must present their action plans and convene every three years to discuss progress towards achieving net-zero emissions. These meetings serve as a platform for states to explain their efforts and advancements along the pathway to carbon neutrality. Targets and measures for reducing emissions are established internally within each country. Due to varying levels of investment and infrastructure development, the rate of progress towards carbon neutrality will naturally differ among regions and countries. This approach recognizes the diverse capabilities and circumstances of member states while fostering collective action towards a sustainable aviation industry.

At the global level, ICAO has initiated the Carbon Offsetting and Reduction Scheme for International Aviation (CORSIA) to target carbon-neutral growth in aviation starting from 2021, with provisions allowing for emission reduction using SAF. The European Union's Emissions Trading System (EU ETS) provides incentives for aircraft operators using biomass-based SAF certified as compliant with sustainability criteria. The revised EU Renewable Energy Directive (RED II) allows SAF to contribute to renewable energy targets, provided they meet sustainability criteria, with a specific multiplier applied to non-food and feed based SAF. However, challenges persist in incentivizing SAF adoption, with CORSIA's economic incentive estimated to be minimal, EU ETS incentives insufficient, and RED II's multiplier possibly inadequate for fuel producers. Several EU countries have implemented or planned policy support measures, such as SAF supply obligations, while initiatives like Bioqueroseno in Spain and AIREG in Germany support SAF development. In Norway and the UK, regulatory schemes aim to increase SAF usage, while various sustainability certification systems, including the Roundtable for Sustainable Biomaterials (RSB), ensure compliance with sustainability standards, with RSB EU RED Standard recommended for EU producers.

Since 2008, several airlines have conducted test flights using bio-based fuels, with over 215,000 commercial flights globally utilizing SAF by December 2019. However, despite increasing interest, current SAF consumption remains low compared to overall aviation fuel usage. In 2018, aviation bio-based fuel production accounted for less than 0.1% of total consumption, according to the International Energy Agency (IEA). In the EU, SAF use represented only 0.05% of total aviation fuel consumption in 2017, as estimated by the European Commission. Production has surged faster in the US due to supportive programs, while in Europe, production and usage have mainly been for demonstration and research purposes. There are promising developments on the horizon, with companies like SkyNRG and Neste expanding production capacities in Europe, aiming to produce significant quantities of SAF annually by 2022. This highlights a growing commitment to increasing SAF production and usage, underscoring the EU's dedication to sustainable aviation.

Several European refineries are poised to produce or shift their output to SAF, primarily focusing on the HEFA process using used oils, animal fats, or tall oil. Estimates suggest that by 2025, annual renewable fuels production in the EU could exceed 7 million tons, with approximately 80% of potential SAF capacity coming from HEFA refineries. This could translate to around 3.66 million tons of SAF production by 2025, covering approximately 6% of total jet fuel consumption. However, demand for SAF is anticipated to increase, with plans in European countries aiming for a significant share of jet fuel use by 2030. The IEA's sustainable development scenario forecasts worldwide SAF consumption of around 30 million tons by 2030. While current potential capacity may meet short-term demand based on existing policy measures, incentives are needed to encourage refineries to shift production towards SAF. Additionally, further production capacity may be necessary if policy-driven demand increases.

Clean Skies for Tomorrow Coalition

Under the auspices of the Clean Skies for Tomorrow coalition, a concerted effort is underway to address five critical areas conducive to the scaling up of SAF production. Firstly, there is a foundational effort to establish a comprehensive fact base, evaluating the feasibility and sustainability of SAF while navigating through disparate studies that present conflicting narratives and unresolved inquiries. Secondly, the coalition is identifying regions endowed with abundant sustainable biomass or low-cost power sources, recognizing their strategic importance in facilitating a global energy transition. Thirdly, emphasis is placed on advocating for policy interventions at a global level to stimulate learning-curve effects and achieve economies of scale, particularly for the broader aviation industry's benefit. The imperative of securing adequate funding for research and development, as well as for scaling up the SAF supply chain, is underscored, with particular attention to aligning investments with evolving investor priorities. Further refining their strategy, the coalition is meticulously analyzing feedstock availability, technology readiness, and production costs, while concurrently devising specific, actionable strategies to upscale SAF production. Commencing with a pilot program in India, they aim to extend these efforts to other regions progressively. Immediate priorities include implementing policy interventions, establishing an SAF marketplace, and initiating transactions and pilots. Concerted efforts are being made to blueprint a financing model for this transition, engaging aviation stakeholders and the finance community in substantive dialogue to ensure its feasibility.

Costs of SAF

One significant challenge lies in the cost of SAF, which can range from two to eight times higher than conventional aviation fuel, making it economically challenging for widespread adoption. Complex production processes and high feedstock costs further contribute to this issue. Existing policy measures like the EU Emissions Trading System (ETS) are not robust enough to stimulate demand effectively. While HEFA pathways offer lower investment costs, concerns arise over feedstock availability and competition with the road sector for resources. Fischer-Tropsch (FT) synthesis pathways, although benefiting from abundant feedstock, entail higher capital costs due to complex production processes. Additionally, the authorization process for SAF presents substantial barriers, with significant costs and lengthy approval timelines. Industrial-scale demonstrations are crucial to gaining trust from stakeholders, including aircraft operators and ground equipment owners.

The scalability of SAF production is hindered by the limited availability of conventional feedstocks, such as waste oils. It is therefore imperative for producers to expand their utilization of diverse SAF-production technologies beyond current methodologies. There is an intricate interplay between technological advancement, feedstock availability, and production costs. The task will require insights from engineering, economics, and environmental science among other technological disciplines to face the challenges and opportunities associated with scaling up SAF production. The advances must include input parameters such as renewable electricity and green hydrogen, on the cost dynamics of SAF production.

Airlines are implementing operational enhancements aimed at optimizing efficiency and asset utilization. This includes efforts to increase load factors, ensuring that each flight maximizes revenue passenger kilometers and operates at optimum capacity. Picture it as ensuring a bus is fully occupied for a single tour rather than running multiple half-full journeys at different times. The economic and financial benefits of a single full journey are evident, with reduced fuel consumption, fewer drivers needed, and optimal asset utilization. To achieve this, airlines must adeptly manage their operations to maintain high load factors and adjust schedules accordingly. They are expediting their transition from older, less efficient aircraft to newer models boasting enhanced fuel efficiency. They're also embracing innovative solutions such as electric ground equipment and wingtip design modifications to minimize environmental impact. There's also a concerted effort to optimize flight routes, making them more direct and fuel-efficient. This includes lobbying for access to previously restricted airspace, allowing for more efficient routing through what is currently designated military airspace.

Airlines may seek to implement various initiatives aimed at enhancing fuel efficiency and reducing carbon emissions within their own operations. These measures include incentivizing pilots to adopt more fuel-efficient flying and taxiing techniques, as well as imposing stricter operational weight limits to minimize fuel consumption.

Achieving greater efficiency in airspace usage requires collaboration among multiple stakeholders. Programs like the Single European Sky and NextGen in the United States aim to modernize air traffic control infrastructure, potentially reducing emissions by up to 10 percent. The actual emission savings for individual airlines may vary depending on their utilization of the affected airspace based on their locations, base and route network.

Hydrogenated esters and fatty acids (HEFA) and Fischer-Tropsch (FT) are two technologies crucial for producing sustainable aviation fuel (SAF). HEFA utilizes waste lipids and purpose-grown plants to achieve substantial GHG emission reductions of as much as 73%-84%. Fischer-Tropsch converts syngas into hydrocarbons with an impressive emission reduction potential of 85%-94%. Both technologies offer high conversion rates and potential for further optimization, holding great promise for sustainable aviation.

Synthetic Paraffinic Kerosene Produced from Hydroprocessed Esters and Fatty Acids (HEFA-SPK)

Synthetic Paraffinic Kerosene Produced from Hydroprocessed Esters and Fatty Acids (HEFA-SPK) is a promising alternative fuel pathway currently at an advanced stage of development. The process involves hydroprocessing vegetable oils and animal fats, where hydrogen is utilized to convert unsaturated compounds into more stable paraffins and cycloalkanes, thereby enhancing fuel stability and reducing reactivity. This process, akin to hydrotreated vegetable oil (HVO) production, incorporates an additional isomerization step to lower the fuel freezing point. With an impressive energy conversion efficiency of approximately 76%, HEFA boasts the highest efficiency among bio-jet fuel routes. Its simplicity and maturity have facilitated its commercial use, albeit limited by feedstock availability. While the production cost of HVO ranges between €1100 and €1350 per ton, transitioning to HEFA incurs only a modest additional cost attributed to the isomerization step. The main challenge lies in sourcing feedstocks, as UCO and tallow resources are relatively small globally, and the availability of virgin vegetable oil is constrained by land and sustainability concerns.

Ongoing research into novel crops like camelina, carinata, and oil-bearing algae, as well as the exploration of fermentation processes to produce lipids, holds promise for expanding feedstock options for HEFA production. Advancements in fermentation processes, utilizing microorganisms to convert sugars and organic materials into lipids, present opportunities to diversify feedstock options for SAF production, including agricultural and food waste. Expanding feedstock options not only increases SAF availability but also reduces reliance on limited resources like used cooking oil, enhancing the sustainability of SAF production.

Alcohol-to-Jet Synthetic Paraffinic Kerosene (ATJ-SPK)

Alcohol-to-Jet Synthetic Paraffinic Kerosene (ATJ-SPK) is a method that transforms alcohols into jet fuel through a series of reactions including dehydration, oligomerization, hydrogenation, isomerization, and distillation. The alcohol source can be conventional, derived from fermentation of sugar or starch crops like sugarcane, corn, and wheat, or advanced, originating from lignocellulosic feedstocks such as woody and grassy materials. While most developers focus on upgrading conventional alcohols, larger demonstration plants are being planned to utilize advanced alcohol routes. Certified blends of ATJ-SPK up to 50% have been endorsed by ASTM International since 2016. These routes have the advantage of versatility, converting various alcohol types from diverse sources into jet fuel and other hydrocarbons. The ATJ method offers logistical flexibility as the catalysis plant need not be co-located with alcohol production, enabling convenient transport and storage of alcohol. The selectivity of jet fuel production remains a challenge, as does the opportunity cost of using alcohol directly in other transport applications versus converting them to jet fuel, which incurs additional capital expenditure and efficiency losses. Jet fuel costs via this route are higher than ethanol feedstock costs on an energy basis, with variations depending on ethanol input prices.

Synthesised Isoparaffins Produced from Hydroprocessed Fermented Sugars (HFS-SIP)

The use of genetically modified microorganisms in the production of hydrocarbons or lipids from sugar is another process under research. This process, known as direct sugars to hydrocarbons (DSHC), encompasses three main routes currently under development. The first involves heterotrophic algae or yeast converting sugars into lipids within their cells. The second utilizes genetically modified yeasts to consume sugars and excrete long-chain liquid alkenes like farnesene. Then genetically modified bacteria consume sugars and excrete short-chain gaseous alkenes such as isobutene. While biological routes predominantly use conventional sugar feedstocks, pilot projects are exploring the use of cellulosic sugars. Routes utilizing conventional sugar feedstocks are at a more advanced stage compared to those based on cellulosic feedstocks. One specific route involves the production of farnesane from sugar, certified as hydroprocessing of fermented sugars (synthetic iso-paraffinic fuels), and can be blended with fossil kerosene up to 10%.

Fischer-Tropsch Synthetic Paraffinic Kerosene (FT-SPK)

Gasification with Fischer-Tropsch (Gas+FT) synthesis transforms biomass or solid waste into valuable fuels like jet fuel. The process involves several steps, including feedstock pretreatment, gasification, syngas clean-up, and catalysis. The resulting jet fuel, FT-SPK, can be blended with fossil kerosene. While mature routes exist for coal and natural gas, the bio-based Gas+FT route is advancing. Challenges include scaling down processes for biomass systems, catalyst design, and addressing system efficiency. Co-processing FT waxes at oil refineries is a potential option.

Pyrolysis and Upgrading

Pyrolysis turns biomass or waste into bio-crude oil, an intermediate for fuel production. Fast pyrolysis is advanced, but refining bio-crude into fuel is in the early stages. Challenges include high water, acidity, and viscosity of pyrolysis oil. Research is ongoing for upgrading methods.

Aqueous Phase Reforming

The APR process converts biomass-derived oxygenates into hydrogen, CO_2, and a mixture of hydrocarbons through catalysis and condensation reactions. This mixture undergoes hydroprocessing, isomerization, and distillation. While APR using conventional sugars is at TRL 5–6, bio-crude derived from lignocellulosic sugars has been produced and upgraded to bio-kerosene at laboratory scale. Aviation kerosene from APR is undergoing ASTM certification as hydro-deoxygenated synthetic kerosene (HDO-SK). Unlike other processes, APR operates in wet conditions, reducing dewatering costs for certain feedstocks. However, it has low selectivity to liquid hydrocarbons and short catalyst lifetimes, making it costly. APR is also explored for biochemicals production, potentially leading to higher-value products.

Hydrothermal Liquefaction

Hydrothermal liquefaction (HTL) involves heating biomass and water at high pressures to produce bio-crude. The near-supercritical water catalyzes biomass depolymerization. HTL oil, with its higher molecular weight distribution, is ideal for diesel production, but can also be upgraded for gasoline and jet fuel. HTL is effective for processing wet biomass like sewage sludge and algae, and some lignocellulosic feedstocks. Testing for refinery upgrading is underway but hasn't reached ASTM certification. HTL oils have lower water content, higher energy content, and greater stability compared to pyrolysis oils, making them cheaper to transport and requiring less extensive upgrading. Challenges include high pressure and corrosive conditions during operation.

Power-to-Liquid with Fischer-Tropsch Synthesis

The PtL FT route produces liquid fuels by combining a carbon source with hydrogen from electrolysis. It requires electricity, water, and concentrated CO_2. While some systems are demonstrated at small scale, high-temperature PtL uses solid oxide electrolyzers. CO_2 sources like biogas upgrading or industrial waste streams are available, while direct air capture is in earlier stages. FT synthesis is established at large scale but in demonstration stages for small-scale applications. FT-SPK produced through PtL is ASTM certified with iron or cobalt catalysts. Operating costs are high due to electricity expenses, and initial capital costs are also steep. Developers are exploring different FT catalysts for economic viability and exploring plant location constraints due to CO_2 requirements. Despite being in the early stages, PtL garners interest for its potential to produce low-GHG emission fuels with fewer feedstock constraints.

Scaling up Power-to-Liquids (PtL) for sustainable aviation hinges on three key factors. First, ensuring feedstock security requires abundant renewable energy and cost-effective carbon capture technologies. Second, PtL needs technological advancements to reduce production costs and infrastructure development to facilitate large-scale deployment. Revenue certainty is crucial, achieved through government policies like carbon pricing or carbon offsetting mechanisms that incentivize airlines to adopt PtL fuels. It's important to address these factors sequentially, from securing sustainable feedstocks to creating economic incentives, thereby PtL can overcome the challenges of scaling up and become a viable solution for powering a cleaner future of air travel.

Electro-fuels

Electro-fuels, also known as power-to-jet fuels, which have garnered increased interest as potential sustainable aviation drop-in fuels. These fuels are created by using electricity to produce hydrogen through electrolysis, which is then combined with carbon to form a liquid hydrocarbon suitable for use in internal combustion engines. Considered renewable fuels of non-biological origin (RFNBO), electro-fuels utilize electricity from renewable sources in the production process. A 2016 study by Ludwig-Bölkow-Systemtechnik GmbH identified Fischer-Tropsch (FT) synthesis and Methanol (MeOH) synthesis as main pathways for electro-fuels. Several demonstration plants are in development or planned in Finland, Germany, Norway, Canada, supported by EU-funded research projects. Despite promising technology readiness, the production process remains costly, with estimates suggesting electro-fuels are three to six times more expensive than kerosene due to high conversion losses and transportation costs. Prices are expected to decrease by 2050, driven by economies of scale and declining renewable electricity costs.

SAF Benefits

SAF offers a hefty reduction in greenhouse gas (GHG) emissions, with potential reductions of up to 80% compared to fossil jet fuel over the fuel's life cycle. It significantly decreases harmful non-CO2 emissions such as NOx, SO2, and particulate matter, contributing to improved air quality and lessening contrail cirrus climate effects. SAF serves as a drop-in jet fuel, seamlessly integrating with existing aircraft engines and airport infrastructure without necessitating additional investments. It enhances aircraft performance by being free of sulphur, oxygen, and aromatics, burning cleaner in engines due to its high energy content. SAF fully complies with aviation standards, certified under ASTM D7566, and exhibits excellent storage properties, maintaining oxidation stability for many years. It boasts outstanding cold weather performance.

Deploying Sustainable Aviation Fuels (SAF)

It's projected that by 2025, only around 2% of total jet fuel use will be from sustainable sources, even with a significant policy push. Accelerating this transition is crucial to achieving sustainability goals. While the technology exists and many commercial flights have already used SAF since certification in 2011, scaling up production and developing new feedstock sources are essential for SAF to contribute effectively to decarbonization. Sustainable aviation fuel, derived from non-fossil sources, embodies three key elements: sustainability, alternative feedstock to crude oil, and meeting technical and certification requirements for use in commercial aircraft. These fuels, known as "drop-in fuels," can be mixed with conventional jet fuel, utilize existing infrastructure, and adhere to sustainability criteria set by international bodies like ICAO.

Switching to sustainable aviation fuel (SAF) offers a promising solution for reducing emissions in aviation. SAF is produced from feedstocks that either draw in CO2 during production, recycle emissions from waste sources, or capture CO2 directly from the air. While the CO2 emissions from burning SAF in aircraft engines are like fossil fuels, the production process removes CO2 from the atmosphere, creating a beneficial 'loop.' Additionally, SAF has shown improvements in fuel performance, resulting in reduced fuel burn and emissions of particulate matter, leading to better air quality and possibly lower contrail formation. Although lifecycle emissions reductions are not always 100% due to energy needs for processing and transportation, employing renewable energy and alternative transportation methods can significantly improve emissions reduction. The CO2 reductions from SAF can be measured by the percentage of SAF blended with traditional fuel and the emissions reduction factor (ERF), with today's best performing SAF sources having around a 90% ERF. Despite slow progress since SAF approval in 2011, new production facilities are expected to come online soon, yet doubling the production will be necessary for the industry to reach 2% of jet fuel use by 2025. Technologies such as carbon capture and storage (CCS) hold promise for further improving the ERF, with some processes already showing emissions reductions of over 150% and even 200%. For the Waypoint 2050 analysis, a conservative outlook was maintained, limiting the ERF to 100% reduction in CO2, allowing room for future improvements without relying heavily on CCS.

Concerns about the availability of feedstock for sustainable aviation fuel (SAF) at scale have been addressed by independent assessments, indicating an abundance of sustainable sources to meet industry demands beyond 2050. Traditional SAF pathways alone could produce approximately 200 million tons (Mt) annually. Power-to-liquid (PtL) presents virtually unlimited potential, albeit with scalability challenges. There could abe a potential demand of around 445Mt of SAF by 2050, with various feedstocks contributing to availability. These include waste and residue lipids, oil crops, cellulosic cover crops, agricultural residues, woody biomass, municipal solid waste, and industrial waste gases, with total availability projected to reach 198Mt by 2050. Notably, changes in availability from 2020 to 2050 reflect optimization for SAF production, particularly as road markets electrify, while industrial waste gases decrease with the decarbonization of industries. Thus, the outlook suggests sufficient feedstock availability for future SAF production.

A diversified approach is essential, recognizing that no single solution suffices. Various regions present distinct opportunities based on available feedstocks, which can be tailored to local conditions. For instance, some areas boast ample agricultural waste, while others grapple with municipal waste disposal. Analyzing potential SAF feedstocks reveals a range of options, including waste and residue lipids, oil crops and trees, cellulosic cover crops, agricultural residues, woody biomass, municipal solid waste, and industrial waste gases. Each feedstock type has its unique challenges and prospects. For instance, municipal solid waste offers significant potential, especially in regions with inadequate waste disposal fees, while woody biomass opportunities are region-specific, often tied to existing timber or paper industries. Agricultural waste residues hold promise but require economic viability at scale. Similarly, waste oils and lipids pose challenges in supply, while industrial off gases show real potential for production scale-up, particularly in countries with significant steel industries like China and India. Furthermore, exploring non-food oil crops such as Carinata, Camelina, and Jatropha reveals varying degrees of viability and scalability across different regions. Additionally, cellulosic crops like Miscanthus, Switchgrass, and Reed Canarygrass present opportunities for further analysis and real-world trials. Innovative approaches like power-to-liquid hold unlimited potential but require significant technological advancement. Thus, a comprehensive understanding of feedstock availability and development potential is crucial for advancing sustainable aviation fuel initiatives.

Rotational cover crops offer a promising avenue for sustainable aviation fuel (SAF) production. These crops, grown during fallow periods or winter in fields usually reserved for food crops, enrich the soil, enhance water absorption, and reduce erosion. They aid in nitrogen restoration and carbon sequestration, contributing to soil health and increased food crop yields. However, the analysis adopted a conservative approach, excluding significant arable land from SAF production to prioritize food production and underestimating the potential of early-stage technologies like algae.

Regarding SAF production capacity, the analysis anticipates a shift from bio-feedstocks to power-to-liquids (PtL) production, driven by constraints on arable land and the increasing maturity of PtL technologies. While bio-feedstocks initially dominate, PtL emerges as the primary source by 2050, accounting for over half of SAF production. Economic factors, such as the production cost, influence this transition.

Sustainability considerations include environmental and social limitations on feedstock availability, while fairness constraints balance SAF production against other sectors' needs. Economic limitations dictate the volume of feedstock viable for SAF production at economically sustainable prices.

Aviation's transition to SAF must consider factors like fuel cost and logistical feasibility. Access to capital markets and government policy choices are critical enablers. While ample bio-feedstock is available, other sectors also vie for these resources, necessitating careful policy frameworks. Aviation, recognized as a 'hard to abate' sector, requires priority access to feedstock resources.

In the ongoing flight plan towards sustainable aviation fuel (SAF), rigorous safety and certification processes have been established. Engineers, chemists, and aviation fuel experts collaborate to test and analyze each pathway, ensuring compliance with industry standards set by ASTM International. Once approved, these pathways enable the production of SAF, which can be blended with fossil fuel for use in flights.

Currently, seven pathways have been approved, with eight more undergoing testing for future approval. Each approved pathway expands the potential for SAF supply. However, there's a blending limit of 50% SAF with fossil fuel due to the absence of certain components in SAF, necessary for the functioning of older aircraft engines. Newer engines, though, can operate with SAF blends up to 100%. While low SAF production volumes don't currently pose an issue with the blend limit, it's anticipated that this limit will eventually increase to 100%.

Sustainability is a fundamental consideration in SAF development. Lessons learned from past biofuel initiatives in road transport have guided the aviation sector in avoiding similar pitfalls. The Sustainable Aviation Fuels Users Group, alongside organizations like the Roundtable on Sustainable Biomaterials and standards set by ICAO, ensure adherence to sustainability criteria. This robust framework underpins the sustainable scaling up of SAF production.

Approved pathways for sustainable aviation fuel (SAF) production encompass a range of processes utilizing various feedstocks, from Fischer-Tropsch Synthetic Paraffinic Kerosene to High Hydrogen Content Synthetic Paraffinic Kerosene. Each pathway, approved by ASTM International, undergoes rigorous testing and analysis before being deemed safe for use in passenger flights. Currently, there are seven approved pathways, with more in the pipeline for future approval. Sustainability is a core consideration, with criteria ensuring minimal impact on biodiversity, reduced greenhouse gas emissions, and positive socio-economic impact. Harmonized global standards are essential to facilitate investment and ensure sustainability across the aviation industry. Scaling up SAF production requires concerted efforts, drawing parallels to successful transitions observed in renewable energy sectors like ethanol, biodiesel, wind, and solar. With proper frameworks and investment, the aviation industry can achieve a sustainable shift to SAF in the coming years.

Scaling up the power-to-liquid (PtL) option for sustainable aviation fuel (SAF) presents a significant opportunity, with its scalability theoretically unlimited. However, its success requires advancements in technology and substantial cost reductions. The main challenge lies in ensuring a robust renewable energy supply to power PtL production, necessitating considerable investment in solar, wind, and potentially nuclear energy. Although the share of global electricity from low carbon sources is increasing, it must accelerate to meet climate goals. The development of PtL could serve as a catalyst for accelerating the transition to renewable energy across various sectors. SAF production scenarios are compared with historical trends in alternative energy sources, such as ethanol and biodiesel production, solar, and wind electricity generation, providing insights into potential growth trajectories. Despite challenges, achieving scaled-up SAF production is feasible, particularly with a concerted focus on renewable energy expansion.

An analysis of various sustainable aviation fuel (SAF) pathways indicates a promising trend of cost reduction, primarily driven by economies of scale and feedstock input optimizations. The production cost includes the value of carbon reduction, allowing for a direct comparison with fossil fuel costs. With the addition of carbon pricing ($100 per ton in 2030, rising to $200 per ton by 2050), the cost difference between SAF and fossil jet fuel is expected to narrow. This underscores the potential impact of government support in fostering the long-term availability and adoption of SAF. The projected reductions in SAF costs across different pathways, such as Hydroprocessed Esters and Fatty Acids (HEFA), Alcohol-to-Jet (ATJ), Fischer-Tropsch Synthetic Paraffinic Kerosene (FT-SPK), and Power-to-Liquid (PtL), offer optimism for the aviation industry's sustainability goals. Notably, advancements in technology and feedstock management are anticipated to drive significant cost reductions, making SAF more economically competitive. However, the integration of carbon capture and storage, while reducing CO_2 emissions, may marginally increase fuel costs. This analysis underscores the importance of continued innovation and policy support in achieving a sustainable and cost-effective transition to SAF.

Costs considerations and Investments in the future

The transition to sustainable aviation fuel (SAF) presents both challenges and opportunities for the aviation industry and beyond. While current SAF costs remain higher than fossil jet fuel, analysis suggests a potential for significant cost reduction over time, especially when factoring in the cost of carbon. However, government support during the 2020-2030 period will be crucial in laying the groundwork for this transition. Investing in SAF not only yields environmental benefits but also nurtures the growth of a new industry. This industry encompasses diverse feedstocks, ranging from agricultural waste to algae farms, and will require substantial investment and construction. Estimates suggest the need for 5,000 to 7,000 facilities globally to meet aviation industry climate targets, with an investment of approximately $1 - $1.45 trillion required to build sufficient SAF capacity. This investment will not only create new jobs but also contribute to energy security and independence across nations. There exists a great opportunity to leverage multi-stakeholder initiatives and harness expertise from various sectors and for countries to create optimal opportunities for aviation biofuel production and create millions of jobs in SAF production, construction, and supply chain sectors.

The Energy Supply.

There is the necessity of integrating low-carbon electricity and green hydrogen into the plans. These resources are essential for producing power-to-liquid sustainable aviation fuel (SAF) and potentially powering aircraft directly. Analysis suggests that by 2050, aviation could consume between 8% and 18% of planned low-carbon electricity production and 23-56% of green hydrogen supply, depending on the scale-up of power-to-liquid technology. However, these figures represent upper-bound estimates, and actual requirements may be lower. To accelerate the energy transition, technological advancements, and improved economics for SAF are imperative. Policy frameworks play a crucial role in this phase, incentivizing airlines to adopt SAF and closing the cost gap between SAF and fossil fuels. While incentives are temporary, they are vital for kickstarting SAF production until economies of scale bring costs down. The aviation industry has committed to ambitious emission reduction goals, with SAF being a cornerstone of these efforts. Airlines must engage in test flights, make substantial SAF offtake agreements, and demonstrate leadership in setting up policy infrastructure. Governments can support SAF projects, join sustainability forums, encourage direct SAF purchases by passengers, and foster research to explore higher blend rates. Together, we can navigate this flight plan towards a sustainable energy future for aviation.

The Kerosene Project at Helmholtz-Zentrum Berlin. Developing Efficient Catalysts for Sustainable Aviation Fuel Production

At the Helmholtz-Zentrum Berlin (HZB), scientists are actively engaged in research and development efforts aimed at advancing Sustainable Aviation Fuel (SAF) production. One of their key projects is the "Kerosene Project," which focuses on developing highly efficient catalysts for converting biomass and other sustainable feedstocks into SAF. Catalysts play a crucial role in the production process of SAF, as they accelerate chemical reactions and improve the overall efficiency and yield. The Kerosene Project researchers are specifically working on optimizing catalysts for the following processes.

Hydrodeoxygenation (HDO) process removes oxygen from biomass-derived molecules, converting them into hydrocarbons suitable for jet fuel.

Fischer-Tropsch synthesis (FTS) process converts synthesis gas (a mixture of carbon monoxide and hydrogen) derived from biomass or other sustainable sources into liquid hydrocarbons that can be used as SAF.

The researchers at HZB are employing advanced techniques and materials to develop catalysts with improved performance and selectivity. Their goals include,

- Increasing the activity and stability of the catalysts will allow for faster reaction rates and longer catalyst lifetimes, ultimately reducing production costs.
- Improving the selectivity of the catalysts means ensuring that the catalysts primarily produce the desired hydrocarbons for SAF, minimizing unwanted byproducts.
- Developing catalysts that are resistant to poisoning and deactivation will further enhance the lifespan and efficiency of the catalysts.

The Kerosene Project aims to make these improved catalysts available to SAF producers by 2025. This will significantly contribute to scaling up SAF production and making it more cost-competitive with conventional jet fuel. Developing efficient and robust catalysts will allow the researchers at HZB to play a vital role in accelerating the transition towards sustainable aviation. In addition to catalyst development, the Kerosene Project also focuses on optimizing the overall SAF production process, including feedstock selection, reactor design, and process integration. This holistic approach aims to maximize efficiency, reduce costs, and minimize the environmental impact of SAF production.

Despite promising potential, several hurdles limit the widespread adoption of Sustainable Aviation Fuel (SAF). These challenges fall into three categories: technical (meeting performance standards), environmental (ensuring true sustainability), and commercial (achieving cost competitiveness). A particularly significant obstacle is specification approval, a lengthy and expensive process that discourages potential SAF producers.

Latin America and Sustainable Aviation Fuels. Addressing the Risk of Falling Behind

There exists a clear risk of Latin America falling behind in the global race for Sustainable Aviation Fuel (SAF) production. Currently, there are no significant SAF producers in the region, while Europe, Asia, and the USA are actively developing and scaling up production capacities. This situation poses a potential disadvantage for Latin American airlines and could hinder the region's efforts to decarbonize its aviation sector.

It's important to note that Latin America possesses several advantages that could enable it to become a major player in the SAF market. For example, it has abundant biomass resources. The region boasts vast agricultural land and diverse biomass sources, such as sugarcane, soybean, and agricultural residues. These resources can be utilized to produce SAF through various pathways, including the HEFA (Hydroprocessed Esters and Fatty Acids) and ATJ (Alcohol-to-Jet) technologies.

Favorable climate and land availability

The climate in many parts of Latin America is conducive to growing energy crops for SAF production. The availability of land allows for the expansion of dedicated energy crops without compromising food security.

Growing demand for sustainable solutions

There is increasing awareness and demand for sustainable practices in the region, including within the aviation sector. This creates a favorable environment for investments in SAF production and infrastructure.

To capitalize on these advantages and overcome the current lag, several actions are needed. Governments in Latin America need to develop supportive policies and incentives to attract investments in SAF production facilities and research and development. This includes tax breaks, subsidies, and loan guarantees, as well as establishing clear regulations and standards for SAF production and use. Fostering collaboration between governments, airlines, fuel producers, and research institutions is crucial to share knowledge, best practices, and resources. This can accelerate the development and deployment of SAF technologies and infrastructure in the region. It is critical to ensure that SAF production in Latin America relies on sustainable feedstocks that do not compete with food production or contribute to deforestation. Utilizing waste biomass, agricultural residues, and dedicated energy crops grown on marginal lands can ensure sustainability and minimize environmental impact. In addressing these challenges and leveraging its inherent advantages, Latin America can become a significant contributor to the global SAF market. This will not only benefit the region's aviation sector but also contribute to global efforts to combat climate change and transition towards a more sustainable future. It's important to remember that the development of a robust SAF industry is a complex undertaking requiring collaboration and commitment from various stakeholders. While Latin America currently faces a gap in SAF production, the region has the potential to emerge as a leader in this crucial field with the right policies, investments, and partnerships.

Major Petroleum Companies and Sustainable Aviation Fuel (SAF)

While traditionally focused on fossil fuels, several major petroleum companies are recognizing the need to transition towards more sustainable practices, including within the aviation sector.

Neste has established itself as a true pioneer in the realm of sustainable aviation fuel (SAF). Their flagship product, Neste MY Sustainable Aviation Fuel™, is a game-changer, offering a drop-in replacement for fossil jet fuel while dramatically reducing greenhouse gas emissions by up to 80%. Made from 100% renewable raw materials sourced with the utmost attention to sustainability, Neste MY SAF is compatible with existing aircraft and infrastructure, making it a readily available solution for airlines committed to reducing their environmental impact. Neste's commitment goes beyond production, as they actively work to expand the global availability of SAF, partnering with major airports like San Francisco International, Los Angeles International, and Amsterdam Schiphol. Their efforts have garnered the trust of leading airlines such as Air France-KLM, Lufthansa, and Delta, as well as cargo carriers like DHL and Amazon Prime Air. Looking towards the future, Neste has ambitious plans to significantly increase SAF production, aiming to reach a capacity of 1.5 million tons annually by early 2024, further solidifying their position as a driving force in sustainable aviation.

BP is taking steps to drive the adoption of Sustainable Aviation Fuel (SAF). With ambitious goals to significantly expand its biofuel production, BP is targeting an output of approximately 100,000 barrels per day by 2030, with a particular focus on SAF. To achieve this, BP has planned five major biofuel projects around the world, located in Australia, the Netherlands, Spain, Germany, and the United States. Together, these projects have the potential to produce approximately 50,000 barrels per day of SAF by 2030. It is working with stakeholders across the energy supply chain, including governments, NGOs, and other companies, to explore and implement different pathways for SAF production. It is exploring advanced technologies such as gasification, Fischer-Tropsch and alcohol-to-jet processes.

Shell is also making significant contributions to the development and adoption of Sustainable Aviation Fuel (SAF). Through their joint venture with Cosan, Raízen, Shell is actively involved in SAF production, utilizing a combination of waste products and sustainable feedstocks. This innovative fuel blend offers a practical solution for existing aircraft, contributing to the decarbonization of the aviation industry. Shell is exploring diverse feedstocks and made a strategic acquisition of EcoOils, a company specializing in recycling waste oils, ensuring a sustainable supply chain for SAF production. They also invested in LanzaJet, a leader in sustainable fuels technology, with the aim to advancing alcohol-to-jet (AtJ) fuel technology. Raízen's ethanol, a key feedstock for SAF, has received the ISCC CORSIA certification, ensuring compliance with rigorous international standards set by the International Civil Aviation Organization (ICAO).

ExxonMobil is taking a different approach to Sustainable Aviation Fuel (SAF) by focusing on algae biofuels. Their research program, in collaboration with Synthetic Genomics Inc. (SGI), aims to develop the technology to produce 10,000 barrels of algae biofuel per day by 2025. This ambitious project involves extensive outdoor field studies in California, where they cultivate naturally occurring algae strains in controlled environments to gain valuable insights into key engineering parameters. ExxonMobil and SGI have achieved a breakthrough by modifying an algae strain to produce more than double the oil content without hindering its growth. This focus on maximizing energy-rich fat production holds immense potential for biodiesel production. Recognizing the importance of diverse solutions, ExxonMobil continues to explore various pathways for SAF production, including waste-based feedstocks and alcohol-to-jet (AtJ) fuel technology.

Chevron is also engaged in advancing the production and use of Sustainable Aviation Fuel (SAF). Its El Segundo refinery has achieved a significant milestone by becoming the first in the U.S. and one of the first in the world to co-process biofeedstocks with conventional petroleum to produce gasoline, jet fuel and diesel fuel with renewable content and a lower carbon footprint. Chevron sees SAF as a key solution for carbon reduction in jet fuel, with the potential to reduce emissions by up to 80% compared to conventional jet fuel. Their first test batch of SAF at the El Segundo refinery demonstrated a 59% reduction in emissions on a lifecycle basis. Chevron aims to build capacity to produce 100,000 barrels per day of renewable fuels by 2030. Chevron, Delta Air Lines, and Google have joined forces to advance sustainable aviation fuel (SAF) and enhance industry transparency.

Feedstocks

There are several challenges to scaling up any sustainable aviation fuel (SAF) production pathway. Some feedstocks may be difficult to collect in sufficient quantities, and some technologies require further development to become practical. Demand for SAF needs to increase significantly, even though it is expected to be more expensive than fossil fuels for a long time to come. Progress will require not only scientific advances, but also significant and rapid changes in global attitudes and behaviors, including consumer preferences for more sustainable travel options and government policy support.

In the CORSIA framework, sustainable aviation fuel (SAF) production relies on a range of feedstocks that can be categorized into five different types: primary and co-products, by-products, wastes and residues. Primary and co-products, like the main feedstocks, have significant economic value and elastic supply, while by-products, wastes and residues provide secondary materials with varying degrees of economic value and supply elasticity. CORSIA assigns an indirect land use change (ILUC) value of zero to by-products, wastes and residues, reflecting their minimal environmental impact. In addition, primary and co-products may also qualify for this exemption, if they adhere to prescribed low land use change risk methodologies. The International Civil Aviation Organization (ICAO) continuously evaluates new SAF feedstocks for inclusion in the CORSIA framework, ensuring ongoing adaptation to new innovations and sustainability criteria.

A thorough understanding of the feedstock landscape and technology options is critical to optimizing the production of sustainable aviation fuel (SAF). SAF production typically begins with the selection of one of five primary feedstock categories, each of which requires specific ASTM-recognized production technologies. There are two main methods of SAF production: standalone units and co-processing. Standalone units convert sustainable feedstocks into synthetic kerosene (SK), which is then blended with conventional jet fuel. Conversely, co-processing involves the simultaneous processing of sustainable and fossil feedstocks in refineries. Adherence to approved technology pathways and standards, such as ASTM D7566, is fundamental to the certification of SK.

First-generation biofuels are derived from familiar crops such as corn, soybeans, sugar cane, and rapeseed, with established production processes based on fermentation and chemical reactions. These offer advantages such as existing infrastructure and lower initial costs, but raise concerns about the food versus fuel dilemma, land use change, and greenhouse gas emissions. With second generation biofuels, the focus shifts to non-food sources such as switchgrass and agricultural residues, requiring more complex production processes that are still under development. They address food-fuel conflicts and promote more sustainable land use, but face challenges of higher production costs and technical difficulties in cellulosic conversion. Third-generation biofuels are exploring unconventional sources such as algae and jatropha, with promising characteristics such as rapid growth and potential for carbon sequestration. However, large-scale production is still in the early stages, and ongoing research is focused on optimizing cultivation, harvesting, and conversion processes. Despite the potential for minimal land use impact and high yields, technical challenges remain in achieving commercial viability and efficient conversion.

Currently, the sustainable fuel industry remains niche, primarily due to the considerable price premium of sustainable fuels over petroleum-derived jet fuel. Production expansions in the 2025-2030 period should triple overall fuel production capacity, with SAF expected to account for about 5 million metric tons in 2025, predominantly from the HEFA pathway. Despite this growth, a significant portion of the planned capacity is not tailored for aviation fuel, posing technical challenges.

To meet 2030 decarbonization targets, demand for SAF must rise sharply, prompting stakeholders across the value chain to adapt. Fuel producers face pathway-specific challenges. HEFA fuels, produced by companies like Neste, ENI, and World Energy, are expected to see a significant capacity increase from roughly 200,000 metric tons in 2020 to over 16 million metric tons by 2025. These companies are increasingly on the lookout for global feedstock supplies that are cost effective and sustainable.

For significant progress to be made, governments must actively support and incentivize the production and sourcing of sustainable aviation fuels (SAF). This requires a concerted effort to align policies and investments towards sustainable solutions. Interestingly, while the oil majors may seem unlikely allies in the transition to SAF, their resources and infrastructure could play a crucial role in scaling up production. Nonetheless, significant challenges persist in achieving the necessary supply volumes to meet industry demands. Innovation is imperative in overcoming these hurdles and realizing the potential of SAF on a large scale.

The multi-stakeholder approach is paramount in devising effective solutions. For instance, optimizing air traffic control (ATC) operations to minimize delays and inefficient routings could substantially reduce fuel consumption significantly. This underscores the importance of collaboration between industry stakeholders, governments, and technology experts in implementing practical measures to mitigate climate impact in aviation.

Optimizing bio/synthetic fuel production for sustainable aviation fuel (SAF) holds immense potential, with the capacity to surpass projected jet fuel demands by 2030. However, scaling up SAF faces challenges, particularly in securing sustainable feedstock. The complex market landscape, including diverse feedstock types and ethical considerations, requires stakeholders to navigate carefully. This section aims to enhance understanding of global feedstock availability, crucial for informed decision-making in SAF production.

Prioritizing feedstocks meeting high GHG reduction criteria and with minimal controversies is crucial.

Sustainable aviation fuel (SAF) requires a diverse range of feedstocks, each meeting stringent sustainability criteria. This report evaluates feedstocks yielding at least 60% GHG savings, as outlined by the Roundtable on Sustainable Biomaterials. Edible oils and sugars are excluded due to their high CO_2 emissions and potential impact on food security. Industrial CO_2 capture raises concerns about incentivizing fossil fuel use, while recycled carbons may serve as bridging feedstocks until alternatives like direct-air-captured carbon become more viable.

In evaluating the practical availability of feedstocks for energy production, including aviation fuel, rigorous sustainability criteria are applied. These criteria, informed by standards set by the Committee on Aviation Environmental Protection (CAEP) and the Roundtable on Sustainable Biomaterials (RSB), ensure that feedstocks with significant emissions footprints or indirect land-use change factors are excluded. The assessment considers competitive uses of feedstocks outside the energy sector, such as animal feed production, to avoid potential conflicts. However, logistical and viability factors are currently excluded from the analysis but may significantly impact overall assessments and require further research. Practical availability is evaluated against sustainability criteria such as soil health, carbon stock preservation, and conservation considerations. Additionally, recycled carbon is considered as a bridging feedstock until more sustainable alternatives become available.

Economic viability is another crucial aspect, varying depending on local conditions and the transportability of feedstocks. It's essential to exclude feedstocks that could compromise soil health or have competing demands outside the energy sector, while also considering the potential impact on biodiversity and ecosystem services.

Primary feedstock sources include sustainable oils and lipids suitable for Hydroprocessed Esters and Fatty Acids (HEFA) processes, as well as cellulosic waste such as agricultural and forestry residues or municipal solid waste for alcohol-to-jet and gasification/Fischer-Tropsch routes. These sources are positioned competitively, with most offering substantial CO_2 reduction compared to fossil jet fuel.

Sustainable oils and lipids for HEFA processes encompass waste and residue lipids like used cooking oil, animal fat, fish oil, and other byproducts. Despite challenges in collection, these sources could meet a significant portion of SAF demand, accounting for approximately 5% of total 2030 jet fuel demand. However, certain feedstocks, such as palm oil-related products, raise sustainability concerns due to ethical and environmental considerations. Extending the HEFA feedstock base involves utilizing oil trees on degraded land and oil cover crops. Jatropha, an oilseed-bearing tree, and oil cover crops can potentially yield substantial feedstock volumes, contributing to SAF production.

Various feedstock sources offer significant opportunities. Cellulosic cover crops, like miscanthus, can utilize 80% of available land, yielding 120 million metric tons of SAF annually. Agricultural residues, forest residues, wood-processing waste, and municipal solid waste collectively provide around 1.5 billion metric tons of feedstock, capable of producing nearly 290 million metric tons of SAF. This abundance highlights the feasibility of achieving substantial SAF production, supporting not only aviation but also decarbonization efforts in other sectors. Scaling up SAF production could optimize collection systems and ensure steady feedstock supplies, enhancing the overall sustainable energy sector. Each regional ecosystem will have unique dynamics, with some feedstocks being globally tradeable while others may be more economically viable locally.

A growing number of countries and regions are implementing clear strategies to manage used cooking oil (UCO), preventing its improper disposal, or blending with virgin oil. India engages in education, enforcement, and ecosystem management—while Brazil has cooperatives collecting UCO from various sources. China's Sustainable Oil Alliance is developing a national collection scheme, and efforts in Singapore, Japan, and the USA involve companies collecting UCO for reuse in sustainable aviation fuels (SAF).

Gas/FT and AtJ technologies hold promise for SAF production but face scale and maturity challenges. Operational small sites exist, with larger-scale implementation ongoing. Technical barriers include syngas control and oligomerization. Robust local feedstock chains are vital, requiring investments in collection and processing. Progress depends on validating technologies and investing in infrastructure.

Aviation consulting firm Avcox is currently researching solutions to the coffee waste challenge in Central and South America, particularly in Nicaragua. Seeing an opportunity to make better use of coffee processing plant waste, it's advocating the development of advanced processes to convert coffee by-products into biofuels, bioproducts and feedstocks.

The current production of Sustainable Aviation Fuel (SAF) is nowhere near enough to meet the needs of the aviation industry. In fact, there isn't enough SAF being produced today to even fuel the airlines for a single day. This highlights the urgent need for a massive ramp-up in production to achieve the ambitious decarbonization goals set for the sector.

Essentially, we are witnessing the creation of an entirely new SAF market. This market requires significant development and investment to reach its full potential. Currently, there are only a handful of commercial-scale SAF production facilities operating globally. Significant investments are needed to build new facilities and expand existing ones. SAF production is currently more expensive than conventional jet fuel. This is due to various factors, including the limited production capacity, the cost of feedstocks, and the technological maturity of some SAF production pathways. Ensuring access to sufficient and sustainable feedstocks is crucial for scaling up SAF production. This involves utilizing waste biomass, agricultural residues, and dedicated energy crops grown on marginal lands to avoid competition with food production and deforestation. The existing infrastructure for conventional jet fuel needs to be adapted or expanded to accommodate SAF. This includes storage, transportation, and blending facilities.

Despite these challenges, there is a growing momentum and commitment from various stakeholders to develop the SAF market. Governments are implementing supportive policies and incentives, airlines are committing to purchasing larger volumes of SAF, and fuel producers are investing in new technologies and production facilities.

Gasification/FT costs are mainly driven by capital expenditure, but the process offers flexibility with various feedstock types, including low-cost options like municipal solid waste. Over time, as the scale increases and capital requirements decrease, cost savings are expected. Meanwhile, AtJ production costs rely on ethanol prices and scale effects, particularly for second-generation crops and residues. For SAF to be commercially viable, carbon costs and blending mandates are crucial, expected to rise significantly over time. Success depends on supply-demand dynamics, with HEFA likely sufficient until low-cost synthetic fuels become widely available. While SAF can be transported using existing infrastructure, maximizing efficiency suggests using it close to production sites. Virtual SAF purchases can stimulate production where it's most suitable, aiding global emission reduction efforts. HEFA is projected to remain the most efficient pathway until 2030 due to its proven technology and relatively low capital requirements, with potential cost reductions expected over time as feedstock costs decline.

Using municipal solid waste (MSW) as feedstock in fuel production involves significant capital expenditure (capex), comprising over 80% of production costs, with a projected decrease over time. MSW, valued for its removal from urban waste streams, offers low-cost feedstock, though rising demand may elevate its value over time. Gasification of forestry residues and cellulosics requires smaller capex but variable feedstock costs. Introducing carbon capture could further reduce emissions, albeit at an additional cost.

In PtL pathways, operating and input factor costs currently make up most production expenses, ranging from 80% to 90%. Specific processes like reverse-water-gas-shift and co-electrolysis have varying electricity costs, which are expected to decrease notably over time. Projections suggest a significant drop in solar power costs by 2030 and 2050. Similarly, hydrogen costs are anticipated to decline over the same period. Industrial CO2 feedstock prices may also decrease. With these cost reductions, SAF production expenses in PtL pathways are expected to decrease significantly over the coming decades.

Co-processing

Co-processing offers a steppingstone towards sustainable aviation fuels (SAF). It works by blending a small percentage of renewable feedstocks like vegetable oils or waste fats with conventional crude oil in existing refinery infrastructure. This approach leverages existing technology for faster SAF adoption and potentially lower costs, but results in a final jet fuel blend with a limited SAF content. Despite this limitation, co-processing plays a crucial role by allowing airlines to access sustainable fuel while dedicated, large-scale SAF production facilities are developed. This strategy prioritizes rapid adoption while ensuring the long-term goal of higher renewable content in jet fuel for a more sustainable aviation future.

Book and Claim System

The Book and Claim System is a mechanism that allows purchasers to buy Sustainable Aviation Fuel (SAF) even when it's not physically available at their location. Suppose Purchaser A wants SAF but can't access it directly due to geographical constraints or costs. Meanwhile, Purchaser B has already used SAF elsewhere and can verify its sustainability benefits. Through the Book and Claim System, Purchaser A can "book" the sustainability attributes of SAF from Purchaser B, even if they're not directly connected in the supply chain. These sustainability benefits (like greenhouse gas emission reduction) are tracked separately via a dedicated registry. Although Purchaser A may not physically use SAF, their purchase supports global supply development and demonstrates market demand.

It is a mechanism designed to simplify and incentivize the use of Sustainable Aviation Fuel (SAF). It allows airlines and other fuel users to purchase and claim the environmental benefits of SAF even if it is not physically delivered to their location. This system helps overcome the current limitations of SAF infrastructure and encourages wider adoption of this sustainable fuel.

The SAF Book and Claim system is a mechanism designed to simplify and incentivize the use of Sustainable Aviation Fuel (SAF). It allows airlines and other fuel users to purchase and claim the environmental benefits of SAF even if it is not physically delivered to their location. This system helps overcome the current limitations of SAF infrastructure and encourages wider adoption of this sustainable fuel.

Here's how the Book and Claim system works.

1. SAF Production and Booked Volumes

SAF producers generate SAF at designated production facilities. The produced SAF is tracked and accounted for in a central registry system.

For each unit of SAF produced, a corresponding SAF certificate is issued. This certificate represents the environmental attributes and carbon reduction benefits of the SAF.

2. Book and Claim Transactions

Airlines and other fuel users can purchase SAF certificates from producers, even if the physical SAF is not delivered to their specific location. This allows them to "book" the environmental benefits of SAF.

When airlines use an equivalent amount of conventional jet fuel, they can "claim" the environmental benefits associated with the purchased SAF certificates. This claim is verified and accounted for in the registry system.

Benefits of the Book and Claim System

The system simplifies SAF transactions and allows airlines to claim environmental benefits even when physical SAF delivery is not feasible. This incentivizes wider adoption of SAF and supports the growth of the SAF market. It allows airlines to purchase SAF from various producers and claim the benefits at different locations, increasing flexibility and optimizing logistics. The central registry system ensures transparency and accountability in SAF transactions, tracking the production, purchase, and claiming of environmental benefits.

Here is another example,

An airline operating in Europe wants to use SAF but cannot access it directly at its hub airport. Through the Book and Claim system, the airline can purchase SAF certificates from a producer in the United States. When the airline uses conventional jet fuel for its flights, it can claim the environmental benefits associated with the purchased SAF certificates. This allows the airline to contribute to the use of SAF and reduce its carbon footprint even though the physical SAF was used elsewhere.

The SAF Book and Claim system is a valuable tool for accelerating the adoption of SAF and decarbonizing the aviation industry. It simplifies transactions and ensures transparency, while encouraging wider participation in the SAF market and helps airlines achieve their sustainability goals. It's important to note that the Book and Claim system is still under development and evolving. Different models and approaches are being explored to ensure the system's effectiveness and integrity.

Renewable Transport Fuel Obligation (RTFO) UK

The Renewable Transport Fuel Obligation (RTFO) in the United Kingdom is an order that regulates renewable fuels used for transport in the UK. Its primary goal is to encourage the production and use of renewable fuels that do not harm the environment. Under the RTFO, suppliers of relevant transport fuel must demonstrate that a percentage of the fuel they provide comes from renewable and sustainable sources. Who Is Affected? Fuel suppliers in the UK are impacted by the RTFO if they supply at least 450,000 liters of relevant transport fuel annually. This includes both fossil fuels and renewable fuels.

The RTFO covers not only road fuels but also fuels used in non-road transport applications, such as non-road mobile machinery (NRMM) and tractors.

Renewable fuels used in aircraft and non-biological renewable fuels used in maritime applications fall under its scope.

Even if a company supplies less than 450,000 liters of fuel per year, they can still register under the RTFO. In doing so, they become eligible to claim RTFCs. RTFCs are certificates that track fuel produced from eligible renewable sources, from supplier to end-use consumer. Companies can trade or sell RTFCs to meet their obligations under the RTFO. The RTFO guidance provides support for fuel suppliers, independent verifiers, and others involved in supplying fossil and renewable fuels for relevant transport modes in the UK.

NEW TECHNOLOGY, ELECTRIC AND HYDROGEN

Technology

In aviation, we accelerate innovation in airframe design and explore electric and hydrogen propulsion. Governments must fund research and enforce standards like the ICAO CO2 Standard. An energy strategy with sustainable aviation fuel, hydrogen, and low-carbon electricity is essential. Agencies should prepare for certifying next-gen aircraft with unconventional designs and energy sources. Collaboration across industries is crucial for sustainable aviation tech.

Efforts to enhance in-flight energy efficiency through advancements in propulsion, airframes, structures, and systems are ongoing regardless of the type of fuel used for flights. New-generation aircraft have historically achieved a 20% reduction in energy use compared to older models, and further improvements are anticipated. Transitioning to the latest aircraft technologies, such as the Airbus A320neo and Boeing 737-Max, will contribute to initial energy savings. Future advancements in technology, including more efficient engines, lighter materials, and improved aerodynamics, could lead to an additional 15-20% improvement by 2050.

Propulsion technologies, such as higher bypass ratio engines and innovative combustion systems, aim to enhance propulsion efficiency while reducing emissions. Revolutionary propulsion systems, like open fan engine architecture, may provide even greater energy savings. Aerodynamic improvements, such as longer and thinner wings with smart wing tip devices, and the integration of composite materials and additive manufacturing techniques, are expected to reduce aircraft weight and drag, further improving fuel efficiency.

Systems enhancements, including the adoption of more electric flight control systems and the integration of systems within the aircraft structure, will contribute to weight reduction and energy savings. The gradual replacement of existing aircraft with more advanced models is projected to mitigate CO2 emissions by 2050, resulting in significant energy savings both in-flight and on the ground.

The challenges of design advancements

Presently, conventional tube-and-wing configurations have yielded notable improvements in energy efficiency, yet further enhancements are becoming progressively intricate and economically demanding. This complexity arises from the intricate interplay of various design parameters; for instance, while ultra-high bypass ratio engines hold promise for reducing specific fuel consumption, their integration introduces additional weight and drag, potentially nullifying anticipated benefits. Similarly, endeavors to minimize aerodynamic drag through higher aspect ratio wings necessitate careful consideration of accompanying weight augmentations and requisite adjustments in engine specifications to maintain optimal operational performance. It's imperative to juxtapose these engineering refinements with the overarching trend of escalating air traffic. Despite incremental gains in efficiency, the sheer growth in air travel magnifies emissions output, thereby complicating efforts to achieve commensurate reductions. This dichotomy underscores the imperative for innovative solutions that transcend incremental improvements. Researchers and engineers are actively exploring revolutionary aircraft architectures poised to transcend the limitations of current designs. One such paradigmatic shift is exemplified by the Transonic Truss-Braced Wing concept, which envisages substantial energy efficiency gains through meticulous wing elongation supported by an intricately engineered truss system. However, the realization of such ambitious designs necessitates meticulous evaluation of multifaceted challenges, ranging from fuel storage logistics to aerodynamic compromises inherent in structural modifications.

The aviation landscape is replete with promising concepts, such as blended wing bodies, which offer a plethora of benefits including enhanced cargo capacity and reduced noise emissions. Nonetheless, their widespread adoption is impeded by formidable obstacles pertaining to scalability and passenger preferences.

Hydrogen

The utilization of hydrogen in aircraft comes in two forms: as a power source for electric-driven planes via fuel cells, or through combustion in gas turbines, akin to conventional jet fuel. While hydrogen aircraft have long been studied, recent momentum, driven by environmental concerns and a recognition of aviation's decarbonization imperative, has spurred significant advancements. Companies like ZeroAvia and Universal Hydrogen are leading the charge with plans to retrofit existing aircraft, aiming for operational hydrogen-powered planes by 2025 and beyond. Airbus and GKN Aerospace are pioneering larger-scale hydrogen aircraft, with entry into service slated for the mid-2030s. Despite their relatively small impact on emissions by 2040, hydrogen-powered aircraft hold promises for substantial reductions by 2050 and beyond, contingent upon overcoming technological hurdles and advancing our understanding of their environmental footprint. Charting a course toward zero-emission aviation by 2050 entails achieving critical milestones outlined in the hydrogen and electric aircraft roadmap, offering a potential mitigation of up to 6.5% of total CO2 emissions.

Hydrogen and battery-powered aircraft offer promising solutions, with the potential to unlock significant CO2 savings by 2050. However, realizing this potential requires the development and enhancement of several enabling technologies. These include thermal management systems for handling high-temperature fuel cells, mega-watt scale electric motors for longer flights, and low-temperature fuel cells with increased power density. Liquid hydrogen (LH2) tanks must be optimized to minimize boil-off and leakage, while advancements in hydrogen combustion technology are necessary to reduce non-CO2 emissions. Dry wings, devoid of fuel storage, also present aerodynamic advantages but require further research and optimization. Notable efforts in these areas include the ENABLEH2 project and advancements by Heart Aerospace in full-electric aircraft design.

A variety of technologies contribute to improving aircraft fuel efficiency and reducing emissions, focusing on advancements in airframe and propulsion systems. Over the next three decades, the industry is expected to adopt various paths as new technologies mature. Continuous improvement within aircraft production cycles was also considered. These efforts aim to pave the way for a more sustainable future in aviation.

In exploring the future of aircraft evolution, various scenarios are considered. Firstly, the Baseline scenario involves replacing older aircraft with current or soon-to-enter-service models, maintaining conventional tube and wing designs with turbofan engines, powered by either conventional or sustainable aviation fuel. The Conservative scenario introduces a new generation of aircraft, still adhering to traditional designs with turbofan engines, utilizing conventional or sustainable aviation fuel. The New Configurations scenario envisions revolutionary aircraft designs such as the strut-braced wing or blended wing body, alongside innovative open rotor engine concepts, powered by conventional or sustainable aviation fuel. The Towards Electrification scenario anticipates a shift towards electric propulsion systems, with battery systems for smaller aircraft and hybrid systems for larger ones, expected to enter service between 2035 and 2040, requiring coordinated efforts across the aviation sector. Finally, the Aspirational Technology scenario envisages a revolutionary leap towards zero-emission aircraft, potentially hydrogen-powered for narrow-body segments starting from 100 to 200 seats, alongside electrification for smaller aircraft and hybridization for larger ones, with an earlier transition around 2030, necessitating coordinated sector-wide efforts. These scenarios collectively outline potential pathways for advancing aircraft technology towards a more sustainable future in aviation.

Airframes

The advancements in aircraft design to reduce fuel consumption and emissions for the next generation of traditional aircraft before 2035 are to be considered. These potential technologies, if introduced early, could significantly slow aviation's impact on climate change. However, achieving reductions beyond 30-35% in fuel burn with current airframe-engine configurations may pose challenges as efforts intensify. Notably, many of these evolutionary technologies can be retrofitted onto existing aircraft or integrated into new models as they come off the production line, resulting in continual efficiency improvements of around 2-3% over a decade. Key advancements include geared turbofan engines, high-pressure-ratio core engines, very high bypass ratio engines, composite structures for wings and fuselages, wingtip devices, riblets, active load alleviation, structural health monitoring, fuel cells for onboard power, and advanced fly-by-wire systems. While some technologies are already in operation, others are nearing readiness for entry into service, offering promising avenues for enhancing aircraft efficiency and sustainability.

Alternative aircraft configurations beyond the traditional 'tube and wing' are explored to achieve significant emissions reductions. These configurations include the canard, blended wing body (BWB) or hybrid wing body (HWB), strut-braced wing, box-wing, variable camber with new control surfaces, and laminar flow control technology. Canard configurations feature a small foreplane placed in front of the main wing, offering potential reductions in drag. BWB/HWB designs integrate wings and fuselage for improved lift-to-drag ratios, with potential civil applications expected by 2035-40. Strut-braced wings utilize structural support for larger spans, reducing induced drag and engine requirements, possibly entering service by 2030-35. Box-wing configurations minimize induced drag and fuel consumption, potentially available by 2035-40. Variable camber technology adjusts wing curvature for optimized lift, while laminar flow control technology maintains turbulence-free airflow over surfaces, each with potential applications in new aircraft designs, advancing steadily in readiness levels.

Propulsion

In aviation propulsion systems, two main types are currently utilized, turbofans and turboprops, both compatible with traditional jet fuel or sustainable alternatives. Revolutionary concepts are under exploration for emission reduction, including open rotor engines, electric propulsion, hybrid-electric propulsion, and hydrogen propulsion. Open rotor engines enhance bypass ratios for fuel savings, with entry into service expected around 2030. Electric propulsion utilizes motors powered by batteries or fuel cells, with small electric aircraft already flying and larger ones planned for the 2030s. Hybrid-electric propulsion combines combustion and electric engines, enabling emissions reductions of up to 40%, with small aircraft expected in this decade and larger ones from 2040. Hydrogen propulsion offers carbon-free fuel for combustion or fuel cells, with entry into service projected around 2035, contingent on addressing challenges like availability and infrastructure. Each technology presents unique benefits and readiness levels, contributing to the ongoing evolution of aviation propulsion.

The introduction of radical new technologies presents several challenges that must be carefully addressed. While aviation is known for innovation, it also adheres to stringent safety standards, requiring extensive testing and certification before new aircraft can be commercialized. These challenges include the need to develop new certification procedures for novel airframe configurations and propulsion systems to ensure safety. Airlines, as significant investors, require trust in new technology to minimize downtime for maintenance and ensure operational reliability. Additional infrastructure, such as high-power electricity or green hydrogen supply, will be needed, potentially altering refueling times and storage requirements. Adjustments in air traffic management procedures may also be necessary to accommodate differences in aircraft performance. Moreover, human support infrastructure, from flight crews to ground handlers, will require re-training. The aviation industry's global adaptation to emerging energies and technological solutions will incur significant costs in the early stages. The introduction of new aircraft types will necessitate building public trust.

Electrification

The aviation industry is witnessing a surge in electrification, with numerous electric aircraft concepts in development, primarily for small-scale operations such as personal transportation and air taxis. These electric aircraft, with their speed, reliability, and quieter operation, could serve as viable alternatives in congested urban areas or for medical emergencies. While not initially considered in the broader analysis, these smaller electric aircraft pave the way for larger commercial-sized models. Next in line for electrification are commuter aircraft in the 9-19 passenger class, with prototypes already in development and expected for service post-2025. Under ambitious scenarios, larger aircraft in the 50-100 seat category, including some turboprop types, could adopt electric propulsion by 2030-35, significantly reducing emissions and enhancing regional connectivity. However, scaling electric technologies for larger aircraft poses challenges, particularly regarding battery energy density, weight considerations, fire safety, and sustainability throughout the battery life cycle. Additionally, transitioning to electric-powered aviation requires significant changes in technology, infrastructure, and operational practices, departing from the current reliance on liquid jet fuel. Despite these challenges, analysis suggests a growing demand for electricity in aviation, reaching approximately 110 TWh by 2050 and 250 TWh by 2060, representing a small but increasing portion of global aviation energy demand.

The transition to all-electric aircraft, especially for larger models exceeding 100 seats, poses considerable technical challenges. Current analysis focuses on the more realistic 51-100 seat segment, where significant hurdles persist. For instance, for a 70-seat turboprop aircraft on a 200 nautical mile flight, the required battery mass exceeds the aircraft's payload, necessitating substantial advancements in battery energy density. Even with optimistic projections, batteries remain far less energy-dense than traditional jet fuel, limiting their viability for larger aircraft. Additionally, high discharge rates during critical flight phases like take-off demand specific power capabilities beyond current battery technology. While smaller aircraft under 19 seats show promise for electrification, their impact on global aviation fuel use remains minimal. Should this segment shift entirely to electric power, it could create additional demand for electricity, albeit significantly lower than larger aircraft. However, the adoption of hybrid solutions or partial electrification may temper this demand. Ultimately, the feasibility and extent of electrification depend on advancements in battery technology, market dynamics, and regulatory frameworks.

Plugin Hybrid Electric Propulsion aircraft

In the pursuit of electric aviation, hybrid electric propulsion (HEP) emerges as a pragmatic solution, offering a viable interim step toward full electrification. HEP integrates internal combustion engines or fuel cells with electric motors and batteries, presenting several advantages over traditional propulsion methods. These include heightened aircraft efficiency, improved reliability, power distribution, and flight range, as well as reductions in emissions and noise, while also expanding accessibility to smaller airports. The demand for electric energy in HEP aircraft hinges on the power architecture, with series, parallel, and series/parallel hybrid designs accommodating energy storage capabilities, particularly in plugin hybrid electric aircraft. The configuration and operations of these aircraft dictate the demand for electric energy, with the hybridization factor—a balance between battery and fuel energy—varying across different architectures. Based on studies exploring hybrid electric systems, a scenario involving hybrid systems for larger aircraft suggests an additional electricity demand ranging from approximately 20 to 300 TWh by 2050.

Projections suggest a substantial demand for electricity. By 2050, the introduction of fully electric aircraft in the 50-100 seat range could necessitate around 110 TWh of electricity. Factoring in the electrification of 9-19 seat aircraft and a portion of energy demand from plug-in hybrid electric propulsion aircraft, the total electricity demand might escalate to 470 TWh in 2050. This assessment excludes smaller-scale electrification for urban air mobility or sub-9-seat applications. In the broader context, the aviation sector's demand for electric energy could represent approximately 0.1 to 1% of global renewable electricity production in 2050 across various scenarios. Evaluating the requirements and costs associated with electric aviation, considerations extend to operators, airports, and original equipment manufacturers (OEMs). Operators might find operating costs of electric aircraft competitive with jet fuel costs, with projected total electricity costs ranging from $3.9 billion to $8 billion by 2050. Meeting the potential demand for all-electric aircraft may necessitate around 3,800 aircraft in the 51-100 seat segment by 2050, potentially expanding services to smaller and remote communities. Logistical challenges, including turnaround time during recharging, could incur increased operating costs or revenue loss, although solutions such as swappable battery packs may offer mitigation with attendant logistical and certification considerations.

For future all-electric aircraft to significantly mitigate CO_2 emissions, a substantial increase in battery energy density is imperative. Currently, lithium-ion battery cells, the frontrunners in energy storage, offer around 250 Wh/kg, far below the 12,000 Wh/kg of jet fuel. To meet the demands of short-range electric aircraft, battery pack specific energies of 750-2,000 Wh/kg are required. Predictions suggest that by midcentury, advancements may elevate battery pack specific energy to approximately 800 Wh/kg, assuming a continuation of historical trends. To enable all-electric aviation for larger aircraft, such as regional jets and narrow-body planes with over 100 seats, innovations in aircraft technologies, particularly lightweight high-temperature superconducting electric motors, will be indispensable. Meanwhile, airports must adapt their infrastructure to accommodate electric aircraft operations. Charging methods range from battery plug-in chargers resembling fuel-refilling stations to battery swapping stations. While these approaches address peak charging issues, they introduce logistical complexities and may necessitate modifications to aircraft certification procedures.

Hybrid Electric Aircraft

Hybrid-electric aircraft systems combine electric motors and turbofans to optimize energy consumption and emissions. Major players like Airbus, Siemens AG, and Rolls-Royce are developing projects like the E-Fan X to demonstrate this technology. Boeing and NASA are also collaborating on the SUGAR project for hybrid-electric aircraft. The EU's MAHEPA project involves developing prototypes to gather real-world data on hybrid-electric flights.

Unlike their all-electric counterparts, Hybrid-Electric Vertical Take-Off and Landing (VTOL) aircraft combine both electric and conventional propulsion systems. The advantages are extended range capabilities due to the use of traditional fuel for longer flights, enhancing operational flexibility; increased efficiency by leveraging electric propulsion during takeoff and landing, while relying on fuel for cruising, optimizing energy usage; and adaptability to various mission profiles, offering versatility in flight operations. The complexity of integrating two propulsion systems necessitates sophisticated engineering solutions, posing technical hurdles. Safety concerns arise regarding ensuring seamless transitions between propulsion modes, requiring meticulous design, testing and certification. Dependence on sustainable aviation fuels (SAFs) for traditional propulsion raises questions about fuel availability and infrastructure development. Despite these challenges, ongoing advancements aim to overcome these obstacles, paving the way for the widespread adoption of hybrid-electric VTOL aircraft.

Urban Air Mobility (UAM)

Urban Air Mobility (UAM) is advancing urban transportation with electric and hybrid VTOLs. These versatile aircraft will facilitate short-haul flights, air taxis, and intercity connections, offering convenience and efficiency. For Regional Air Mobility, hybrid-electric regional aircraft will connect smaller cities, gradually transforming regional travel as technology matures. Importantly, these advancements align with environmental goals, as VTOLs contribute to net-zero objectives by significantly reducing emissions. Sustainable Aviation Fuels (SAFs) and electrification emerge as enablers in this endeavor, promising a greener and more sustainable future for aviation.

Promising Technologies

The Turbo-Electric Hybrid Architecture stands out as it cleverly combines gas turbines, or jet engines, with electric generators. These generators power electric motors that drive the aircraft's rotors or fans, offering enhanced efficiency and performance. Another intriguing concept is Boundary Layer Ingestion (BLI), where air from the aircraft's boundary layer near the fuselage is ingested to improve efficiency by enhancing lift and reducing drag. Distributed Propulsion is also gaining attention, employing multiple smaller electric motors distributed across the airframe. This configuration not only enhances safety and redundancy but also enables innovative designs, such as distributed electric fans. Lastly, Fuel Cells are emerging as a promising technology, converting hydrogen or other fuels into electricity, offering the potential for long endurance and zero emissions.

The Companies Working on Electric Flight Technologies

AIRBUS

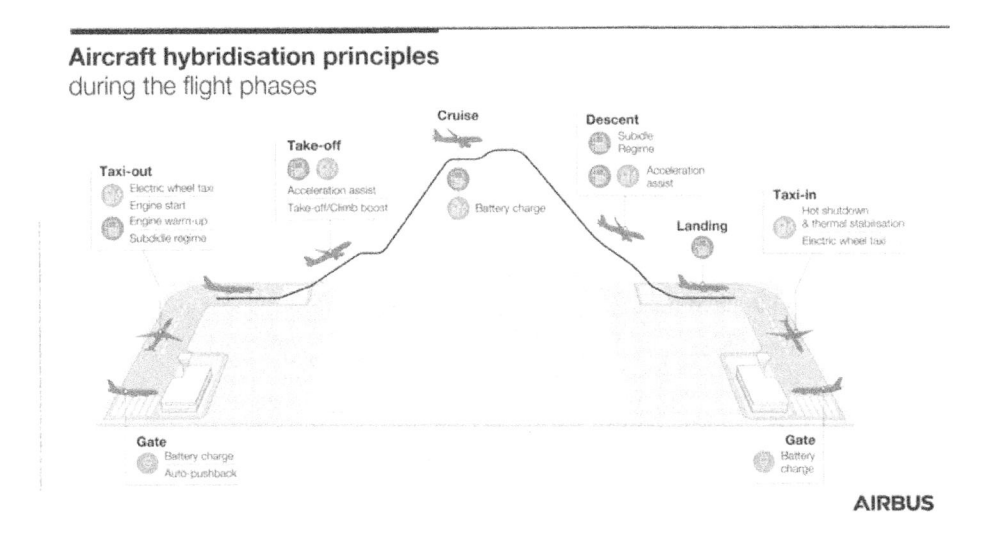

Image by Airbus

Airbus is actively involved in several electric flight projects that focus on various technologies and aircraft types, with the overarching goal of reducing emissions and noise pollution.

Here are some of their key initiatives:

E-Fan X. This project, in collaboration with Rolls-Royce and Siemens, aimed to develop a hybrid-electric propulsion system for regional aircraft. The E-Fan X demonstrator was a modified BAe 146 aircraft with one of its four gas turbine engines replaced by a 2 MW electric motor. Although the project concluded in 2020, it provided valuable insights into hybrid-electric propulsion integration and challenges.

CityAirbus NextGen. This project focuses on developing an all-electric, four-seat eVTOL (electric Vertical Take-Off and Landing) vehicle for urban air mobility. The CityAirbus NextGen features fixed wings, a V-shaped tail, and eight electrically powered propellers. It aims to offer a clean, quiet, and efficient mode of transportation within cities, potentially reducing traffic congestion and emissions.

ZEROe. This ambitious project explores various concepts for zero-emission aircraft, targeting entry into service by 2035.

There are three main aircraft concepts are being considered, the turbofan, a conventional design propelled by hydrogen combustion via modified gas turbine engines; the turboprop, a regional aircraft utilizing hydrogen fuel cells and electric motors for propulsion; and the blended-wing body, an innovative design integrating wing and fuselage for potential aerodynamic and efficiency enhancements.

Electric and hybrid-electric propulsion systems have the potential to significantly reduce carbon dioxide and other harmful emissions compared to traditional jet fuel engines. Electric motors are significantly quieter than combustion engines, which can significantly reduce noise pollution around airports and improve the quality of life for communities near airports. eVTOL vehicles like CityAirbus NextGen can offer new, sustainable transportation options within cities, potentially reducing reliance on cars and ground infrastructure.

These projects are still under development, and several challenges remain. Battery technology needs further advancements to achieve the desired range and performance for larger aircraft. I infrastructure for hydrogen production and distribution needs to be developed to support hydrogen-powered aircraft.

BOEING

Like Airbus, Boeing is also investing in electric flight technologies to contribute to a more sustainable future for aviation.

Boeing is a major investor in Wisk Aero, a company developing autonomous, all-electric eVTOL aircraft for urban air mobility. Wisk's Cora aircraft is a two-seater with a 40 km range and can operate without a pilot. This technology has the potential to revolutionize urban transportation by offering a safe, quiet, and emission-free alternative to ground transportation.

Boeing is also actively researching various electric and hybrid-electric propulsion technologies through partnerships with universities, research institutions, and other companies. These efforts focus on improving battery technology, electric motor efficiency, and overall system integration for future electric aircraft.

Airbus and Boeing are taking somewhat different approaches to electric flight. Airbus is focusing on developing hybrid-electric and hydrogen-powered aircraft for regional and short-haul flights, while Boeing currently appears more invested in eVTOL technology for urban air mobility.

NASA

NASA is working on the X-57 Maxwell project, an experimental aircraft designed to demonstrate the benefits of distributed electric propulsion. The X-57 features 14 electric motors and aims to achieve significant improvements in efficiency, noise reduction, and emissions.

Wright Electric

The Wright Spirit Project, spearheaded by Wright Electric, endeavors to revolutionize regional aviation by converting existing aircraft, notably the BAe 146, to electric propulsion, aiming to expedite the adoption of electric flight by retrofitting existing models rather than developing entirely new designs. Central to this initiative are several key components: firstly, the conversion process itself, which entails replacing the BAe 146's conventional jet fuel engines with electric motors, necessitating significant modifications to the aircraft's structure, electrical systems, and control mechanisms. Secondly, collaboration with regional airlines and aircraft operators plays an important role in identifying suitable BAe 146 candidates for conversion, ensuring project viability, and acquiring essential operational insights. The benefits of such conversion are manifold, including expedited implementation due to the faster and potentially less costly nature of retrofitting compared to crafting new electric aircraft designs, leveraging existing infrastructure and ground facilities already in place for the BAe 146, thus streamlining the introduction of electric planes without necessitating extensive infrastructure overhauls, and offering a lower initial investment option for airlines, as converting existing aircraft may prove more financially feasible than acquiring entirely new electric models, thus catalyzing broader adoption of electric aviation. The project is not without its challenges and technical intricacies abound in ensuring the safety, performance, and range of the retrofitted aircraft, demanding meticulous engineering and system integration efforts, while grappling with the ongoing battery limitations pervasive in electric aviation projects, necessitating advancements in high-energy-density battery technology to achieve commercially viable flight capabilities. Regulatory hurdles loom large, as obtaining approval for converting existing aircraft to electric propulsion mandates rigorous testing and certification to meet stringent aviation safety standards, potentially entailing protracted and intricate processes.

Bye Aerospace

Bye Aerospace is a company focused on developing and manufacturing all-electric aircraft for various applications, including flight training, air taxi services, and cargo transportation. Their primary goal is to create environmentally sustainable and cost-effective aircraft solutions. Here are some of their key projects:

They are developing an eFlyer family series that includes two-seat and four-seat electric aircraft designed for flight training and personal transportation. Their eFlyer 2 is already FAA-certified and offers significant cost savings and noise reduction compared to traditional training aircraft.

The eFlyer 4 is under development and aims to provide a versatile platform for personal and commercial use.

Aero Electric Aircraft Corporation (AEAC)

The Aero Electric Aircraft Corporation (AEAC) specializes in converting existing general aviation aircraft to electric propulsion, offering conversion kits with components like electric motors and batteries. They ensure safety standards through STC certification and collaborate closely with aircraft owners for tailored solutions, aiming to promote sustainability and cost-effectiveness in the aviation industry.

Dufour Aerospace

Dufour Aerospace, a Swiss company, is pioneering innovative electric aircraft with applications in passenger transport, cargo delivery, and aerial surveying. Their distinctive approach integrates fixed-wing aircraft design with vertical take-off and landing (VTOL) capabilities, providing efficiency, range, and operational flexibility. The flagship project, Aero3, is a tilt-wing eVTOL aircraft tailored for regional passenger transport and cargo delivery, featuring a fixed wing for efficient cruise flight and tiltable wingtips with propellers for VTOL operations, combining the speed and range of fixed-wing aircraft with helicopter-like flexibility. Dufour Aerospace is also developing a hybrid-electric propulsion system for the Aero3, merging a combustion engine with electric motors and generators to enhance range and operational adaptability compared to purely battery-powered eVTOLs.

Eviation Alice

The Eviation Alice is a groundbreaking all-electric commuter aircraft designed for regional flights, offering a range of up to 440 nautical miles and a cruising speed of 250 knots. Powered by two magniX magni650 electric motors, the Alice boasts zero direct carbon emissions, advanced composite airframe design for weight reduction, and lower operating costs compared to traditional combustion engine aircraft. With its potential to revolutionize short-haul air travel, the Alice represents a significant step toward a more sustainable aviation industry.

Faradair

Faradair, a UK-based company, is pioneering innovative and sustainable aircraft concepts for regional air mobility and special missions, with a focus on accessibility to remote communities and versatile operations. Their flagship project, the BEHA M1H, is a hybrid-electric aircraft featuring a unique "triple box-wing" design and hybrid propulsion system, enabling Short Takeoff and Landing (STOL) capabilities, quiet operation, low emissions, and mission versatility for passenger transport, cargo delivery, medical evacuation, and aerial surveying. The hybrid-electric propulsion system, combining a combustion engine with electric motors and generators, offers extended range, operational flexibility, and reduced emissions.

Ampaire

Ampaire is dedicated to advancing hybrid-electric propulsion systems for aircraft, aiming to enhance sustainability and accessibility in aviation. Their technology combines a combustion engine with electric motors and batteries to offer cost-effective and environmentally friendly solutions for regional air travel and beyond.

Joby Aviation

Joby Aviation is at the forefront of developing electric vertical take-off and landing (eVTOL) aircraft for commercial passenger transportation, aiming to revolutionize urban and regional mobility with fast, quiet, and sustainable air taxi services. Their eVTOL aircraft, designed for four passengers and a pilot, features six tilting propellers for vertical takeoff and landing and efficient forward flight, boasting a range of up to 150 miles and speeds of up to 200 mph. Notably quieter than helicopters and traditional airplanes, thanks to electric motors and specially designed propellers, Joby Aviation's aircraft is ideal for urban environments, contributing to reduced noise pollution. Operating with zero emissions, it presents a sustainable transportation solution, potentially mitigating air pollution and greenhouse gas emissions in urban areas. With plans for on-demand air taxi services utilizing vertiports in densely populated areas, Joby Aviation collaborates with partners like Uber and Toyota to develop infrastructure, regulations, and public acceptance for eVTOL operations, signaling a transformative shift in transportation paradigms.

Embraer

Embraer SA, a Brazilian aerospace leader, focuses on sustainable aviation through research and partnerships, exploring electric and hybrid-electric propulsion. Their Energia concept includes hybrid-electric regional aircraft and fully electric urban models. EmbraerX explores eVTOLs for urban mobility. Challenges include battery tech and regulatory hurdles, necessitating collaborative efforts for progress.

Pipistrel

Pipistrel, a Slovenian aircraft manufacturer renowned for high-performance, fuel-efficient, and eco-friendly aircraft, leads in electric aircraft development, achieving notable milestones. Their electric aircraft lineup includes the Alpha Electro and Velis Electro, both EASA-certified two-seat models for flight training, and the Nuuva V300, an eVTOL cargo aircraft poised to revolutionize short-haul logistics. Pipistrel's innovation integrates lightweight composites, high-efficiency electric motors, and aerodynamic optimization for superior performance and sustainability.

Magnix

Magnix is a pioneering company specializing in electric propulsion systems for aircraft, renowned for their high-power electric motors and controllers. These systems offer exceptional power-to-weight ratios, efficiency, and scalability, catering to various aircraft sizes from small trainers to regional planes. Magnix collaborates extensively with aircraft manufacturers and industry stakeholders to integrate their propulsion systems, fostering the rapid advancement of electric aviation technology. Their achievements include powering the world's first commercially certified all-electric aircraft, the Harbour Air eBeaver, and the largest all-electric aircraft, the Eviation Alice, marking significant milestones in the electrification of aviation.

GE Aviation

While renowned for traditional combustion engine technology, GE Aviation actively explores electric and hybrid-electric propulsion systems, alongside sustainable aviation fuels and advanced materials, to enhance fuel efficiency. Collaborating with diverse partners, including universities and research institutions, accelerates the advancement of sustainable aviation technologies. Their focus on hybrid-electric propulsion systems incorporates innovative features like open fan architecture and advanced materials such as ceramic matrix composites, offering potential benefits in fuel efficiency and emissions reduction. Additionally, GE Aviation develops digital solutions like data analytics and flight optimization software to aid airlines in operating aircraft more efficiently, further contributing to environmental sustainability.

Dixon Motors Inc

Dixon Motors Inc specializes in high-performance electric motors and controllers, tailored for applications including electric vehicles and aircraft. Renowned for their efficiency and power-to-weight ratios, Dixon's motors hold promise for advancing electric aviation. Their advanced controllers ensure precise motor control, vital for safe aircraft operation. With customizable products and scalability, Dixon Motors caters to diverse aircraft needs, from drones to passenger planes. Their technology finds potential applications in eVTOLs, regional electric aircraft, and retrofitting existing planes with electric propulsion systems, supporting the aviation industry's decarbonization efforts.

Full-Electric Aircraft

Full-electric propulsion in aircraft promises zero emissions and high energy efficiency, leading to growing interest from policymakers. Norway plans to have all short-haul flights electric by 2040. Over 150 electric aircraft programs exist worldwide, mainly focused on urban air taxis and general aviation, which serves as a testing ground. Distributed electric propulsion, like the Lilium Jet, enables vertical take-off and landing. Companies like Kitty Hawk, Uber, and Airbus are developing electric aircraft for air taxi services. Despite benefits, challenges remain, including battery energy density and power-to-weight ratio limitations.

Honda

Honda is actively developing an electric vertical take-off and landing (eVTOL) aircraft, featuring all-electric propulsion for quieter operation and zero emissions, along with autonomous flight capability for reduced pilot workload. Early-stage development includes research, testing, and partnerships with companies like Aernnova for aerodynamics expertise. Envisioned applications range from urban air mobility and regional transportation to emergency response and medical transport, though challenges like battery technology, regulations, and public acceptance remain.

Hyundai

Hyundai is actively developing an electric vertical take-off and landing (eVTOL) aircraft, featuring all-electric propulsion for quiet operation and zero emissions, along with distributed electric propulsion (DEP) design for redundancy and safety. Autonomous flight capability and a focus on passenger experience underline Hyundai's commitment to innovative mobility solutions. In the development and testing phase, Hyundai has unveiled concept designs and prototypes, collaborating with various partners through its dedicated Urban Air Mobility (UAM) division. Envisioned applications include urban air mobility for on-demand air taxi services, regional transportation for faster connections, and cargo delivery in urban areas.

Vertical Aerospace

Vertical Aerospace, a UK-based company, is developing their VX4 model featuring piloted and autonomous flight capabilities, electric propulsion for zero emissions, and a lift-and-cruise configuration for efficiency. The company is targeting urban air mobility, regional transportation, and cargo delivery applications. They have formed extensive partnerships with industry leaders like Honeywell, Rolls-Royce, Microsoft, leasing companies and airlines which has further bolstered their progress.

Lilium

Lilium, a German company, is advancing regional air mobility with its unique eVTOL aircraft. The Lilium Jet boasts 36 electric jet engines for zero emissions and quieter operation, housed in tilting ducts for vertical take-off and landing. With a capacity of seven passengers and a pilot, and a range of up to 250 km, it offers efficient regional transportation. Lilium aims for autonomous flight capability, currently testing their Phoenix 2 prototype. Targeting late 2020s for commercial operations, Lilium envisions applications including regional air mobility, airport shuttles, and on-demand air services. It has formed collaborations with industry leaders like Honeywell, Collins Aerospace, and also engaged in partnerships with companies like Azul Brazilian Airlines and Ferrovial.

EHang

EHang, a Chinese company, leads in autonomous aerial vehicles (AAVs) with their eVTOL aircraft for passenger and cargo transportation. Notable for their autonomous flight capability, they employ electric propulsion for zero emissions and quieter operation, utilizing multi-rotor designs for stability. With a focus on urban air mobility, EHang targets applications like air taxi and airport shuttle services, tourism, and emergency response. Having achieved regulatory approval in China for their EH216 model, EHang is actively progressing towards commercialization and establishing urban air mobility operations, aiming to revolutionize transportation in urban environments.

Archer Aviation

Archer Aviation, a US-based company, pioneers eVTOL aircraft for urban air mobility and regional transportation. Their eVTOLs feature electric propulsion for zero emissions and quieter operation, along with a lift and cruise configuration optimizing efficiency. With the Midnight model capable of carrying four passengers and a pilot, Archer targets various applications like urban air mobility and airport shuttle services. Currently undergoing flight testing and certification, Archer aims for FAA certification and commercial operations by 2025. Partnering with United Airlines, Stellantis, and Honeywell, Archer demonstrates commitment to safe, sustainable, and efficient air travel solutions.

Volocopter

Volocopter, a German company, pioneers eVTOL aircraft for urban air mobility and air taxi services. Their eVTOLs feature electric propulsion, multi-rotor design for stability, and a focus on both piloted and autonomous flight. With applications in passenger and cargo transportation, Volocopter targets urban environments to alleviate traffic congestion. Currently undergoing certification with EASA, they aim to launch commercial services soon. Partnerships with companies like DB Schenker and Fraport underscore their commitment to logistics and infrastructure development.

EVTOL

Disruptive propulsion technologies are essential, especially for Vertical Take-Off and Landing (VTOL) aircraft. These innovations, like electric propulsion, redefine traditional methods, making flight quieter, more efficient, and environmentally friendly. They enable VTOL aircraft to navigate urban areas, offering new possibilities for transportation. Embracing these advancements leads us toward a future of sustainable and accessible aviation.

In Electric Vertical Take-Off and Landing (eVTOL) aircraft, propulsion relies solely on electricity for powering these aircraft, eliminating the need for traditional fuel-based engines. They operate with zero emissions, as electric motors produce no direct emissions, and have considerable reduced noise levels compared to traditional engines. However, challenges persist, notably in energy density and weight. Batteries, the primary energy storage component, face limitations in storing sufficient energy for long flights due to their limited energy density, while their weight affects the aircraft's payload capacity and range, as heavier aircraft require more energy to lift off and fly. These challenges are actively being addressed through ongoing research and development efforts aimed at making electric propulsion more efficient, sustainable, and viable for future aviation endeavors.

Hydrogen

Hydrogen offers a promising avenue toward sustainability. Its versatility extends from serving as a crucial component in sustainable aviation fuels to potentially becoming a direct energy source for aircraft propulsion. Liquid hydrogen, especially, garners attention as a major alternative energy carrier, with significant advancements in flight testing and product development. Collaborations with the automotive industry are expected to yield technological synergies, particularly in cryogenic composite tanks and fuel cells. Moreover, the use of green or blue hydrogen, produced with low carbon electricity or with carbon emissions captured and stored, promises environmental benefits by reducing carbon emissions, particulate matter, and NOx. Hydrogen fuel cells, particularly for smaller aircraft, show promise in mitigating contrail formation. Depending on the aircraft's size and system, hydrogen propulsion could reduce climate impact by 70-90% compared to traditional counterparts. However, substantial work lies ahead to translate these advancements into commercial viability.

Transitioning to hydrogen in civil aviation entails significant aircraft and infrastructure alterations. Despite the challenges, the potential for hydrogen as a widespread clean energy source fuels interest in its aviation applications. It's important when utilizing hydrogen for propulsion that it is sourced sustainably. While hydrogen boasts a higher gravimetric energy density than kerosene, its lower volumetric energy density necessitates airframe redesign to accommodate highly insulated tanks for storing liquid hydrogen (LH2). Another major hurdle lies in the development of entirely new aircraft systems to accommodate liquid hydrogen, which necessitates storage at extremely low temperatures and requires special tanks due to its unique volume-to-energy ratio. For short-haul flights, hydrogen fuel cells powering distributed electric engines could be viable, albeit with a minor increase in cost per passenger, offering a significant reduction in emissions. For longer flights, aircraft would require special tanks and stretched fuselages to carry the same payload, resulting in a range penalty. These aircraft would likely be equipped with hydrogen combustion engines, which, while beneficial for reducing CO_2 and NOx emissions, could increase water vapor emissions. Liquefaction of hydrogen poses another challenge, requiring a considerable investment of energy. It's unlikely that hydrogen would be the preferred option for medium- and long-range aircraft before 2050 due to the additional volume required and the heavy tanks, which could be too costly compared to sustainable aviation fuels. However, advancements in technology or materials could alter this assessment, potentially paving the way for blended-wing style fuselages capable of housing larger tanks. Infrastructure requirements, implementation challenges, and fleet turnover constraints must also be considered when assessing the potential contribution of liquid hydrogen to aviation's decarbonization pathways.

Requirements

Transitioning to hydrogen as a non-drop-in fuel for aircraft propulsion would mark a significant departure from the current reliance on jet fuel, necessitating changes in technology, energy sources, infrastructure, and operations that have been optimized for decades. Hydrogen is envisioned to potentially be used in the 101-210 seat segment of aircraft, with a projected entry into service by 2035 and a ramp-up to 100% of new deliveries by 2042. This scenario predicts a substantial increase in demand for hydrogen, reaching approximately 43 MtH2 in 2050 and 79 MtH2 in 2060, representing about 20% and 33% of global aviation energy demand, respectively. However, it's essential to note that this projection represents a high-end assessment, and conventional propulsion systems may continue to be used alongside hydrogen-powered aircraft. The potential demand for hydrogen from global aviation in 2050 could represent 8-15% of future global hydrogen production, with various scenarios highlighting the crucial role of hydrogen in reducing greenhouse gas emissions and facilitating the energy transition. Several studies have explored the potential role of hydrogen in future decarbonization scenarios for the aviation sector, estimating its impact on CO2 emissions reduction and forecasting varying levels of hydrogen demand, albeit with some differences in assumptions and projections.

Costs

Transitioning to hydrogen-powered aviation entails various requirements and costs across the aviation sector. Operators would face costs associated with procuring hydrogen, which are expected to decrease over time as production becomes more efficient. The total investment required to meet aviation demand for hydrogen could range from approximately $170-370 billion by 2050, depending on production costs. Additionally, operators would need to invest in a substantial number of new aircraft, with potential increases in capital expenditure and maintenance costs due to the integration of LH2 tanks and other complexities. Turnaround time-related costs may also increase, impacting revenue and operational efficiency. Airport infrastructure would require significant investment to accommodate hydrogen distribution and refueling, with considerations for timing, synchronicity, and optimization of infrastructure. Despite these challenges, there are opportunities for synergies with other sectors and the development of hydrogen hubs to facilitate the transition to hydrogen-powered aviation.

Current hydrogen production primarily relies on fossil fuels, but there's a shift towards green hydrogen produced through electrolysis from renewable electricity. Meeting the demand for green hydrogen would require a significant increase in renewable electricity generation, far surpassing the electricity needs of electric and hybrid-electric aircraft.

Hydrogen-powered aircraft, especially narrow-body ones, would require cryogenic hydrogen, necessitating liquefaction. The energy demand for producing liquid hydrogen adds to the overall electricity requirements. Financing and investment risks are high in scaling up hydrogen production and related aviation infrastructure.

Regulatory agencies face the challenge of certifying new technologies, particularly disruptive ones like hydrogen-powered aircraft. The certification process is complex and lengthy, requiring careful timing to ensure safe entry into service.

While hydrogen offers promise for reducing CO2 emissions in aviation, it also emits water vapor, adding complexity to environmental considerations. Addressing uncertainties in non-CO2 emissions is crucial for mitigating the environmental impact of hydrogen-powered aircraft.

In hydrogen production, various "colors" symbolize different pathways and their environmental implications. Black and brown hydrogen are derived from coal, emitting CO2 and CO during extraction. Grey hydrogen, sourced from natural gas, emits CO2 into the atmosphere. Blue hydrogen, extracted from fossil fuels, captures and stores CO2 underground, though some may escape during processing. Pink hydrogen, generated from water using nuclear power, releases oxygen as a byproduct. Green hydrogen, produced using renewable energy like solar and wind power, also releases oxygen and is anticipated to become the primary source over time. This transition is crucial for reducing carbon emissions and advancing sustainable energy solutions, with blue hydrogen serving as a potential transitional source.

Hybrid propulsion systems utilizing direct electricity or electricity generated from aircraft engines could become viable options for regional and short-haul flights by around 2030, expanding to medium-haul routes by approximately 2035, and reaching long-haul flights by 2045.

The widespread implementation of these technologies depends on several factors, including further research breakthroughs, the accessibility and reliability of energy sources, and the economic feasibility of integrating these new designs into existing fleets. As technological innovations continue to emerge, our assumptions may evolve accordingly. For instance, advancements in battery technology may enable electric propulsion for larger aircraft with extended range, while government initiatives promoting a hydrogen economy could accelerate the adoption of hydrogen-based propulsion systems.

It's important to provide context by considering factors such as seating configuration, flight durations, and the share of CO2 emissions associated with different flight segments. This comprehensive approach will guide our efforts towards achieving significant reductions in CO2 emissions from air transport while ensuring the feasibility and sustainability of the solutions we pursue.

Smaller commuter and regional planes, typically serving routes with fewer than 100 seats, could be the initial adopters of electric, hybrid, and hydrogen propulsion systems. These aircraft often connect smaller communities to larger hubs or provide essential links between secondary and tertiary cities. Turboprop aircraft, known for their fuel efficiency, could serve as a steppingstone for introducing these innovative technologies.

The progression would likely involve starting with electric aircraft in the 9-50 seat range, followed by scaling up to regional aircraft with 50-100 seats, such as the ATR and DeHavilland models. These advancements could offer lower carbon alternatives for routes where building extensive rail infrastructure may not be feasible in the short term. Norway aims to electrify its domestic air travel fully by 2040, with commercial electric services expected by 2030.

Transitioning to sustainable aviation fuels (SAF) presents a more straightforward path, requiring minimal investment in distribution systems. SAF can be blended gradually into existing jet fuel supplies, with blending facilities situated off-airport. However, adopting hydrogen and electric battery options would necessitate significant shifts in energy supply systems. Special considerations include establishing hydrogen refueling infrastructure at airports and developing high voltage charging stations for electric aircraft.

Addressing various logistical challenges, such as refueling times, storage facilities, and safety protocols, will be essential for the successful integration of these new technologies. While the current fossil fuel-based infrastructure is highly efficient, transitioning to greener energy carriers requires a systemic approach to ensure adequate supply and address potential limitations as the global economy moves toward carbon-free energy.

To propel aviation towards a greener future, concerted efforts are required from policymakers, industry players, and partners across various sectors. Industry should actively support initiatives like Clean Aviation in the EU and the FAA CLEEN project in the US, accelerating collaboration globally to leverage new talent and resources. Manufacturers should explore emerging non-drop-in energy sources and innovative design concepts to accelerate product cycles and market penetration of climate-friendly technologies by 2050, forming partnerships with non-aviation sectors such as battery technology and hydrogen. Establishing incubators for aviation environmental efficiency startups can encourage innovation without constraints faced by larger manufacturers. Airports should anticipate future needs by incorporating clean energy infrastructure such as electricity, hydrogen, and battery recharging facilities into expansion plans. Governments should ensure ongoing funding for collaborative R&D projects, such as the Clean Aviation Partnership project in the EU, while prioritizing research on environmentally friendly aviation and expanding efforts to mitigate climate impacts beyond CO2 emissions. A portion of funds collected from market-based measures should be allocated towards aircraft and propulsion technology research to accelerate CO2 reduction efforts, alongside the adoption of the ICAO CO2 Standard into national legislation. Developing wider hydrogen economy strategies and ensuring sufficient infrastructure for low-carbon electricity are also crucial steps towards achieving long-term CO2 emissions reduction goals across the economy. Through these collective actions, the aviation industry can accelerate its transition towards a more sustainable and environmentally friendly future.

The energy industry must plan strategic energy needs, develop a worldwide hydrogen supply structure, and prioritize the development of sustainable aviation fuel (SAF) pathways. Collaboration between the automotive and aviation sectors is essential to leverage synergies in developing clean energy solutions, while close cooperation with the hydrogen sector is necessary to include potential aviation demand for hydrogen in green hydrogen scale-up planning.

Hydrogen Turbofan

The European Commission commissioned Airbus for the 'Cryoplane' study, aimed at exploring the conceptual design of an aircraft powered by hydrogen-fueled turbo-engines and cryogenic tanks for LH2 storage. The study revealed a 10% increase in energy consumption compared to a kerosene aircraft, attributed to the additional weight of hydrogen tanks. Recent studies suggest that optimizing airframe and engine design for hydrogen aircraft could yield energy savings of up to 12% on long-haul flights, but short-haul flights may experience increased energy consumption. Turbo-engine modifications are necessary due to differences in combustion gases and properties between hydrogen and kerosene, impacting various engine components. Additionally, adopting hydrogen as aviation fuel necessitates redesigning the fuel supply chain, including storage, and refueling infrastructure.

Airbus is dedicated to advancing hydrogen propulsion technologies through its ZEROe program, aiming to develop hydrogen-powered commercial aircraft by 2035. The program explores turbofan and turboprop engines, as well as fuel cell technology, with projects including converting an A380 into a hydrogen demonstrator and collaborating on infrastructure development and technology partnerships. Airbus also extends its focus to helicopters and collaborates with airlines. Challenges include technological maturity, infrastructure development, and cost considerations, but Airbus remains committed to overcoming these hurdles to drive sustainable aviation forward.

Hydrogen Fuel Cell Aircraft

Hydrogen holds promise for aviation use in fuel cells (FCs), including proton exchange membrane fuel cells (PEMFC) and solid oxide fuel cells (SOFC). These FCs convert chemical energy into electrical energy, capable of powering onboard equipment or electric propulsion systems.

FCs could supplement or replace traditional auxiliary power units (APUs) onboard aircraft, providing power for electrical and pneumatic loads during stationary periods and backup power during cruising. The Boeing Company reported that hydrogen SOFC-powered APUs could reduce fuel consumption for onboard energy by 40% during cruising compared to traditional APUs. However, it's essential to note that auxiliary units represent only a small portion of total aircraft energy consumption.

Various projects have explored hydrogen FC aircraft, primarily focusing on small, low-speed aircraft. For instance, the HyFlyer project by ZeroAvia aimed to decarbonize medium-range six-seater aircraft using a hydrogen PEMFC system. Similarly, NASA funded a project by CHEETA to develop an aircraft powered by a LH2 PEMFC system, demonstrating cryogenic hydrogen's potential for larger aircraft.

NASA

To revolutionize single-aisle airplanes, a major source of aviation emissions, NASA is launching a public-private partnership aiming for a 25% fuel efficiency improvement by the early 2030s. Through cost-shared research with US companies, NASA is fostering innovation in high-risk, high-reward technologies to maintain US competitiveness. The Sustainable Flight National Partnership brings together NASA, the FAA, and industry to develop and demonstrate groundbreaking technologies like hybrid-electric propulsion systems, ultra-efficient wings, and advanced engine designs. Additionally, collaboration with the Department of Energy focuses on next-generation battery technology for electric aircraft. Aligned with the national Sustainable Aviation Fuel Grand Coalition, NASA will also use its expertise to analyze sustainable aviation fuels, ensuring compatibility with current and future airplanes for a cleaner aviation future.

Future Propulsion Fuels

The major aircraft engine manufacturers are engaged in research and development initiatives aimed at achieving sustainable aviation through various approaches, including:

1. **Improving Engine Efficiency**

GE Aviation

Developing next-generation engines like the GE9X and CFM LEAP, offering significant fuel burn reductions compared to their predecessors. Exploring open fan architectures and advanced materials like ceramic matrix composites for further efficiency gains.

The GE9X Engine is a high-bypass turbofan engine exclusively designed for the Boeing 777X family of aircraft. Here are some notable features,

Derived from the General Electric GE90, the GE9X incorporates advanced materials like ceramic matrix composites (CMCs) and boasts a larger fan. These enhancements contribute to a remarkable 10% improvement in fuel efficiency compared to its predecessor, the GE90. The GE9X generates 110,000 pounds of thrust, slightly less than the GE90-115 variant. It first ran on the ground in April 2016 and powered the 777-9's maiden flight in early 2020. The GE9X received its Federal Aviation Administration (FAA) type certificate in September 2020, marking a significant milestone in aviation technology.

CFM LEAP Engine: The CFM LEAP (Leading Edge Aviation Propulsion) engine, produced by CFM International (a joint venture between GE Aerospace and Safran Aircraft Engines), is another remarkable achievement:

The LEAP incorporates technologies developed as part of the LEAP56 program. It aims to overcome limitations associated with conventional ceramics by embedding long multi-strand ceramic fibers into the matrix. Enhancing crack resistance, elongation, and thermal shock resistance, the LEAP achieves better performance. Its continuous-length ceramic fibers bridge cracks without fracturing, avoiding abrupt brittle failure. The LEAP's architecture includes variable pitch compressor blades, modulating stator vanes, and advanced low-pressure turbines.

These innovations contribute to a remarkable 16% reduction in fuel consumption. Airbus and CFM plan to perform joint flight tests using an A380 testbed aircraft equipped with the open fan engine. The goals include evaluating propulsive efficiency, aerodynamics, and noise levels.

Rolls-Royce

Focusing on the "UltraFan" engine design, featuring a geared turbofan architecture and advanced technologies for improved efficiency and lower emissions. Investigating electrification of aircraft systems to reduce engine load and fuel consumption.

Rolls-Royce is making significant strides in revolutionizing aircraft propulsion. The UltraFan represents a paradigm shift in engine design, aiming for unparalleled efficiency and sustainability. At its core, the UltraFan features a geared design, which optimizes power delivery at high-bypass ratios. This innovative approach allows for a larger fan diameter (140 inches) while maintaining a relatively small core. The result? Greater fuel efficiency and reduced emissions. Rolls-Royce employs carbon titanium fan blades within a composite casing, significantly reducing weight. The combination of lightweight materials and advanced fan system technology contributes to a remarkable 25% improvement in fuel burn compared to the first-generation Trent engines. UltraFan offers 40% less NOx (nitrogen oxides) and 35% less noise during cruise. Additionally, it virtually eliminates nvPM particulates. (non-volatile particulate matter. These are tiny solid particles or liquid droplets suspended in the air that do not evaporate readily.) The UltraFan is prepared to run on 100% Sustainable Aviation Fuel (SAF). SAF provides a lifecycle carbon reduction of at least 80% compared to traditional jet fuel.

Pratt & Whitney

Continuously improving the GTF (Geared Turbofan) engine family, offering double-digit fuel burn improvements. Exploring hybrid-electric propulsion systems for regional and short-haul aircraft. The GTF Advantage engine builds upon the mature dispatch reliability of the GTF family, offering up to 17% lower fuel consumption compared to prior engines like the V2500. This translates to significant cost savings for airlines. With sea level takeoff thrust up to 34,000 pounds per engine, the GTF Advantage delivers enhanced performance. On traditional fuel, it emits up to 17% less CO2 than its predecessors. Successful tests on 100% Sustainable Aviation Fuel (SAF) demonstrate even lower lifecycle emissions. Drawing from over 26 million hours of GTF service experience, the GTF Advantage engine ensures high durability at entry into service. Airlines benefit from seamless upgrades. New and base model engines are fully interchangeable, providing operational flexibility.

All major manufacturers are actively involved in testing and promoting the adoption of SAFs, which can be produced from various sustainable feedstocks like used cooking oil, plant oils, or even captured carbon dioxide. These fuels offer significant lifecycle greenhouse gas emission reductions compared to conventional jet fuel.

Contrails

Aircraft contrails, also referred to as condensation trails, are the visible cloud-like streaks left in the wake of jet aircraft flying at high altitudes. These formations occur when the hot exhaust gases from aircraft engines mix with the cold air at cruising altitudes, typically between 30,000 and 38,000 feet, causing the water vapor in the exhaust to condense into tiny ice crystals. Although approximately 65% of jets at cruising altitudes produce contrails, most dissipate within minutes due to atmospheric conditions. Contrails mainly consist of ice crystals but can also contain pollutants such as sulfur compounds, soot particles, and nitrogen oxides from aircraft exhaust. They play a significant role in global warming by creating clouds that trap heat in the atmosphere at the critical altitude where airliners fly, potentially contributing more to global warming than carbon dioxide or other fuel emissions. The emerging field of study called "effective radiative forcing" measures the total warming effect, considering contrails alongside CO_2 emissions. Cirrus clouds formed from persistent contrails can linger longer and have a more lasting impact on climate. Airlines are increasingly acknowledging the environmental impact of contrails, presenting a new challenge beyond the traditional focus on carbon emissions. Carriers like American and Southwest are collaborating with aviation companies and research institutions to study the worst contrails for global warming, as the airline industry aims to reduce its emissions footprint, though achieving these goals remains a technological challenge.

Contrails' impact on the climate varies significantly based on several factors. Weather conditions, including temperature, humidity, and air pressure, greatly influence their behavior. In cold and humid environments, contrails tend to persist longer, forming persistent contrail clouds, whereas in dry or warmer conditions, they dissipate quickly. Daytime and nighttime conditions affect contrail behavior differently.

Contrails influence radiative forcing by disrupting the balance between incoming solar radiation and Earth's emitted heat. Persistent contrail clouds function like a blanket, trapping heat within the atmosphere. During the day, contrail cirrus clouds exhibit dual effects on climate. They reflect incoming sunlight, which contributes to cooling, yet they also trap heat emitted from Earth's surface, leading to warming in the lower atmosphere. At night, they still contribute to warming by trapping outgoing infrared radiation. The presence of underlying clouds can also alter contrail behavior; they may merge with existing cloud layers under overcast skies, whereas they stand out more distinctly against clear skies. Contrails formed over land or water exhibit varying effects, interacting with local weather patterns over land and dissipating more rapidly over water. They can be classified into short-lived, persistent, and spreading types, each with its own duration and impact on climate dynamics.

Research on aircraft contrails encompasses a comprehensive approach, integrating various observation methods and laboratory investigations. Ground-based observations play a pivotal role, with strategically positioned cameras and sensors actively monitoring contrail activity. EUROCONTROL's contrail observatory, located atop their Innovation Hub near Paris-Orly Airport, exemplifies this approach, employing state-of-the-art cameras from Reuniwatt to capture both visible and infrared spectrums. These observations yield crucial data aiding in contrail formation comprehension and the formulation of avoidance strategies. Satellites provide a global perspective, allowing researchers to track contrails across vast regions. Integrating ground-based and satellite data enhances our ability to analyze contrail behavior, especially when covering extensive areas. In situ observations involve direct measurements within contrails, facilitated by specialized instruments onboard research aircraft. These measurements, encompassing composition and particle size, validate models and enhance our understanding of contrail formation processes. Laboratory studies simulate contrail conditions under controlled settings, investigating factors such as temperature, humidity, and exhaust composition to inform prediction models accurately. Models like CoCiP (Contrail Prediction Model) utilize air traffic data and numerical weather predictions, aiding in contrail behavior simulation and refinement through comparison with observed data. Through this multifaceted approach, researchers continue to advance our understanding of contrails, crucial for both environmental and aviation considerations.

Environmental advocates and climate-focused organizations argue that contrails contribute more to global warming than the carbon dioxide emitted from jet engines. Consequently, the aviation industry has ramped up its research endeavors to gain a deeper understanding of contrails and explore potential mitigation strategies. Several initiatives highlight the multifaceted nature of contrail studies. Boeing and NASA collaborated on flight tests in October, conducted from Everett, Washington. A NASA DC-8 research plane trailed a Boeing 737 MAX 10 to closely scrutinize its exhaust and analyze contrail formation, primarily examining whether sustainable aviation fuel (SAF) could mitigate contrails. Google partnered with Breakthrough Energy, a climate action group founded by Bill Gates, to conduct experiments aiming to assess pilots' ability to avoid contrail-inducing airspace. A small-scale trial involving American Airlines preceded plans for a larger endeavor with multiple carriers, including Alaska Airlines.

Scientific uncertainties persist regarding contrail impacts. David Lee, a prominent climate researcher and chair of the U.N. Intergovernmental Panel on Climate Change's aviation working group, published a new assessment challenging the consensus on contrails' significant climate influence. Co-authored by U.K. climate researchers, the paper underscores the uncertainty surrounding aviation's non-CO_2 impacts, including contrails and engine emissions' effect on cloud formation. Lee warns that efforts to mitigate contrails may yield limited efficacy or unintended consequences due to this uncertainty, potentially exacerbating fuel consumption and CO_2 emissions.

Contrail formation involves complex processes, with water vapor condensing around aerosols emitted by jet engines, resulting in ice crystals at high altitudes. While contrails exhibit a cooling effect during the day by reflecting sunlight, they also trap surface heat, akin to the greenhouse effect induced by CO_2. Researchers continue to delve into contrail behavior, considering variables such as weather conditions, time of day, and underlying surface features, highlighting the intricate nature of contrail science and mitigation approaches.

Deploying Sustainable Aviation Fuel (SAF) on flights known to produce warming-type contrails presents a logical step forward in addressing aviation's environmental impact. Contrails can have varying effects on the climate, with persistent contrails contributing to global warming by trapping heat in the atmosphere, particularly the "warming kind" that enhances the greenhouse effect by trapping outgoing infrared radiation.

Given these effects, using limited stocks of SAF and prioritizing them on flights prone to producing warming-type contrails offers a potential solution. This approach requires careful consideration and research. Identifying flights with warming-type contrails necessitates detailed monitoring and assessment of specific conditions such as altitude, temperature, and humidity. Implementing SAF on targeted flights also poses logistical challenges, including fuel availability and cost. A holistic approach is essential, combining ongoing research into contrail behavior and climate effects with optimized flight planning to avoid contrail-inducing regions when feasible.

The Rocky Mountain Institute (RMI) has been actively engaged in researching and addressing the climate impact of aircraft contrails. Through initiatives like the Contrail Impact Task Force, RMI collaborates with leaders from the aviation industry, the tech sector, and academia to measure and tackle the climate challenge posed by contrails. While the precise warming effect of aviation-induced cloudiness caused by contrails remains uncertain, there's a growing consensus that their impact on climate could be comparable to aviation CO_2 emissions. RMI brings together experts to explore opportunities for addressing the warming impact of certain contrails, recognizing that collaboration can lead to better understanding, prediction tools, and mitigation strategies.

Non-CO_2 factors like contrails also contribute to atmospheric warming. Efforts to mitigate contrails include exploring tools to avoid their formation and identifying opportunities for reduction. In a milestone trial conducted by RMI, involving 70 test flights over six months, small altitude adjustments were made to 35 flights to avoid contrails. The result showed a statistically significant 54% reduction in contrail formation in the rerouted flights, with only a 2% increase in fuel usage and CO_2 emissions compared to controlled flights. Airlines such as Delta Airlines, in collaboration with the Massachusetts Institute of Technology (MIT) and RMI, are increasingly acknowledging contrails as an environmental concern and are actively studying which flights create the worst contrails.

Imperial College London has also conducted significant research on the impact of aircraft contrails on the climate. While most contrails last only a few minutes, some can linger for up to eighteen hours, contributing to the formation of clouds. Previous studies suggest that contrails and the clouds they help form have a warming impact on the climate comparable to aviation's cumulative CO_2 emissions, known as 'radiative forcing'. However, unlike CO_2, which persists for centuries, the impact of contrails is short-lived and can be swiftly reduced.

Recent research led by Imperial College London indicates that small altitude changes could significantly mitigate the climate effects of aviation contrails. By adjusting the altitudes of less than two percent of flights, contrail-linked climate change could be reduced by up to 59 percent. Specifically, altering flight altitudes by just 2,000 feet could lessen the impact of contrails. Combining this altitude adjustment with the use of cleaner aircraft engines could further reduce the harm caused by contrails to the climate by up to 90 percent. Lead author Dr. Marc Stettler emphasized the potential of this method to swiftly improve the overall climate impact of the aviation industry. The research is published in the journal Environmental Science & Technology, underscoring Imperial College London's contributions to addressing contrails' impact on climate change and proposing practical solutions to mitigate their effects.

Trinity College Dublin

Trinity College Dublin, in partnership with Ryanair, has announced the establishment of the Ryanair Sustainable Aviation Research Centre in April 2021, marking a significant milestone as the first initiative of its kind in Ireland. With a donation of €1.5 million, Trinity has put together a multi-disciplinary research team to explore sustainable aviation fuels, zero carbon aircraft propulsion systems and noise mapping. This effort aims to inform EU and international aviation policy while catalyzing future investment in sustainability within the industry. Embedded in Trinity's E3 initiative, which is dedicated to engineering, the environment, and emerging technologies, this partnership aligns with the university's commitment to addressing global challenges, including those facing the aviation sector.

INFRASTRUCTURE AND OPERATIONAL EFFICIENCIES

Improvements in Operations and Infrastructure

Enhancements in operations and infrastructure wield significant potential for reducing CO_2 emissions and aligning with the 2050 carbon goal. While these improvements may not singularly achieve the target, they offer swifter implementation compared to aircraft-level technologies, making them noteworthy contributors, especially in the short term. Aircraft operations, focusing on weight reduction, aerodynamic enhancements, and efficiency systems, play a pivotal role initially, though their impact diminishes over time as efficiency measures reach saturation. Similarly, infrastructure enhancements, including structural changes in air traffic management and energy-saving measures at airports, contribute to emissions reduction. Fuel consumption optimization remains a challenge, driven by both economic and environmental concerns. Manufacturers are urged to design and deliver aircraft with enhanced fuel efficiency and environmental performance, complemented by operational measures throughout the aircraft's lifecycle. Collaboration among airframers, infrastructure providers, airports, and aviation authorities are crucial in facilitating efficient aircraft operation. Drawing from sources such as

ICAO reports, IATA Technology Roadmap, and others, the exploration of potential emissions reductions from operations and infrastructure improvements forms a crucial aspect of ongoing research initiatives in aviation.

Aviation sustainability advancement forecasting high-level presents a formidable challenge, given the multitude of initiatives worldwide and varying efficiency enhancement prospects. Congestion within the airspace system poses a hurdle to delivering improvements efficiently, as squeezing more flights into finite airspace compromises operational efficiency measures. The net enhancement from aircraft operations and infrastructure is dependent on traffic growth. Substantial investment is imperative to accommodate escalating connectivity demands arising from traffic growth. Load factors profoundly influence fuel-efficient aircraft utilization, with recent years witnessing substantial improvements despite anomalies due to the pandemic. Integrating multiple factors like regulatory restrictions, traffic management, and maintenance, efficient aircraft operations require meticulous planning. Retrofitting winglets, lightweight equipment, seating, and cargo containers, last-minute fuel and water uplift, and electric taxiing are tangible strategies for reducing emissions and enhancing efficiency. Thinner paint for liveries and exterior maintenance further contribute to weight reduction and aerodynamic efficiency. Performance improvement packages, fuel efficiency management systems, and reduced engine taxiing are additional measures aiding in emissions reduction and fuel conservation. Engine wash systems and meticulous interior cleaning ensure engine health and weight maintenance. Awareness and training programs for aircrews and engineers serve as strategies in promoting eco-friendly operational practices, underscoring the collaborative effort needed to move towards a greener aviation future.

Infrastructure initiatives

Fixed electrical ground power at gates, coupled with pre-conditioned air, enables airlines to minimize auxiliary power unit usage, thereby reducing CO_2 emissions by over 100,000 tons annually and diminishing aircraft noise. Airport collaborative decision-making (A-CDM) fosters information exchange among stakeholders, leading to more accurate turn-around information, minimizing delays, and saving over 102,700 tons of CO_2 annually across European airports. Surface congestion management tools, like virtual departure queues, optimize departure processes, saving 48,000 tons of CO_2 yearly at major airports. Performance-based navigation (PBN) utilizes GPS and satellite technology to enhance airspace capacity and reduce emissions, offering significant fuel savings. Required navigation performance (RNP) specifications facilitate precise flight paths, enhancing safety and efficiency, saving 39,000 tons of fuel and 124,556 tons of CO_2 annually in the USA alone. Space-based navigation provides global aircraft tracking, improving airspace capacity and enabling more fuel-efficient routes. Continuous climb and descent operations (CCOs and CDOs) minimize fuel burn, emissions, and noise, delivering environmental and economic benefits. Expansion of 'perfect flight' partnerships sets an optimum standard for flight efficiency, serving as a catalyst for emission reduction efforts.

4D Trajectory-based Operations (TBO) integrate time into the traditional 3D aircraft trajectory, aiming to optimize flight paths while ensuring accurate arrival times. Flexible tracks and free-route airspace capitalize on improved navigational capabilities, allowing for more direct and efficient flight routes, potentially saving up to 500,000 tons of CO_2 annually over Europe alone. Flexible use of military airspace can significantly reduce emissions by allowing civil aircraft to fly more direct routes, although it requires close civil-military cooperation. Formation flight, demonstrated through projects like fello'fly, leverages the wake of leading aircraft to improve efficiency for following planes, potentially reducing fuel consumption by 5-10% per trip. Initiatives like the Single European Sky (SES) and SESAR in Europe, as well as NextGen in the United States, aim to modernize airspace management, improve safety, and enhance environmental performance by reducing fragmentation, increasing automation, and implementing advanced technologies.

The potential for operational and infrastructure improvements within the flight plan is subject to various interdependencies that can introduce inefficiencies compared to ideal conditions. Factors such as safety considerations necessitate deviations from optimal routes to maintain aircraft separation, while adverse weather conditions may require route adjustments for safety and comfort. Capacity constraints at airports or within airspace can lead to aircraft holding or ground delays, increasing congestion and reducing efficiency. Collaborative decision-making and improved data utilization can mitigate these issues by implementing measures earlier in each flight, such as delaying aircraft until capacity is available. Emerging airspace users like unmanned aerial vehicles pose future capacity challenges. Noise abatement procedures around airports can affect flight paths, and airline practices and military airspace restrictions can also impact routing efficiency and fuel consumption. Institutional factors like fragmented airspace and differing operating procedures between regions may require political will to resolve for optimal routing and efficiency within the aviation system.

To enhance the efficiency of operations and infrastructure within our flight plan, several recommendations and actions have been proposed. These include rebuilding air traffic volumes based on perfect flight principles post-Covid-19 shutdowns, implementing fixed electrical ground power and pre-conditioned air at appropriate aircraft stands by both airports and airlines, and exploring opportunities for assisted taxiing to reduce engine use for ground movements involving various stakeholders. Additionally, weight-based efficiency measures like tablet computers, lighter cabin equipment, and seating are encouraged, along with accelerating the full implementation of Airport Collaborative Decision Making (A-CDM) and more efficient continuous approach and departure procedures. Investigating new approach technologies and retrofitting applicable aircraft with aerodynamic efficiency devices are also highlighted, as well as supporting trajectory-based operations (TBO) and collaborating with local communities on new airspace design. Expediting the testing and certification of new efficiency measures, encouraging efficiency actions throughout the aviation system, and increasing intermodal operations with rail operators are further emphasized. Finally, working with local authorities and transport providers to boost the share of passengers using public transport to reach airports completes the comprehensive strategy aimed at accelerating efficiency and sustainability in aviation.

Governments are urged to implement flexible military airspace usage, adopt ICAO's Aviation System Block Upgrades, develop regulatory systems for harmonized standards, fund intermodal planning, and ensure a balanced comparison of transport modes. The energy industry should collaborate with airports to ensure low-carbon energy supplies.

Airlines

Airlines are setting voluntary targets, primarily centered on environmental sustainability, aiming to curtail carbon emissions against established benchmarks. These internal objectives drive investments in initiatives such as purchasing offsets to mitigate unavoidable emissions, aligning with broader environmental commitments. A burgeoning consumer consciousness regarding carbon footprints impels airlines to offer sustainable travel options, meeting the demands of both passengers, corporate and cargo customers. This customer-centric shift encourages the adoption of practices like biofuel-powered flights and carbon offset programs, enhancing airlines' appeal to environmentally conscious travelers, and advancing overarching sustainability objectives. Regulatory mandates impose legal obligations, compelling airlines to adhere to specified environmental standards and emissions targets. Compliance with these mandates is non-negotiable, prompting airlines to invest in technologies and practices that mitigate their environmental impact. Thus, fostering collaboration among airlines, regulators, and customers is imperative.

In the value chain of Sustainable Aviation Fuel (SAF), the role of airlines is quite important. The best role for airlines in this context depends on their strategic approach and risk tolerance. One school of thought advocates for airlines to actively engage in sourcing strategies, ensuring a reliable and sustainable supply of SAF. This may involve various approaches, such as long-term off-take contracts to secure supply, co-investing in production plants for vertical integration, or fostering partnerships with SAF producers. These strategies come with inherent risks, including regulatory uncertainties and technological challenges. Regarding the perception of supply and demand dynamics, airlines' beliefs shape their sourcing strategies. If airlines perceive a shortage in the SAF market, they may proactively engage in securing supply through long-term contracts or investment in production facilities. Conversely, if they anticipate sufficient supply, they may adopt a more conventional approach as fuel customers. The uncertain nature of SAF technology at scale complicates accurate economic predictions, making strategic decisions challenging. Working with regulatory complexities, including fragmented mandates and the need for harmonization, is crucial for the sustainable development of SAF. Stable regulations and de-risking investments in sustainable production plants are essential for fostering industry growth and innovation. Ultimately, partnerships, strategic sourcing, and regulatory stability play pivotal roles in shaping the airline industry's involvement in the SAF value chain.

Environmental actions by airlines

KLM is focused on shaping the future of sustainable aviation through a series of innovative initiatives and strategic collaborations. At the heart of its efforts is an innovation ecosystem, led by a dedicated Radical Innovation team within the corporate office. This team focuses on three critical areas: strategizing innovation portfolios for Horizon 2 and 3 projects, facilitating knowledge sharing through the KLM Innovation Ecosystem, and providing training on various innovation methodologies.

It harnesses internal expertise and partners with respected institutions such as the Technical University of Delft and the University of Amsterdam, KLM distinguishes itself as an airline committed to pioneering innovation in the aviation sector. One outstanding collaboration is with Delft University of Technology on two groundbreaking projects such as the Flying V, an energy-efficient aircraft design, and Flying Vision, a carbon-neutral flight technology initiative that aims to achieve sustainable flying by 2050.

KLM's commitment to sustainability extends to circular additive manufacturing, where the Radical Innovation Team has developed a process to turn recycled plastic bottles from flights into 3D printed tools for aircraft maintenance. This innovative approach not only reduces waste, but also improves operational efficiency. Its innovation labs are exploring disruptive technologies such as automated 3D scanning of cargo, autonomous robotic operations, and smart workspaces to drive meaningful change and shape the future of aviation.

In terms of onboard renewables and recycling strategies here's a summary of the various airlines' efforts to cut down on single-use plastics onboard:

British Airways (BA)

- Replaced plastic stirrers with bamboo alternatives.
- Reduced plastic packaging in amenity kits.
- Switched to paper wrapping for bedding and blankets.
- Replaced plastic wrapping with paper envelopes for headsets in economy cabins.
- Uses water bottles made from 50% recycled plastic.
- Eliminated plastic bags onboard.

Virgin Atlantic

- Replaced plastic cutlery with pressed cardboard cutlery.
- Switched to bamboo stirrers.
- Implemented weight reduction strategies to minimize onboard waste.
- Strives to eliminate single-use plastics wherever possible.
- Replaced plastic water bottles with canned wine or crew service for pouring drinks.

Delta Airlines

- Testing new paper cups to replace plastic cups for hot, cold, and alcoholic beverages.
- Eliminated over 4.9 million pounds of single-use plastics annually.
- Plans to eliminate plastic straws, utensils, wrapping, and stirrers.

Ryanair

- Pledged to become plastic-free on all flights in 2023.
- Switched to biodegradable cups, wooden cutlery, and paper packaging.
- Aims to be 100% free from single-use plastic by 2025.

American Airlines

- Exploring recycled plastic alternatives to reduce or eliminate single-use plastics.
- Increased use of sustainable cutlery kits made of bamboo.
- Phased out plastic straws and stirrers, opting for biodegradable and wooden options with a future transition to bamboo utensils.
- Implemented BioNatur Plastics products to reduce long-term plastic waste.

United Airlines

- Phased out plastic straws and cocktail picks, replacing them with paper alternatives.
- Uses blankets made from recycled plastic bottles and recycles plastic bottles sold on flights.
- Exploring the use of beeswax lids and compostable cutlery.

Lufthansa Group

- Following the principles of "reduce-reuse-recycle-replace" for product development and service.
- Using PaperWise material made from agricultural waste for packaging onboard delights.
- Aims to replace single-use plastic articles with sustainable materials by 2025.
- Using compostable cutlery made from bamboo.
- Introduced a new type of cargo film containing 10% recycled plastic and being thinner to save weight.

Air France

- Reduced 1,300 tons of single-use plastic annually onboard.
- Swapped plastic cups with paper and cutlery with bio-sourced materials.
- Involved in biofuel testing partnerships for sustainable aviation fuel.

Aer Lingus

- Introduced birchwood cutlery packs, reducing single-use plastics by almost 23 tons per year.

- Replaced newspapers and magazines with digital alternatives.

Qantas

- Aims to have zero single-use plastics on all flights before 2027.
- Transitioning to compostable or recyclable packaging for all inflight products.
- Removed or replaced more than 200 million single-use plastics since 2019.
- Introduced compostable hot meal boxes, wooden cutlery, bamboo drink stirrers, and paper products for amenity kits.
- Collaborating with suppliers to increase the use of recycled and renewable materials.

Japan Airlines (JAL)

- Replacing plastic fixtures and fittings in the cabin with sustainable materials.
- Aims to eliminate all new petroleum-derived single-use plastics in the cabin and lounge by 2025.
- Introduced paper cup lids, muddlers, containers, lids, and tray mats.

Korean Air

- Replaced single-use plastics with eco-friendly paper products in 2019.
- Partnering with SK Energy to adopt carbon-neutral jet fuel.

Qatar Airways

- Qatar Airways takes a multi-step approach to sustainability in aviation:
- They reduced single-use plastics onboard by ditching plastic cutlery wrap and using eco-friendly hot drink spoons.
- Committed to being environmental leaders, they're the first Middle Eastern airline with top-level IATA eco-accreditation. Their hub airport aims for high sustainability ratings.

China Airlines

- China Airlines they're actively reducing single-use plastics onboard.
- By 2025, they aim for a significant drop in disposable, non-degradable plastic consumption compared to 2020 levels.
- Specific actions include replacing disposable plastic tableware with recyclable alternatives and piloting on-board garbage sorting programs.

China Southern Airlines

China Southern Airlines is a leader in eco-friendly practices within China's aviation industry, as evidenced by their "Green Airline of the Year" award.

- China Southern significantly reduced plastic consumption by eliminating disposable plastic straws, stirrers, tableware, cups, and packaging bags across terminals, lounges, and domestic flights.
- They promote "On-Demand Dining" services to minimize food waste.

Air India

Air India has achieved an 80% reduction in the usage of single-use plastics on board all flights worldwide.

- Replacing plastic zip lock bags for cutlery with paper packaging.
- Substituting plastic straws with paper straws and plastic stirrers with wooden ones.
- Introducing reusable linen bags on board.
- Introducing 100% compostable PET lids.
- Ensuring all waste bags are completely compostable.

LATAM Airlines Group

- LATAM got rid of single-use plastics on all its flights.
- LATAM plans to achieve zero waste to landfill by 2027.

A4A

Airlines for America (A4A) champions the U.S. airline industry, advocating for policies to improve safety, security, and industry robustness. Collaborating with stakeholders, including airlines, labor, Congress, and the Administration, A4A works to enhance aviation for travelers and shippers. Airlines for America (A4A) pushes for several policies to promote a sustainable and efficient aviation industry. These include tax credits for cleaner jet fuels, modernization of air traffic control systems to reduce fuel burn, continued research into new technologies like electric planes, and international carbon offset programs. A4A also supports emerging technologies like carbon capture to further reduce the industry's environmental impact. By advocating for these measures, they aim to balance environmental responsibility with economic growth for the airline industry.

Operational Efficiencies

Air traffic management (ATM) improvements can significantly reduce fuel burn and emissions in aviation. Existing systems in the US, like NextGen, have already made strides in efficiency, but future efforts will focus on optimizing flight paths throughout the entire journey, from takeoff to landing. This includes using precise, 4D trajectories (including time) and leveraging data sharing to enable airlines to choose the most fuel-efficient routes. Investments in research and technology development, particularly for oceanic airspace with limited tracking capabilities, are crucial for further improvements and accommodating future growth in air travel. To tackle aviation emissions, the US government sees sustainable aviation fuels (SAF) as a key solution.

SAF are basically eco-friendly jet fuels made from renewable sources like waste materials, resulting in at least 50% less greenhouse gas emissions compared to regular jet fuel. To ramp up SAF production, the US is taking a multi-step approach. First, a government-led initiative called the SAF Grand Challenge is working to bring down costs, improve environmental benefits, and boost production to meet all US aviation fuel needs by 2050. Second, policies like the proposed Sustainable Aviation Fuel tax credit aim to make SAF cheaper and encourage domestic production. The government is exploring bulk purchases of SAF by the military and others to create a stronger market for this eco-friendly fuel. The strategy is to make SAF a more affordable and attractive option, ultimately leading to a broader use of the fuel.

The International Civil Aviation Organization (ICAO) is a key forum for international leadership in reducing aviation's environmental impact. Countries contribute to ICAO's technical committees and policy making bodies, promoting ambitious yet achievable standards for aircraft emissions. A key achievement is the Carbon Offsetting and Reduction Scheme for International Aviation (CORSIA), a global market-based measure to address CO2 emissions. Countries also collaborate through bilateral agreements to share best practices and promote environmentally friendly aviation technologies. Leadership in ICAO and collaboration among member states are crucial for achieving ambitious climate goals for aviation.

A4E

As part of the European Green Deal vision, A4E aims to minimize its environmental impact and contribute to a more sustainable European economy. Their initiatives include a comprehensive roadmap called "Destination 2050," which outlines a clear path to achieving net zero CO2 emissions for intra-European and departing flights by 2050. A4E airlines have also pledged to decarbonize air transport, making Europe the world's first carbon-neutral continent by 2050. Collaboration with policymakers, cross-sector efforts, and a focus on SAF deployment are key components of their sustainability drive.

Airports

ACI

While airports are responsible for a smaller portion of CO2 emissions than jet fuel combustion, they too are actively engaged in the fight against climate change. Airline services and route networks ultimately decide the success or failure of any airport. As global environmental concerns grow, navigating air service development towards sustainable aviation will be a key challenge going forward for all stakeholders including airports. The FAA for instance is taking action to reduce greenhouse gas emissions and working on making infrastructure more resilient. To achieve this, it offers grant programs to support these goals. Support programs such as Voluntary Airport Low Emissions and Zero Emission Vehicle provide funding for electric ground support equipment, solar energy systems, and electric vehicle infrastructure. In addition, an Energy Efficiency Program helps airports identify and implement energy-saving measures.

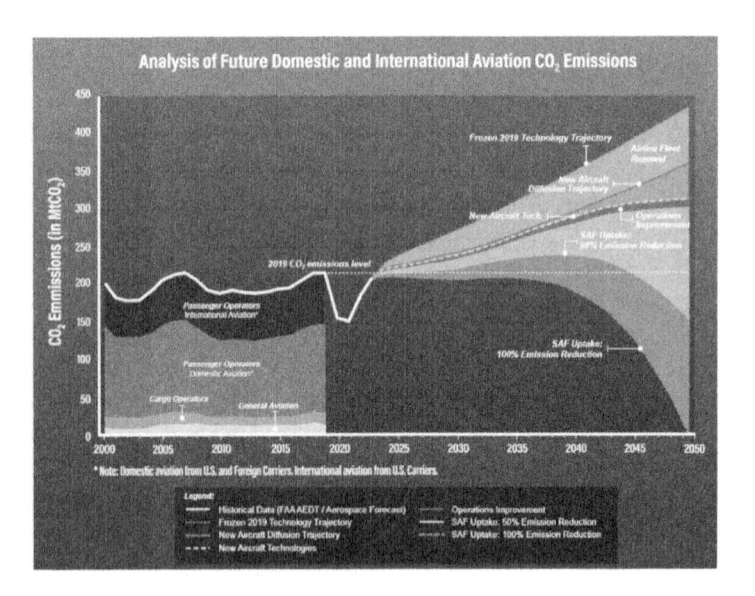

Image from FAA.gov

Chicago O'Hare International Airport

O'Hare International Airport, managed by the Chicago Department of Aviation (CDA), has made significant strides in promoting sustainability. At the heart of their efforts is the Sustainable Airport Manual (SAM), a document that provides guidance for airport design, construction, operations, and maintenance projects. Developed with input from over 200 stakeholders, including airports, airlines, and sustainability experts, the SAM offers airport-specific strategies. It includes the first airport rating system for sustainability projects, with 291 ratings completed for O'Hare and Midway projects. Endorsed by the U.S. Green Building Council (USGBC), the Federal Aviation Administration (FAA), and the U.S. Environmental Protection Agency (USEPA), the SAM ensures that sustainability principles are integrated into every aspect of airport development.

O'Hare 21 for example, is a transformative plan aimed at revolutionizing O'Hare International Airport, one of the busiest airports in the world. The collaborative effort between the City of Chicago and airline partners seeks to elevate O'Hare's status by enhancing its infrastructure, capacity, and passenger experience. Key components include terminal expansion, concourse modernization, runway enhancements, state-of-the-art amenities, and sustainability integration. Collaborations Under the O'Hare 21 plan, the City of Chicago and airline partners are investing $8.5 billion to transform O'Hare. This initiative aims to expand capacity, improve connectivity, and enhance customer service at passenger terminal facilities. Sustainability strategies from the SAM are being seamlessly incorporated into all O'Hare 21 design, construction, operations, and maintenance projects. Additionally, the CDA collaborates with the U.S. Department of Energy's National Renewable Energy Laboratory (NREL) to advise on environmentally sustainable initiatives. Their joint efforts emphasize energy-efficient practices and sustainable infrastructure.

ACI Europe

ACI Europe representing the European airport community has taken steps to support the goals of the Paris Agreement to combat climate change. They reaffirmed their commitment to reducing carbon emissions from airport operations, as outlined in previous agreements and initiatives such as Airport Carbon Accreditation. Recognizing the urgent need for action on climate change, informed by scientific reports including those from the UN IPCC, they emphasized the importance of limiting global warming and achieving net zero emissions by 2050. This aligned with the European Commission's vision for a climate-neutral economy by 2050 and the EU Green Deal. European aviation, including airports, aimed to achieve net zero CO_2 emissions by 2050, as outlined in the "Destination 2050" roadmap. The resolution stressed the necessity for European airports to address both local and global environmental impacts sustainably, aiming for the full decarbonization of air transport over time. This involved reducing emissions as much as possible and investing in carbon removal and storage to achieve net zero emissions.

There are several key commitments by ACI Europe and its members regarding carbon emissions reduction in the aviation sector. They express their continued support for the ATAG 2050 net zero carbon goal, aiming for global civil aviation operations to achieve net zero carbon emissions by 2050. They also articulate their commitment to achieving net zero carbon emissions from airport operations within their control by 2050, with an emphasis on reducing absolute emissions and investing in carbon removal and storage. Member airports are individually committing to these goals, with over 270 European airports already committed to the 2050 target, and 128 aiming to achieve it by 2030. ACI Europe members pledged to provide a detailed Net Zero roadmap by May 31, 2024, and call on the EU and European governments to accelerate the clean energy transition to support airports in achieving their Net Zero commitment. They urge all ICAO Member States to align international aviation's climate target with the Paris Agreement and provide concrete implementation policies to guide states toward achieving net zero emissions.

ATAG

The Air Transport Action Group (ATAG) is a non-profit organization that brings together various stakeholders from the air transport industry globally. Its membership includes key players such as airframe and engine manufacturers, airlines, airports, air navigation service providers, and others, totaling around 40 organizations worldwide. ATAG aims to ensure the continued development of air transport while adhering to climate commitments, notably the Paris Agreement. Its primary mission is to lead the industry towards achieving net-zero carbon emissions for air transport by 2050. Through collaborative efforts, ATAG facilitates initiatives such as the commitment to fly net zero by 2050 and projects like Waypoint 2050, which explores strategies for achieving long-term climate goals in aviation. Additionally, ATAG coordinates representation and input to international governmental meetings concerning aviation and climate issues, such as those held by the International Civil Aviation Organization and the UNFCCC Conference of the Parties.

ATAG, with the backing of its members, engages in a variety of activities to promote unity and progress within the aviation industry. They advocate for collaborative action and develop cohesive positions to advance the industry's shared vision. Additionally, ATAG contributes expertise to governmental and UN processes, facilitating coordinated industry representation at pertinent meetings. Through conducting studies, they gather reliable data on air transport's contributions to various aspects such as job creation, trade, connectivity, tourism, and disaster response, ensuring informed decision-making. ATAG establishes cross-sector working groups to address aviation's significant challenges collectively. They also prioritize education by creating accessible resources, including the www.aviationbenefits.org website, publications, and videos, freely available to the public. ATAG develops toolkits for members to enhance their communication efforts on specific issues. Lastly, they host informative sessions like the Global Sustainable Aviation Summits and Forums, fostering collaboration among aviation sectors, governments, environmental groups, and other stakeholders.

Other Regions

Masdar City in Abu Dhabi is pioneering a sustainable aviation future with the world's first commercial-scale Methanol to Jet (MTJ) facility. This project captures carbon dioxide, combines it with green hydrogen from renewable sources, and converts it into jet fuel, significantly reducing the environmental impact of air travel. The MTJ facility positions the UAE as a leader in sustainable aviation solutions, serves as a springboard for wider adoption of cleaner fuels, and thrives within Masdar City's innovation ecosystem to propel the future of sustainable flight.

OFFSETS AND CARBON CAPTURE

Offsetting Carbon Reductions

The path towards net-zero emissions in aviation necessitates exploring additional measures, even with advancements in technology and operations. This is where offsets and carbon capture technologies come into play. They act as balancing tools, compensating for emissions that are challenging to eliminate entirely.

Airlines, for example, emit a certain amount of carbon dioxide during flights. To "offset" this emission, they can invest in projects elsewhere that reduce or remove an equivalent amount of carbon dioxide from the atmosphere. These projects might involve initiatives like planting trees, investing in renewable energy sources, or capturing methane gas from landfills. Airlines can compensate for their emissions and contribute to global emission reduction efforts through supporting such endeavors.

Carbon capture technology directly captures carbon dioxide emissions from various sources, including power plants or directly from the air. The captured CO2 can then be stored underground or even utilized to create products like synthetic fuels or building materials. While still under development, carbon capture technologies hold promises for the future of aviation by offering a way to remove emissions from the atmosphere.

Both offsets and carbon capture play a role in achieving net-zero aviation emissions. They are not intended to replace direct emission reductions through fuel efficiency and technological advancements but rather serve as complementary tools to bridge the gap.

Ensuring the credibility of offset projects and their genuine contribution to emission reductions is crucial. Carbon capture technologies are still evolving and can be expensive. The focus lies in making them more affordable and scalable for wider adoption. While offsets and carbon capture can address current emissions, the goal remains to transition to sustainable aviation fuels and zero-emission aircraft to eliminate emissions altogether.

Governments and policymakers play a crucial role in supporting initiatives such as the ICAO Carbon Offsetting and Reduction Scheme for International Aviation (CORSIA). It is essential to ensure the continued evolution of CORSIA and to set long-term CO2 goals through ICAO. Avoiding duplication of market mechanisms and basing domestic measures on CORSIA principles are vital steps forward. Collaboration with fellow governments to conclude UNFCCC Article 6 discussions and promoting the development of carbon capture and removal opportunities are also key priorities.

Sustainability pledges, particularly those related to carbon offsetting, are becoming increasingly common across industries. However, it's crucial that these pledges are not merely symbolic but are grounded in tangible actions and genuine efforts to mitigate environmental impact. The challenge lies in ensuring the transparency and effectiveness of carbon offset projects. Often, the intricacies of offsetting practices can be overlooked, leading to uncertainties about their actual environmental benefits. There is a risk of greenwashing, where companies may engage in superficial or misleading sustainability efforts to enhance their image without making substantial progress.

To address these concerns, it's imperative to scrutinize offsetting projects rigorously and ensure they genuinely contribute to emissions reductions beyond what would have occurred naturally or through regulatory compliance. This requires transparency in project selection, implementation, and verification processes. Additionally, there should be mechanisms in place to identify and eliminate instances of greenwashing or insincere commitments. In the corporate sphere, sustainability efforts should extend beyond superficial gestures by integrating genuine environmental stewardship into core business strategies and operations. This necessitates a cultural shift where sustainability is ingrained in corporate values rather than merely being a checkbox exercise for marketing purposes.

A challenge arises from the uneven distribution of growth of air traffic across the globe. As political landscapes shape technological and policy responses to climate change, emerging economies emerge as important players. Their burgeoning demand for air travel necessitates equitable access to the opportunities enjoyed by established economies.

Approximately 80% of air transport emissions stem from flights exceeding 1,500 kilometers in length, leaving us with limited alternatives. Yet, since the dawn of the jet age, advancements in technology have propelled us forward, enhancing fuel efficiency by over 80%. This progress, embodied in the development of innovative airframes and engines, forms the backbone of our endeavors to reconcile growth with environmental responsibility.

Overcoming these challenges requires a coordinated effort on a global scale. International rules, administered through institutions such as the International Civil Aviation Organization (ICAO), serve as our compass in this endeavor. Here, we must support economic growth while curbing CO_2 emissions. The aviation industry has assumed a leadership role, advocating for the adoption of global climate standards and leading efforts to establish long-term goals for emissions reduction.

Operational and infrastructure enhancements, coupled with advancements in fleet utilization, have paved the way for a significant reduction in CO_2 emissions.

There is sometimes hesitance to transition to newer technologies when fuel prices are at low levels as airlines make the economies of the older aircraft work. The transition towards embracing radical new technologies demands significant financial commitments from commercial aerospace entities, alongside robust support from research institutions and governments alike. From conception to certification, the pathway to integrating novel technologies into the aviation ecosystem is arduous but essential. It entails not only the development of prototypes but also their refinement into commercially viable products, ready to navigate the rigorous testing and certification procedures essential for ensuring safety and reliability in the skies.

While CO_2 garners much of the spotlight due to its enduring presence in the atmosphere and its significant role in driving long-term climate change, it is but one constituent of the complex cocktail expelled from the exhaust of jet engines. The aggregate impact of aviation extends beyond CO_2 emissions, encompassing various greenhouse gases and particulate matter.

CO_2, comprising a modest 5% to 6% of the exhaust, while water vapor, nitrogen oxides, unburned hydrocarbons, carbon monoxide, sulfur oxides, and assorted compounds constitute the rest. These emissions intermingle, influencing the delicate balance of Earth's atmospheric composition.

It's crucial to understand that not all gases contribute equally to climate change. While carbon dioxide (CO_2) holds sway as the most notorious greenhouse gas due to its longevity in the atmosphere, gases like methane, originating from agricultural and waste sources, wield a stronger but fleeting influence on climate.

Among the visible manifestations of aircraft activity are contrails, wispy streaks trailing through certain atmospheric regions. Composed of ice crystals formed from the condensation of water vapor emitted during the combustion process within engines, these ephemeral trails resemble natural clouds.

Understanding the climate implications of contrails remains a complex endeavor, shrouded in uncertainties despite strides in research. Recent investigations suggest that while contrail-induced cirrus clouds may exert a cooling effect during the day, they could conversely contribute to nighttime warming, echoing the behavior of conventional clouds.

Interestingly, strategies exist to mitigate contrail formation, such as altering flight paths to avoid super-saturated cold air zones or adjusting cruising altitudes. However, these maneuvers come with trade-offs, potentially increasing fuel consumption and CO_2 emissions. Yet, the imperative to minimize any surplus CO_2 emissions persists.

Airlines and aviation experts are collaborating with research teams to delve deeper into contrail impacts. While prospects seem promising for mitigating contrails with minimal CO_2 repercussions, the overarching challenge lies in acquiring reliable meteorological data and streamlining flight routes in congested airspace.

Technological advancements offer promising solutions to address both CO_2 and non-CO_2 impacts of aviation. Sustainable aviation fuels, devoid of sulfur and aromatic hydrocarbons, hold potential to reduce contrail formation by producing cleaner exhaust. Electric and hydrogen propulsion systems offer avenues for virtually eliminating contrail formation.

Carbon Offsetting

In the flight plan towards carbon neutrality by 2050, we're considering the role of carbon markets and potential evolutions in offsetting emissions. Offset mechanisms, such as out-of-sector carbon reductions and market-based measures, could complement sustainable aviation fuels (SAF) in achieving our industry goals. While SAF aims to cover 90% of our liquid fuel requirements, the remaining emissions to achieve net-zero will likely require out-of-sector carbon reduction measures. However, forecasts for the types of offsets available in 2050 are scarce, as current offset markets may mature by then. Yet, international carbon pricing mechanisms, like those under the Paris Agreement, provide avenues for cooperation among nations to mitigate emissions. Despite existing carbon pricing mechanisms for aviation, such as CORSIA, striking a balance between incentivization policies and airlines' financial capabilities is crucial. Looking ahead, we anticipate a substantial contribution from out-of-sector carbon reduction measures to achieve our decarbonization targets by 2050.

CORSIA

Carbon credit products, such as Verified Emission Reductions (VERs) and Certified Emission Reductions (CERs), are evolving under the Paris Agreement. These credits stem from various projects, including energy efficiency, renewable energy, land use, industrial greenhouse gas offsets, and methane capture. CORSIA, the Carbon Offsetting and Reduction Scheme for International Aviation, established in 2016 by ICAO, aims to offset 80% of the growth in international aviation CO2 emissions from 2020 onwards. Initially voluntary, it becomes mandatory for most countries in later years. CORSIA's phased implementation ensures gradual inclusion of flights and emphasizes real emissions reductions through rigorous criteria for emissions unit integrity.

CORSIA requires airplane operators to offset their CO2 emissions by purchasing and canceling emissions units. Originally, CORSIA planned to use the average annual emissions between 2019 and 2020 as a baseline, but due to the COVID-19 pandemic's impact on aviation, only 2019 emissions will be used for the pilot phase (2021-2023), with subsequent phases basing 85% of emissions on 2019 levels (2024-2035). All international civilian airplane operations fall under CORSIA, except for humanitarian, medical, and firefighting flights. Carbon offsetting allows companies or individuals to compensate for their emissions by financing emission reductions elsewhere, providing a viable option for sectors with limited emissions reduction potential. Carbon markets and offsetting have long been essential for global emission reduction policies, offering effective mechanisms to combat climate change. Various methods, such as renewable energy projects, can be used for offsets, bringing additional social, environmental, and economic benefits.

Several countries have introduced or considered carbon pricing mechanisms, including taxes and emissions trading schemes. CORSIA operates at a global level alongside these regional and city-level initiatives. CORSIA is subject to regular performance reviews, with potential for a future global market-based measure beyond 2035. The International Civil Aviation Organization (ICAO) established the International Standards and Recommended Practices (SARPs) for CORSIA to regulate carbon offsetting. Initially adopted in June 2018, these SARPs were updated in July 2023 to reflect the outcome of a periodic review, taking effect from January 1, 2024. Annex 16, Volume IV, outlines rules for CORSIA administration, including emissions monitoring, reporting, verification, and emissions unit cancellation. Member states must align their national regulations with these SARPs to maintain market integrity and environmental standards. The periodic review, conducted every three years starting in 2022, evaluates CORSIA's impact on states, operators, and aviation, aiming to improve implementation and minimize market distortions. Notably, a review in 2022 led to adjustments in CORSIA's design elements, particularly in baseline calculations. CORSIA, the Carbon Offsetting and Reduction Scheme for International Aviation, applies solely to international flights, excluding domestic flights between two aerodromes within the same state. The categorization of a flight as international disregards the operator's nationality or the airspace used. Even if a flight traverses foreign airspace or is operated by an entity from another state, it's deemed domestic if the departure and arrival are within the same state. Overseas territories are attributed to their respective states for CORSIA purposes. Each stage of a flight with intermediate stops is treated independently, regardless of landing nature. Operators must monitor, report, and verify CO_2 emissions from all international flights annually, with exemptions for state flights, operations with small aircraft, and certain humanitarian, medical, and firefighting operations. State flights encompass military, customs, and police services, discernible in the flight plan or supported by documentation. Humanitarian, medical, and firefighting flights, along with their preceding or following flights for operational purposes, are also exempt from CORSIA. Operators with annual CO_2 emissions exceeding 10,000 tons must report emissions annually, starting January 1, 2019, and develop an emissions monitoring plan for monitoring, reporting, and verification (MRV). This plan outlines operator details, fleet, operations, fuel monitoring methods, emission calculations, and data management. Approval by the administrating authority is necessary, ensuring compliance with MRV requirements. New entrants submit plans within three months of CORSIA scope inclusion. Approval assures satisfactory processes, but any significant plan changes necessitate resubmission. The plan's completeness and alignment with Annex 16 vol. IV are reviewed for adequacy. The plan's approval ensures adherence to MRV requirements. CO_2 emissions in international flights are typically based on actual fuel use, but some operators can use simplified monitoring. Eligible operators use the ICAO CORSIA CO_2 Estimation and Reporting Tool (CERT), which applies CO_2 Estimation Models (CEMs) to estimate emissions based on flight distance or block time. The CERT version must match the reporting year. Operators below specific emission thresholds qualify for simplified monitoring. After 2020, CERT can be used for certain flights based on emission levels. Exceeding thresholds mandates actual fuel use monitoring. Operators can choose to monitor fuel use instead of using CERT.

When operators monitor actual fuel use, they can choose from five fuel monitoring methods, each with specific data requirements. These methods must be applied consistently across all planes of the same type. Operators must use the same method during the baseline period and subsequent compliance cycles, with any changes approved by the administrating authority. While specific data points are required, operators have flexibility in how they collect this data, detailing their methods in their emissions monitoring plan. The plan needs to be approved by the administrative authority, ensuring satisfactory processes. The five monitoring methods include measurements after fuel uplifts, at block-on times, between block-off and block-on, based on fuel uplift volume, and using average fuel burn ratios by airplane type and block hours.

Offsets may undergo significant changes. Historically, they focused on emission avoidance, but future offsets will need to adapt to meet ambitious climate goals. Efforts like the Task Force on Scaling Voluntary Carbon Markets aim to enhance the efficiency and robustness of carbon markets. In the context of meeting climate targets, technologies like direct air capture (DAC) are gaining attention. DAC involves removing CO_2 directly from the atmosphere using large fans and chemical adsorbents. While still in its early stages, DAC shows promise for mitigating emissions, potentially benefiting sectors like aviation. Current DAC costs are high, but technological advancements could lower them. Scaling up DAC will require significant investment in renewable energy, chemical production, and CO2 storage infrastructure. DAC holds potential as a valuable tool in the fight against climate change, provided it can be proven effective and deployed globally.

Forestry Projects

Forestry projects have gained attention as a source of carbon credits, with efforts to protect forests becoming increasingly important in the fight against climate change. Forestry credits have seen a rise in demand, accounting for a significant portion of credits issued in recent years. Challenges such as ensuring permanent protection and avoiding double trading and determining if the projects are genuine and effective must be addressed. Additionally, there's a growing interest in natural climate solutions, including reforestation and peatland rehabilitation, which could not only prevent CO2 emissions but also remove CO2 from the atmosphere. Estimates suggest that these measures could potentially reduce up to 11.3 billion tons of carbon annually by 2050.

On the other hand, Carbon capture and storage (CCS) technology offers a means to capture and store CO2 emissions from fossil fuel use, preventing them from entering the atmosphere. While there's been skepticism about its widespread adoption, CCS is now recognized as a crucial component of global climate strategies by organizations like the IPCC and IEA.

Carbon sequestration, alongside conservation efforts, holds the key to achieving net zero carbon emissions. Despite its acknowledged importance, the deployment of carbon sequestration technology remains limited in scale thus far. Broadly speaking, carbon sequestration efforts fall into two main categories: natural sinks, which encompass natural carbon reservoirs like forests and agricultural lands that can absorb carbon dioxide through activities such as reforestation and afforestation, and carbon capture, utilization, and storage technologies (CCUS).

Carbon sequestration has yet to achieve widespread adoption and the economies of scale necessary for significant cost competitiveness, particularly when compared to other CO2-reducing technologies like renewables. Investments in carbon capture and storage (CCS) plants have been minimal over the past decade, comprising less than 1% of investments in renewable power. Despite this, we are still uncertain about the potential cost reductions if CCS were to benefit from economies of scale like those seen in solar and wind technologies. Much of the cost associated with carbon capture and storage arises from the sequestration process itself, with costs inversely correlated with the concentration of CO2 in the air stream.

CCS can significantly reduce emissions in energy-intensive industries and has gained traction in several countries. Plans for new CCS facilities are underway worldwide, with the next generation of plants expected to have lower costs.

In the long term, CCS could issue CO2 reduction certificates, potentially complementing offsets used by industries like aviation under schemes like CORSIA. This could help ensure a balanced supply of carbon credits, particularly as demand increases.

For aviation, the focus should initially be on reducing emissions within the sector, such as using alternative fuels. Partnerships with future offset providers will be crucial. Airlines should seek early engagement with providers in forestry, natural carbon sinks, and carbon capture opportunities to accelerate action and secure long-term offset agreements. Governments also have vital roles to play. Supporting initiatives like CORSIA and ensuring its continuous evolution to meet environmental ambitions are essential steps. Setting long-term CO2 goals for international aviation and avoiding duplication of market mechanisms are crucial policy proposals. Scaling operations and integrating global carbon prices pose hurdles, as seen in the EU Emissions Trading System's success in transitioning power generation but facing difficulties in establishing a global cap-and-trade market. Ensuring accurate measurement and verification of carbon offsets is crucial, despite consumer distrust, yet projects certified by standards like the Woodland Carbon Code and Peatland Code provide validated carbon credits, offering transparency. Effectiveness and avoiding greenwashing remain concerns, with critics questioning the true impact of carbon offsetting, emphasizing the importance of reducing emissions at the source. Exploring forestry projects such as Forest Conservation (REDD+), Improved Forest Management (IFM), and Afforestation, Reforestation, and Revegetation (ARR) initiatives reveal pathways to maintain carbon stocks, enhance carbon sequestration, and mitigate climate change.

Pursuing out-of-sector carbon reductions requires collaboration among governments. Concluding discussions on UNFCCC Article 6 is imperative for the success of schemes like CORSIA that rely on international carbon credits. Promoting the development of carbon capture opportunities, particularly direct air capture, and robust forestry accounting standards are also vital components of our flight plan toward carbon neutrality.

ICAO Global Coalition for Sustainable Aviation

The International Civil Aviation Organization (ICAO) has taken a significant step towards advancing sustainability in aviation by establishing the Global Coalition for Sustainable Aviation. This collaborative platform aims to accelerate progress towards environmentally responsible practices within the industry. Bringing together stakeholders from various sectors, including governments, airlines, manufacturers, fuel producers, international organizations, NGOs, research institutions, and academia, the Coalition targets several key areas to promote sustainability.

One primary focus of the Coalition is the reduction of greenhouse gas emissions. This involves supporting the development and deployment of sustainable aviation fuels (SAF), enhancing aircraft technology and operations for improved fuel efficiency, and implementing market-based measures like the Carbon Offsetting and Reduction Scheme for International Aviation (CORSIA). Additionally, efforts are directed towards mitigating noise pollution by advocating for quieter aircraft technologies and operational procedures to minimize disturbances to communities surrounding airports. Furthermore, the Coalition addresses the improvement of air quality by tackling emissions of pollutants such as nitrogen oxides and particulate matter through technological advancements and operational enhancements.

Central to the Coalition's mission is fostering collaboration among its members through various initiatives. These include sharing best practices and knowledge, developing common goals and roadmaps, supporting research and development efforts, advocating for policies and regulations that promote sustainable aviation, and raising public awareness about sustainability endeavors within the aviation industry. By facilitating cooperation among diverse stakeholders, the Global Coalition for Sustainable Aviation plays a vital role in driving the transition towards a more environmentally responsible and sustainable aviation sector. It is useful to know who the contributors are and what they are doing. Here is a summary of some of those initiatives.

Air Transat

Air Transat is committed to sustainability in aviation, as evident through its comprehensive "Traveller Care" program, organized around four key pillars. The airline actively reduces its carbon footprint by modernizing its fleet with fuel-efficient aircraft like the Airbus A321neoLR and implementing operational enhancements to optimize fuel consumption. Air Transat explores sustainable aviation fuel (SAF) technologies to significantly mitigate carbon emissions. Air Transat focuses on responsible waste management, minimizing single-use plastics and maximizing recycling and composting efforts, alongside investing in carbon offset projects. Through community engagement initiatives and transparent reporting, it demonstrates its commitment to sustainability.

Airbus

Airbus contributes to the coalition by spearheading the development of zero-emission aircraft concepts, particularly focusing on hydrogen aircraft. Airbus also actively contributes to the ITAKA project, which aims to develop and deploy Sustainable Aviation Fuels (SAF). It's involved in the Fello'fly project, which explores formation flights as a strategy to reduce CO_2 emissions.

Aireg

Aireg, the German Aviation Research and Innovation Initiative, is instrumental in promoting regenerative aviation fuels (SAF) in Germany. Through funding research, fostering collaboration among stakeholders, and raising public awareness, Aireg drives SAF development and adoption. As a result, there's increased investment, pilot projects, and supportive policies, marking significant progress towards a sustainable aviation sector in Germany.

Archer Aviation

Archer Aviation leads the way in sustainable urban mobility with its development of electric vertical take-off and landing (eVTOL) aircraft. These fully electric vehicles not only promise zero emissions but also boast significantly reduced noise pollution compared to traditional helicopters. Offering increased efficiency and lower operating costs, Archer's eVTOLs have the potential to revolutionize urban transportation by bypassing ground traffic congestion. Through partnerships and sustainable practices, Archer ensures that its innovative aircraft contribute to a cleaner and more efficient future for urban mobility.

Avikor

Avikor is revolutionizing access to Sustainable Aviation Fuels (SAF) through a comprehensive platform that connects stakeholders across the aviation industry. It streamlines procurement processes, promoting transparency and collaboration while advocating for supportive policies. Their platform simplifies SAF transactions, enabling airlines and other buyers to make informed decisions about SAF options, fostering trust and encouraging wider adoption. Their efforts contribute to increased SAF availability, reduced costs, and a significant reduction in aviation's carbon footprint, accelerating the industry's transition towards sustainability.

Brasil BioFuels (BBF)

Brasil BioFuels (BBF) is pioneering a sustainable energy matrix in the Amazon through vertically integrated biofuel development. By cultivating oil-rich crops in degraded areas, BBF ensures sustainability while engaging local communities. Advanced biofuel production technologies enable the production of biodiesel, renewable diesel, and biojet fuel, reducing dependence on fossil fuels. BBF's integrated logistics network optimizes transportation, while prioritizing social and environmental responsibility fosters economic development and land restoration. This approach offers a promising pathway towards a cleaner and more sustainable energy future in the Amazon.

C-SAF

C-SAF, or Canadian Sustainable Aviation Fuel, is a collaborative initiative aimed at expediting the commercial production and utilization of low-carbon SAF in Canada. Through funding, partnerships, knowledge sharing, and advocacy, C-SAF strives to bolster SAF adoption across the aviation industry. Through supporting research, development, and infrastructure projects, C-SAF enhances SAF production capacity, driving down costs and increasing availability at Canadian airports.

CFM International

CFM International, a collaboration between GE Aviation and Safran Aircraft Engines, is a key player in reducing CO2 emissions in aviation through engine technology advancements. Their focus on enhancing fuel efficiency and compatibility with Sustainable Aviation Fuels (SAF) has led to significant emission reductions. With a 40% cumulative decrease compared to older technologies, CFM continues to invest in research for even more sustainable engine solutions.

Canadian Advanced Air Mobility Consortium (CAAM

The Canadian Advanced Air Mobility Consortium (CAAM) is at the forefront of advancing Advanced Air Mobility (AAM) in Canada. Through collaborative efforts, CAAM brings together industry players, government agencies, academic institutions, and community organizations to address challenges and opportunities in the AAM sector. They emphasize sustainable practices, advocating for the use of electric propulsion systems and sustainable aviation fuels to minimize environmental impact. CAAM also supports innovation by providing funding and facilitating knowledge sharing between industry and academia, while advocating for policies that promote AAM development and adoption. Furthermore, CAAM engages in public outreach and education initiatives to inform Canadians about the benefits of AAM and address concerns, ensuring widespread acceptance and equitable access to AAM services across the country.

Cranfield University

Cranfield University's EnableH2 project is a pioneering endeavor aimed at researching and developing liquid hydrogen as a sustainable fuel for civil aviation. Through extensive research and development, the project focuses on various aspects, including fuel storage and handling, aircraft design, hydrogen infrastructure, safety, and regulations. Collaboration with industry partners, government agencies, and academia is key to sharing knowledge and resources to accelerate progress. The project also includes demonstrations and pilot projects to showcase the feasibility of using liquid hydrogen in real-world aviation scenarios. If successful, EnableH2 has the potential to significantly reduce greenhouse gas emissions, improve air quality, and contribute to energy independence in aviation.

Earth Day Canada

Earth Day Canada is a prominent environmental organization dedicated to driving ongoing action for the planet. Their efforts extend beyond the annual Earth Day celebration on April 22nd, focusing on empowering individuals, businesses, municipalities, and organizations to make lasting environmental impacts. Through educational programs, community engagement, business support, and advocacy, Earth Day Canada provides comprehensive resources and guidance on topics such as climate change, biodiversity, waste reduction, and sustainable living. They mobilize communities across the country through initiatives like tree planting projects, clean-up events, and advocacy campaigns, fostering collective action towards positive environmental change. It offers guidance and assistance to businesses seeking to adopt sustainable practices, while also advocating for robust environmental policies and regulations at all levels of government.

Eindhoven University of Technology

Eindhoven University of Technology (TU/e) in the Netherlands is leading pioneering research into advanced sustainable aviation fuels (SAF) derived from second-generation biomass. Its focus on low-cost and abundant biomass sources such as agricultural residues and wood waste is driving innovation in thermochemical conversion processes such as pyrolysis and gasification. TU/e is also investigating biomass pretreatment methods and developing advanced catalytic processes to upgrade bio-oil and syngas into high-quality SAF. By optimizing process integration and conducting sustainability assessments, TU/e aims to make SAF production economically viable and environmentally sustainable. Their research has the potential to significantly reduce the cost of SAF, increase production capacity, diversify feedstock sources, and ultimately reduce aviation's carbon footprint, contributing to a greener future for the industry.

Eurocontrol

Eurocontrol, the European Organization for the Safety of Air Navigation, is playing a key role in promoting sustainable air transport across Europe. Working with airlines, airports and air traffic management authorities, Eurocontrol implements initiatives to optimize air traffic management, reduce CO2 emissions and promote the use of sustainable aviation fuels (SAF). By advocating operational improvements, supporting research and development, and fostering partnerships, Eurocontrol's efforts contribute to significant reductions in fuel consumption and emissions, improved air quality, and the long-term competitiveness of the European aviation sector. Its leadership plays a crucial role in accelerating the transition to a more sustainable and environmentally responsible aviation industry in Europe.

Falcon Electric Aviation

Falcon Electric Aviation is pioneering the development of a sustainable and modular electric powertrain for the Cessna 150 aircraft. Their innovative approach involves replacing the traditional combustion engine with a fully electric propulsion system, offering benefits such as zero emissions, reduced noise pollution, and improved efficiency. The modular design of the powertrain allows for flexibility, cost-effectiveness, and scalability across different aircraft types. Committed to sustainability, Falcon sources materials responsibly, optimizes energy efficiency, and plans for end-of-life disposal. This project has the potential to significantly reduce greenhouse gas emissions, lower operating costs, increase accessibility to air travel, and promote innovation in the aviation industry, despite challenges in battery technology, charging infrastructure, and regulatory approvals.

GE Aviation

GE Aviation, a prominent figure in the aviation sector, is dedicated to pioneering sustainable solutions for the industry's future. They're spearheading the development of next-generation engine technologies like open fan architectures and hybrid-electric propulsion systems, aiming to boost efficiency, and cut emissions. Additionally, GE Aviation is actively advocating for the adoption of Sustainable Aviation Fuel (SAF), collaborating across the industry to ensure its safety and performance. They're also focused on achieving carbon-neutral operations by 2030, investing in renewable energy and enhancing energy efficiency. GE Aviation's initiatives not only reduce greenhouse gas emissions but also drive technological innovation and set industry standards for sustainability.

Groningen Airport Eelde (GAE)

Groningen Airport Eelde (GAE) in the Netherlands is at the forefront of sustainable airport operations, focusing on key initiatives to reduce its environmental impact. GAE is exploring hydrogen as a clean fuel source for ground vehicles and potentially aircraft and is investing in a solar farm to generate renewable electricity. In addition, GAE is emphasizing energy efficiency, sustainable materials, and waste management, while providing charging infrastructure for electric vehicles. Their collaborative approach is leading by example, reducing greenhouse gas emissions, improving air quality, and enhancing their competitiveness as a forward-thinking airport.

Honeywell Aerospace

Honeywell Aerospace provides the aviation industry with advanced fuel management software solutions that help airlines optimize fuel consumption and reduce environmental impact. Through data collection and analysis, the software identifies areas for efficiency improvement and provides tailored recommendations such as optimized flight paths, operational procedures, and weight management strategies. Airlines can monitor performance and track the effectiveness of implemented initiatives, resulting in reduced fuel consumption, lower greenhouse gas emissions and improved operational efficiency. Honeywell's software facilitates data-driven decision-making, enabling airlines to improve sustainability while reducing operating costs.

HyPoint

HyPoint is a pioneering hydrogen fuel cell systems tailored for aviation, offering a promising path to zero-emissions flight. With high power density, lightweight design and high efficiency, their systems maximize aircraft performance while emitting only water vapor. Its scalability and modular design allows it to adapt to a wide range of aircraft sizes, from drones to commercial airliners.

Hybrid Air Vehicles (HAV)

Hybrid Air Vehicles (HAV) is innovating airship technology with its Airlanders, offering a unique solution for sustainable transportation. By combining buoyant lift with aerodynamic properties and using fuel-efficient engines powered by Sustainable Aviation Fuels (SAF), Airlanders can achieve up to 90% emission reductions compared to conventional aircraft. Operating at lower speeds and providing point-to-point transportation, they reduce both fuel consumption and the need for airport infrastructure, while their versatility enables multiple applications. HAV's Airlanders have the potential to mitigate climate change, improve air quality, increase access to remote areas and create new economic opportunities, marking a significant step toward greener transportation.

International Airlines Group (IAG)

International Airlines Group (IAG) has set clear targets and a comprehensive strategy for sustainable aviation and carbon net zero by 2050. Its approach includes a low-carbon transition pathway integrated into its business strategy, management incentives aligned with sustainability goals, and transparent carbon disclosure. IAG is investing in key areas such as sustainable aviation fuels (SAF), future aircraft and low carbon technologies to drive industry transformation and reduce carbon emissions.

ISABE

The International Society for Air Breathing Engines (ISABE) serves as a platform for the global exchange of knowledge in air-breathing propulsion technologies, facilitating collaboration among experts through international conferences, publications, working groups, and educational initiatives. It fosters the dissemination of cutting-edge research and technical knowledge, ISABE accelerates innovation, promotes the development of more efficient and sustainable engines, and fosters global collaboration and capacity building.

ISAE-SUPAERO

ISAE-SUPAERO is an aerospace engineering institution in France at the forefront of research efforts to mitigate aviation-related greenhouse gas emissions and promote sustainable aviation practices. Its research spans several innovative solutions, including hydrogen aircraft propulsion and sustainable flight trajectories. By investigating hydrogen internal combustion engines and fuel cell technology, as well as exploring storage methods and infrastructure, ISAE-SUPAERO aims to realize hydrogen's potential as a clean aviation fuel. Its work on flight path optimization, continuous descent operations, and formation flying contributes to minimizing fuel consumption and emissions. ISAE-SUPAERO's research encompasses sustainable aviation fuels, aircraft design, materials, and life cycle analysis, all of which collectively advance the environmental sustainability of aviation.

The International Association for Sustainable Aviation (IASA)

The International Association for Sustainable Aviation (IASA) plays a key role in advancing sustainability in the aviation industry by fostering collaboration among stakeholders worldwide. Through knowledge-sharing platforms such as conferences and workshops, IASA facilitates the exchange of best practices and lessons learned in various sustainability areas, from sustainable aviation fuels to operational efficiency. It promotes industry-wide standards and initiatives and works to ensure a harmonized approach to sustainability while advocating for supportive policies and regulations to incentivize the adoption of sustainable practices. IASA engages in public outreach and education to raise awareness of the importance of sustainable aviation and to build public support for the industry's efforts.

Istanbul Airport

Istanbul Airport (IST), as a major international airport, aligns its sustainability efforts with both national regulations and international standards. It complies with Turkish environmental laws and holds ISO 14001 certification, showcasing its commitment to environmental management. It implements various initiatives like energy efficiency, renewable energy adoption, and waste management, setting a precedent for sustainable airport management in the region.

Joby Aviation

Joby Aviation develops electric vertical take-off and landing (eVTOL) aircraft, offering a sustainable urban transportation solution with zero emissions and low noise levels. Their fully electric aircraft significantly reduce air pollution and noise pollution in cities.

NACO (Netherlands Airport Consultants)

NACO (Netherlands Airport Consultants), a leading international airport consultancy and engineering firm, places sustainability at the forefront of its services, aiming to minimize environmental impact and support airports in achieving sustainability objectives. Through sustainable airport design, operational efficiency optimization, environmental management, and innovation integration, NACO fosters positive outcomes such as reduced energy consumption and emissions, enhanced passenger experience, and global impact in shaping a more environmentally responsible aviation industry.

NESTE

Neste, a global leader in renewable and circular solutions, is aiding the aviation industry in meeting its ambitious emission reduction targets. As the foremost producer of Sustainable Aviation Fuel (SAF), Neste significantly lowers greenhouse gas emissions compared to conventional jet fuel. Through several key initiatives, Neste contributes to a more sustainable aviation sector by producing SAF from renewable and sustainable feedstocks like used cooking oil and animal fat waste. They are continually expanding production capabilities and collaborate across the aviation supply chain to ensure SAF availability worldwide. They also invest in technological innovation, researching new feedstocks and production methods to further enhance SAF sustainability.

Norsk e-Fuel

Norsk e-Fuel, a Norwegian company, is pioneering the production of sustainable aviation fuels (SAF) by harnessing captured carbon dioxide (CO_2) and renewable energy. Their innovative approach involves three key steps, capturing CO_2 from industrial sources, utilizing renewable energy sources like wind and solar power, and employing power-to-liquid (PtL) technology to create SAF. This process results in SAF with up to 85% fewer lifecycle greenhouse gas emissions compared to conventional jet fuel. Notably, Norsk e-Fuel's SAF is a drop-in fuel compatible with existing aircraft engines, facilitating its adoption by airlines and accelerating the transition to sustainable aviation.

Northvolt

Northvolt, a Swedish company, is leading the charge in developing and manufacturing sustainable battery cells with the aim of building the "world's greenest battery." Their approach focuses on several key areas: employing 100% renewable energy in their battery factories, incorporating recycled materials into their cells, and minimizing waste and emissions throughout production. Northvolt's commitment to sustainability extends to producing high-performance battery cells designed for longevity and efficiency, suitable for various applications like electric vehicles and energy storage systems.

Oceania Biofuels

Oceania Biofuels is spearheading the development of a cutting-edge Sustainable Aviation Fuel (SAF) production facility in Gladstone, Australia, leveraging existing feedstock supply chains and proven technology. It uses waste materials such as used cooking oil and tallow. They promote a circular economy while ensuring a sustainable source of feedstock. Partnering with leading technology providers, Oceania Biofuels aims to produce high-quality SAF that meets aviation fuel standards, contributing to greenhouse gas emissions reduction in the aviation sector. Situated strategically near transportation infrastructure, the facility facilitates efficient SAF distribution across Australia and the region, fostering economic growth and job creation in the Gladstone region.

OpenAirlines' SkyBreathe®

OpenAirlines' SkyBreathe® platform is aimed at improving fuel efficiency for airlines, providing a suite of tools to optimize operations and reduce environmental impact. It collects and analyzes data from multiple sources, including aircraft sensors and operational data and SkyBreathe® identifies areas for fuel savings. It provides actionable recommendations for optimized flight paths, operational procedures and aircraft weight management, enabling airlines to reduce fuel burn and greenhouse gas emissions. Pilot engagement is fostered through personalized feedback and fuel-saving tips, while performance monitoring enables continuous improvement.

Pipistrel

Pipistrel, the Slovenian aircraft manufacturer, stands at the forefront of electric and sustainable aviation, notably with its groundbreaking Velis Electro, the world's first certified electric aircraft. This two-seat marvel, certified by the European Union Aviation Safety Agency (EASA), boasts zero tailpipe emissions, reduced noise pollution, and lower operational costs. Pipistrel's dedication extends beyond electric propulsion, as they actively research hydrogen-powered aircraft and other low-carbon concepts, aiming to further mitigate aviation's environmental footprint. Embracing sustainable design and manufacturing practices, Pipistrel pioneers lightweight materials and aerodynamic efficiency, significantly impacting the industry with reduced greenhouse gas emissions, lower noise levels, and enhanced economic viability.

Prometheus Fuels

Prometheus Fuels is revolutionizing the aviation industry with its pioneering technology, employing a process dubbed "combustion in reverse" to produce Sustainable Aviation Fuel (SAF). This innovative method begins with the capture of carbon dioxide (CO2) from diverse sources, including industrial emissions and the atmosphere itself. Pairing renewable electricity, like solar or wind power, the process utilizes electrolysis to split water molecules into hydrogen and oxygen. These elements are then combined in a reactor with captured CO2 to generate synthetic hydrocarbons, effectively reversing the combustion process. The resulting SAF meets stringent aviation fuel standards, offering a host of benefits. Prometheus Fuels' SAF supports circular economy principles while boasting scalability and feedstock flexibility. Moreover, as a drop-in fuel compatible with existing aircraft engines can facilitate seamless adoption by airlines, accelerating the industry's transition to sustainability.

Qatar Airways

Qatar Airways is actively pursuing strategies to minimize its environmental footprint and enhance fuel efficiency, showcasing its commitment to sustainability in the aviation sector. The airline is implementing initiatives aimed at reducing aircraft weight, optimizing flight routes, and minimizing energy consumption during ground operations. It also invests in lightweight materials, optimizing cabin configurations, and employing efficient galley equipment to reduce aircraft weight and improving fuel efficiency. Furthermore, advanced flight planning software enables the identification of optimal routes and altitudes, while direct routings and continuous descent approaches contribute to fuel savings and noise reduction. The airline reviews energy usage during taxiing, promoting single engine taxiing procedures, exploring electric taxiing systems, and utilizing ground power units to minimize emissions. These efforts collectively contribute to reducing fuel consumption, minimizing environmental impact, improving operational efficiency, and positioning Qatar Airways as a leader in sustainability.

Rolls-Royce

Rolls-Royce is driving innovation and collaboration to foster a more sustainable future for aviation. Key elements of their commitment include advocacy for Sustainable Aviation Fuels (SAF), with a focus on accelerating SAF production and infrastructure development. Their in-production engines are certified for 50% SAF blends, with plans to achieve full compatibility. They also invest heavily in next-generation engine technologies like the UltraFan, boasting a 25% fuel efficiency enhancement. Their exploration of open fan architectures and hybrid-electric propulsion systems further underscores their dedication to fuel efficiency and emissions reduction. Embracing electrification and hydrogen, Rolls-Royce actively pioneers projects for electric and hydrogen-powered aircraft, from small-scale electric propulsion to larger-scale hydrogen fuel cell technology. Complementing technological advancements, Rolls-Royce collaborates with airlines and air traffic management to optimize flight operations, alongside investing in carbon offsetting initiatives to counterbalance unavoidable emissions.

Rotterdam The Hague Airport

Rotterdam The Hague Airport (RTHA) is taking a transformative role as an innovation partner for sustainable development, going beyond traditional airport sustainability initiatives to become a driving force for broader environmental progress in the region. Central to their approach is a proactive stance on Sustainable Aviation Fuels (SAF), actively promoting and facilitating their use by airlines operating at the airport, while exploring options for on-site production of SAF. RTHA is also at the forefront of preparing for the rise of electric and hybrid aircraft, investing in infrastructure and regulations to support their operation, and working closely with industry stakeholders to advance their development and adoption. As an innovation hub, RTHA fosters partnerships with startups, research institutions and other stakeholders to incubate and test cutting-edge technologies to accelerate progress in sustainable aviation. In addition, RTHA's commitment extends beyond its borders as it works with regional partners to advance sustainable development initiatives that include transportation, renewable energy, and circular economy practices. This comprehensive approach positions RTHA as a catalyst for change, accelerating the transition to sustainable aviation while promoting economic development and environmental stewardship in the region. Through its visionary leadership and collaborative spirit, RTHA is setting a compelling example for airports worldwide, demonstrating the transformative potential of embracing sustainability as a driver of innovation and progress.

SATAVIA

SATAVIA is harnessing the power of cloud-based data analytics and advanced atmospheric modeling. At the core of its solutions is a sophisticated platform that ingests and analyzes diverse data streams, enabling airlines to optimize operations and minimize environmental impact. Of particular importance is SATAVIA's contrail avoidance flight planning, enabled by state-of-the-art atmospheric models. SATAVIA helps airlines design routes that mitigate contrail formation, thereby reducing their climate impact. This innovation not only curbs emissions that contribute to global warming, but also saves fuel and improves operational efficiency. SATAVIA's approach exemplifies a data-driven strategy for aviation sustainability, providing airlines with tangible tools to navigate toward a greener future.

Sasol

Sasol, a global leader in energy and chemicals, boasts over seven decades of expertise in Fischer-Tropsch (FT) technology, pioneering the conversion of diverse feedstocks like coal, natural gas, and biomass into valuable fuels and chemicals. Sasol contributes significantly to sustainability by diversifying feedstock utilization, exploring sustainable alternatives like biomass, and reducing reliance on finite fossil resources. Their production of cleaner-burning fuels with lower emissions aligns with stringent environmental standards, improving air quality and mitigating climate change. Sasol's active involvement in carbon capture and utilization initiatives further minimizes greenhouse gas emissions, fostering a circular carbon economy.

Signol

Signol harnesses the power of behavioral science and data analytics to revolutionize sustainability efforts by providing personalized performance feedback and targets. Through their platform, operational data from various sources is meticulously collected and analyzed, enabling the identification of areas for improvement. Applying insights from behavioral science, Signol tailors feedback and targets to individuals and teams, making them actionable and relevant. The impacts include reduced fuel consumption and emissions, heightened operational efficiency, increased employee engagement, and data-driven decision-making. Signol's innovative approach empowers organizations to make meaningful strides towards sustainability, leveraging behavioral science and data analytics.

SkyNRG

Central to SkyNRG's mission is the careful management of SAF, from sourcing to distribution, ensuring that it meets stringent sustainability standards. SkyNRG ensures the availability and accessibility of SAF, while managing its blending and distribution to meet specific airline needs. Crucially, its rigorous certification system ensures the sustainability of SAF throughout the supply chain, resulting in real reductions in greenhouse gas emissions. It addresses the cost barrier by co-financing the price gap, making SAF more affordable for airlines and stimulating demand. This strategic approach not only increases SAF availability, but also fosters collaboration and industry leadership.

Skyports

Skyports is leading the development of essential infrastructure for the Advanced Air Mobility (AAM) industry, focusing on the design, construction, and operation of Vertiports, central hubs for air taxi and cargo drone operations in urban environments. Their Vertiports are meticulously designed to ensure safety, efficiency, and environmental sustainability, with optimized landing pads, charging infrastructure, and passenger/cargo facilities. Skyports builds and manages these facilities, maintaining the highest operational standards and facilitating seamless integration with existing transportation systems. It works closely with government agencies to develop standards and regulations essential to the safety and long-term viability of the industry, while engaging communities to foster public acceptance.

Smart Airport Systems

Smart Airport Systems (SAS) is helping improve airport operations with a keen eye on sustainability, driven by three core objectives. First, they prioritize fuel savings for airlines through innovative solutions such as Follow the Greens, which streamlines aircraft taxi routes with dynamic green lights, reducing taxi times and fuel consumption. SAS optimizes ground operations, reducing idle time and unnecessary fuel burn during aircraft turnarounds, while providing airlines with valuable data-driven insights to improve flight planning and fuel efficiency. Second, SAS is working to reduce noise and emissions by working with air traffic management to implement more efficient arrival and departure procedures, advocating the use of ground power units rather than auxiliary power units, and promoting the use of Sustainable Aviation Fuels (SAF). It also drives operational efficiency at airports through collaborative decision making (CDM) initiatives, resource management optimization software, and predictive maintenance analytics that promote real-time information sharing and proactive maintenance practices. While SAS isn't directly involved in the development of new aircraft technologies, its focus on optimizing existing infrastructure and operations demonstrates its key role in advancing sustainable aviation practices and paving the way for a greener future for the industry through collaboration with airports, airlines, and air traffic management.

SmartEnergy

SmartEnergy takes a comprehensive approach to the entire green energy value chain. They specialize in the identification of renewable energy resources, conducting thorough assessments that include solar, wind, hydro, geothermal and biomass options. This includes analysis of resource availability, environmental impact, and economic feasibility. They excel in project development, identifying and nurturing viable green energy projects while navigating factors such as energy demand, grid infrastructure, and regulatory frameworks. They also provide market analysis services, identifying opportunities for green energy integration based on energy market dynamics and government incentives. In the development phase, SmartEnergy helps secure project financing, integrates appropriate technologies, and ensures seamless project management from inception to completion. In the delivery phase, they manage construction, installation, grid integration, and ongoing operations and maintenance, ensuring compliance with quality, safety, and regulatory standards.

The Solar Impulse Foundation

The Solar Impulse Foundation is dedicated to facilitating the transition to a sustainable future by identifying and promoting clean technologies. At the heart of its mission is the Solar Impulse Efficient Solution label, awarded to technologies that meet strict criteria in terms of environmental impact, economic viability, and technological maturity. Leveraging a network of experts and an open platform, the Foundation evaluates and validates solutions in sectors such as energy, transport, and agriculture. They catalyze the adoption of clean technologies by curating a portfolio of labeled solutions and facilitating connections between developers and stakeholders. Through advocacy and awareness initiatives, the Foundation amplifies the importance of clean solutions and bridges the gap between innovators and potential users. While the Foundation does not directly invest in or develop technologies, its role as a catalyst and advocate is critical to accelerating the transition to sustainability.

SpiceJet

SpiceJet, a prominent Indian airline, made aviation history with India's inaugural Sustainable Aviation Fuel (SAF) test flight in February 2023, flying from Dehradun to Delhi. The flight, powered by a blend of 25% SAF and 75% conventional jet fuel, showcased the airline's commitment to environmental sustainability and carbon footprint reduction. Utilizing SAF derived from used cooking oil, the test flight highlighted a promising alternative to fossil fuels, capable of slashing carbon emissions by up to 80% over its lifecycle. In collaboration with CSIR-Indian Institute of Petroleum (IIP), SpiceJet spearheaded this endeavor, backed by government support for SAF adoption and policy exploration.

Starburst

Starburst offers tailored support for startups, including mentorship, funding access, and global networking opportunities, Starburst nurtures emerging technologies from conception to market integration. It facilitates open innovation initiatives, propelling collaboration to tackle industry challenges and pioneer groundbreaking solutions for sustainable aerospace. Through curated events, Starburst cultivates a culture of innovation, fostering knowledge exchange and networking within the aerospace ecosystem.

Sustainable Aviation, UK

Sustainable Aviation (SA) represents a concerted effort within the UK aviation sector to tackle environmental concerns by advocating for Sustainable Aviation Fuels (SAF), promoting noise reduction measures, and championing smarter aviation practices through technological innovation and collaboration. Since its inception in 2005, SA has led initiatives to decarbonize aviation, minimize noise pollution, enhance operational efficiency, leveraging partnerships across airlines, airports, manufacturers, and regulatory bodies.

TU Delft

TU Delft, a leading Dutch university, is driving sustainable aviation research and development on several fronts. Through initiatives focused on aerodynamics, lightweight materials and advanced engine technologies, the university aims to improve aircraft efficiency and reduce fuel consumption. TU Delft is also investing in alternative modes of transportation such as high-speed rail and electric vehicles, while optimizing air traffic management systems to minimize fuel consumption. Working with industry partners, the university is developing sustainable aviation fuels from renewable sources and exploring hydrogen technology for cleaner air operations.

To70

To70, a prominent aviation consultancy firm, is dedicated to shaping sustainable aviation through innovative projects tailored for airports, airlines, and industry stakeholders. Their focus on sustainability spans various areas, including the implementation of Sustainable Aviation Fuel (SAF), carbon management at airports, sustainable airport design and operations, and community engagement for noise mitigation. To70's approach involves conducting feasibility studies, developing SAF blending facilities, and optimizing energy efficiency. They also integrate renewable energy sources into airport operations, promote sustainable ground transportation, and facilitate effective waste management. It engages in noise monitoring, analysis, and mitigation strategies, fostering community collaboration to address noise concerns.

The University of Tennessee Space Institute (UTSI)

The University of Tennessee Space Institute (UTSI) is a leading research institution specializing in aerospace engineering and propulsion technologies, with a particular emphasis on advancing hydrogen combustion research. UTSI's researchers delve into premixed combustion dynamics, employing computational modeling and experimental validation to optimize combustion parameters and predict flame behavior. They focus on developing hydrogen-specific injector designs using advanced manufacturing techniques to enhance fuel-air mixing and combustion efficiency. UTSI investigates flame stabilization mechanisms and lean combustion techniques for stable and efficient hydrogen-air mixtures, crucial for reducing emissions and improving fuel economy. UTSI's research holds promise for the future of sustainable aviation, contributing to the development of hydrogen-powered aircraft with significantly reduced carbon emissions.

Urban Aeronautics

Urban Aeronautics is improving urban air mobility with its innovative rotor design, showcased in the "CityHawk" project. With its internal rotor design, CityHawk offers reduced noise pollution, enhanced safety with minimized risk of blade strikes, and the ability to operate in compact urban spaces. Its optimized aerodynamics and hybrid propulsion system promise high efficiency and extended range, while redundant systems and low-speed flight capability ensure safety in urban environments. Although still in development, Urban Aeronautics' focus on safety and efficiency positions the CityHawk as a promising solution for alleviating urban congestion and improving mobility.

Urban-Air Port (UAP)

Urban-Air Port (UAP) is leading the development of innovative urban air mobility (UAM) infrastructure solutions in the UK, with the aim of decarbonizing cities through a holistic approach. In addition to providing landing and take-off facilities for electric vertical take-off and landing (eVTOL) aircraft, UAP designs and builds modular vertiports with integrated charging infrastructure powered by renewable energy sources. These hubs seamlessly integrate with existing transportation modes, promoting sustainable travel within cities through intermodal connectivity and smart mobility solutions. With a focus on sustainable design and operations,

UAP prioritizes renewable energy integration, energy-efficient design, and zero-emission ground operations. UAP actively engages with local communities to ensure social impact by promoting job creation, economic development, and equitable access to UAM. Through this integrated approach, UAP's Vertiports serve as sustainable transportation hubs, contributing to the overall decarbonization and accessibility of urban mobility.

WasteFuel

WasteFuel is pioneering a transformative project in the Philippines to convert municipal solid waste (MSW) into sustainable aviation fuel (SAF). Through partnerships with local governments and waste management companies, WasteFuel will collect and sort MSW, separating organic waste for processing. Its innovative biochemical conversion technology will then convert this organic waste into biofuels, which will be hydroprocessed to produce high-quality SAF that meets international standards. The locally produced SAF will be supplied to airlines in the Philippines, reducing their carbon footprint and dependence on fossil fuels while addressing waste management challenges. This initiative promises to deliver environmental benefits such as reduced greenhouse gas emissions and improved air quality, as well as economic development and job creation.

World Energy

World Energy is a pioneer in the field of sustainable aviation fuel (SAF) production, leading the commercialization of SAF with a track record spanning more than a decade. Operating the world's first commercial SAF production facility in Paramount, California since 2016, World Energy has demonstrated the viability and scalability of SAF production. Through innovative Hydroprocessed Esters and Fatty Acids (HEFA) technology, they efficiently convert diverse feedstocks such as used cooking oil and agricultural waste into SAF, ensuring a sustainable and adaptable supply chain. World Energy's strategic partnerships with major airlines and collaborations with government agencies underscore their commitment to driving SAF adoption and advocating for supportive policies. With an unwavering commitment to sustainability, including rigorous lifecycle GHG reduction measures and transparent certification processes, World Energy continues to pave the way for a future where SAF plays a central role in the decarbonization of the aviation sector.

ZeroAvia

ZeroAvia is at the forefront of aviation innovation with its pioneering work in zero-emission hydrogen-electric aircraft propulsion. Their mission to decarbonize aviation is driving the development of a 19-seat hydrogen-electric aircraft that will revolutionize regional air travel with its environmentally friendly design. Using hydrogen fuel cells and electric motors, ZeroAvia's aircraft promise zero carbon emissions, reduced noise pollution and lower operating costs, marking a significant step towards sustainable aviation. While the technology is still in development, ZeroAvia's progress underscores its potential to transform the industry and usher in a new era of zero-emission commercial aviation.

oneworld

oneworld, a global airline alliance made up of leading carriers including American Airlines, British Airways, Cathay Pacific, and Qantas, in September 2020 became the first major alliance to commit to carbon neutrality by 2050. This collective target underscores oneworld's commitment to reducing the environmental impact of aviation and promoting sustainability. At the heart of its strategy is a collaborative approach among member airlines, facilitating knowledge sharing and joint initiatives to advance sustainable practices. Key initiatives include increasing the use of Sustainable Aviation Fuel (SAF) through investment and infrastructure development, optimizing flight operations and fleet modernization for efficiency gains, and investing in carbon offsetting programs and carbon capture technologies.

Paris Agreement and Aviation Net Zero Goals

The aviation industry's goal to halve net CO2 emissions by 2050 aligns with the Paris Agreement's aim to limit global temperature rise. While the agreement emphasizes the need to stay below 2°C, with a stretch goal of 1.5°C, achieving this requires significant efforts, especially in hard-to-decarbonize sectors like air transport. Despite challenges, concerted global action, technological innovation, and policy support are essential for aviation to navigate towards sustainability in harmony with the Paris Agreement's objectives.

Tradeoffs and compromise

There are some practical constraints and trade-offs. Accelerating technology development demands significant investment, prompting decisions on resource allocation between traditional fuels and emerging alternatives like electric or hydrogen aircraft. A balanced approach is crucial, considering limitations in bandwidth and resources. Collaboration, policy support, and innovative financing are essential for successful transitions. Key actions include continued technology investment, policy frameworks for sustainable fuels, and facilitating a smooth shift to carbon neutrality. The aviation sector cannot rely solely on technological advancements, operations enhancements, or air traffic management improvements. Instead, a multifaceted approach is required, with energy transitions playing an important role.

Traffic Forecasts

In contemplating the future of air travel, we confront pervasive misconceptions regarding its accessibility. While historically associated with the affluent, the increasing affordability of air travel has democratized access, offering opportunities to billions across diverse economic backgrounds and fostering employment within the aviation sector and its ancillary industries.

Predicting future air traffic involves considering a multitude of variables. Historically, global air travel has doubled approximately every 15 years. Various factors influence traffic growth, including demographic shifts, economic conditions, travel costs, capacity constraints, and regional disparities, with the COVID-19 pandemic reshaping long-term forecasts. Industry forecasts anticipate an annual growth rate averaging around 3.1%, resulting in 22 trillion revenue passenger kilometers (RPKs) by 2050, reflecting ongoing demographic changes and economic development. While growth patterns may decelerate in the coming decades, this scenario considers diverse influences, including emerging air markets in Africa, demographic constraints in some regions, and potential demand generation through market liberalization.

OEMS and Defense Companies

Aerospace and defense companies on the original equipment manufacturer (OEM) side, representing approximately 20 percent of the global value pool, have also pledged to objectives in alignment with Science-Based Targets initiative (SBTi). The Science-Based Targets initiative (SBTi) is a global effort enabling businesses to establish ambitious emissions reduction goals in accordance with current climate science. Its purpose is to hasten worldwide efforts to cut emissions by 2030 and achieve net-zero emissions by 2050, providing a framework for companies to take effective climate action. Over 4,000 businesses spanning various sectors have committed to emission reduction targets through SBTi, which are assessed and approved independently. Adopting science-based targets offers several benefits, including enhanced profitability, increased investor confidence, stimulation of innovation, reduced regulatory uncertainty, and bolstered brand reputation. Implementing science-based targets involves committing to setting such targets, developing them according to SBTi criteria, submitting them for validation, communicating them to stakeholders, and disclosing company-wide emissions and progress annually.

The concept of Mitigation Action Commitments and Contributions (MACCs) delineates the strategic roadmap for Original Equipment Manufacturers (OEMs) in the aviation sector, focusing predominantly on emissions pertaining to the use of their sold products. However, OEMs are inextricably tethered to collaborative efforts, particularly with airlines, in enhancing operational efficiencies to diminish downstream decarbonization challenges. This symbiosis entails initiatives such as the aggregation of demand for Sustainable Aviation Fuel (SAF) to curtail fuel consumption in the short term. Concurrently, while revolutionary technologies like hydrogen and electric propulsion hold transformative potential, their widespread adoption remains contingent upon overcoming formidable obstacles, with practical application likely limited to short-haul or low-passenger use cases until approximately 2035. The trajectory toward sustainability in aviation necessitates a concerted and collaborative approach, melding incremental improvements with pioneering endeavors, as the industry navigates toward a cleaner and more environmentally responsible future.

Aircraft manufacturers worldwide are diligently advancing sustainability initiatives to mitigate the aviation industry's environmental footprint. Airbus spearheads innovation with its ZEROe concept aircraft, exploring hydrogen fuel cells and electric propulsion, while fostering partnerships to accelerate sustainable aviation fuel (SAF) adoption. Similarly, Boeing's commitment is evident through investments in SAF research, hybrid-electric propulsion, and collaborative projects like the Sustainable Flight Demonstrator with NASA. Embraer focuses on regional aviation sustainability with its Energia concept, featuring hybrid-electric and fully electric aircraft prototypes, alongside SAF testing and collaboration efforts. Meanwhile, COMAC prioritizes fuel efficiency in its C919 aircraft through advanced aerodynamics and lightweight materials, while actively exploring SAF potential in collaboration with Chinese fuel producers. Mitsubishi Aircraft Corporation tests SAF compatibility for its SpaceJet, aiming to reduce ecological impact through partnerships and adoption. Additionally, Sukhoi Superjet's emphasis on fuel efficiency and Irkut Corporation's integration of advanced aerodynamics and lightweight materials in the MC-21 aircraft reflect concerted efforts toward sustainable aviation practices, including the promotion of SAFs and implementation of eco-friendly manufacturing processes.

IATA Aviation Strategy for Net Zero CO2 Emissions

At the recent 77th IATA Annual General Meeting, airlines committed to achieving net-zero carbon emissions by 2050, aligning with the Paris Agreement's objectives. This decision ensures sustainable flying for future generations, emphasizing the importance of collective efforts and government support. The plan to achieve net-zero emissions involves a multifaceted approach, including sustainable aviation fuel (SAF), new technology like electric and hydrogen propulsion, operational efficiencies, and offsets. Achieving this goal presents a significant challenge, requiring coordinated action across the aviation industry and beyond. Immediate enablers such as the CORSIA scheme will stabilize emissions, paving the way for emissions reductions through in-sector solutions and out-of-sector options like carbon capture and storage. The resolution demands concrete actions and clear timelines from all stakeholders, including fuel producers, governments, manufacturers, and airport operators. Government support through policies and incentives is crucial, particularly in advancing SAF production. The milestones set for SAF production highlight the industry's commitment to sustainability, with a focus on increasing production to meet future demand. Accountability and follow-through from fuel suppliers are essential to ensure the success of these initiatives.

IATA Aviation Strategy for Net Zero CO2 emissions	
65%	Sustainable Aviation Fuel (SAF)
13%	New technology, electric and hydrogen
3%	Infrastructure and operational efficiencies
19%	Offsets and carbon capture

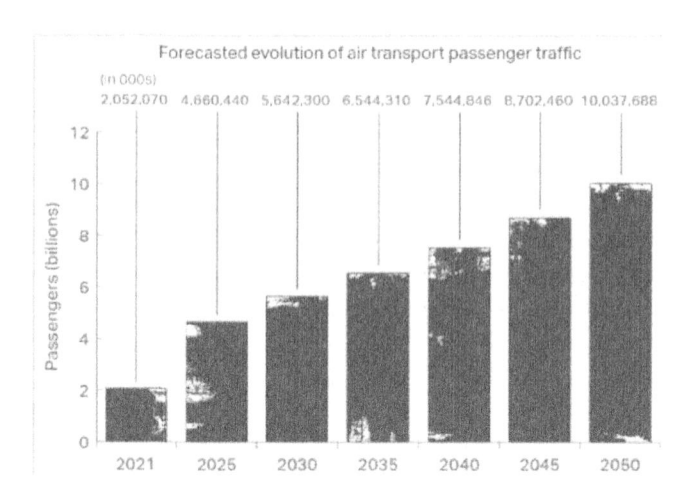

Forecasted evolution of air transport passenger traffic
(in 000s)

Year	Passengers
2021	2,052,070
2025	4,660,440
2030	5,642,300
2035	6,544,310
2040	7,544,846
2045	8,702,460
2050	10,037,688

IATA.org

Clean Skies of Tomorrow Coalition

Despite advancements, aviation faces challenges in reducing emissions, particularly considering industry growth. The efforts at reducing carbon emissions have been outpaced by the growth in the industry. Younger demographics' heightened environmental consciousness underscores the significance of addressing these challenges. While ambitious targets for CO2 reduction have been set, achieving them requires navigating complexities such as reliance on high-energy-density fuels and stringent safety standards. Evaluating alternative energy sources reveals promising but nascent technologies like sustainable aviation fuel and hydrogen, each presenting unique considerations and potential disruptions.

The International Organization for Public-Private Collaboration has led the Clean Skies of Tomorrow Coalition, a broad alliance encompassing stakeholders across the aviation value chain. Recognizing the imperative for consolidated action, the coalition focuses on environmental considerations and collaborates closely with bodies such as the Airports Council International (ACI). Key endeavors include feasibility assessments, cost modeling, and identifying opportunities within general aviation to produce bio-based fleet fuels and e-fuels. While sustainable aviation fuels (SAFs) currently incur higher costs compared to conventional kerosene, policies are deemed essential to bridge this cost gap and stimulate investment. The coalition identifies five critical workstreams, including finance, to mitigate risks and foster the uptake of SAFs. Notably, four pathways for SAF production are identified, each capable of substantial CO2 reduction and potentially blending up to fifty percent with conventional fuel. These pathways encompass various technologies, such as hydroprocessed esters and fatty acids (HEFA) fuel, alcohol to jet, gasification with Fischer-Tropsch, and power to liquid fuels. Production volume, though currently modest, is expected to increase, with ample feedstock availability to potentially meet the aviation industry's demand by 2030.

Choosing Sustainable Aviation Fuel (SAF) as the primary means of decarbonization presents a significant advantage due to its compatibility with existing aircraft technology, eliminating the need for costly redesigns. This allows investments and research efforts to focus primarily on scaling production and reducing costs. Collaboration with other sectors is essential for the successful deployment of SAF, as it can drive down the costs of required technologies such as hydrogen production, direct air capture, and biomass conversion, while ensuring effective resource utilization. To address societal expectations and reach sufficient SAF volumes to meet the industry targets, the pathway to decarbonization needs to be more ambitious, with investments commencing sooner. Individual initiatives should be integrated into comprehensive plans representing all points along the value chain, systematically deployed in areas with favorable policies, market conditions, and access to SAF, thus optimizing the industry's efforts towards net-zero emissions.

Analysis indicates a notable trend of decreasing costs for all sustainable aviation fuel types over time, attributed to scale effects and lower-cost green electricity, albeit with variations among different pathways. Currently, HEFA fuel stands as the most economical option due to its reliance on abundant waste oils, while gasification and alcohol to jet fuels remain slightly costlier but tap into more abundant feedstock resources. Power to liquid fuels currently exhibit higher costs owing to diverse technologies and electricity costs, yet these are expected to decrease significantly in the future. Despite these cost reductions, sustainable aviation fuels are not projected to match the cost of fossil jet fuel, necessitating demand stimulation measures such as CO2 costs or emission trading. Scaling up sustainable aviation fuel production necessitates technological maturity, supportive regulatory frameworks, financial investments, and an efficient marketplace to facilitate uptake. Transitioning to hydrogen propulsion in aviation presents significant potential for decarbonization, with various technology options explored, including fuel cell-powered or hydrogen-burning aircraft. Challenges remain in understanding the full climate impact, particularly regarding non-CO2 emissions, and further research and development efforts are required to realize hydrogen's potential in aviation decarbonization.

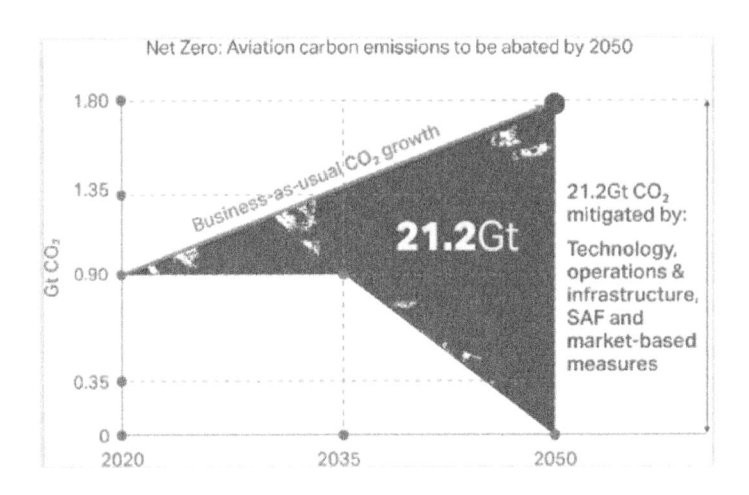

Net Zero: Aviation carbon emissions to be abated by 2050

21.2Gt CO$_2$ mitigated by: Technology, operations & infrastructure, SAF and market-based measures

IATA.org

FAA and NASA

The United States' Aviation Climate Action Plan provides a comprehensive approach and policy framework for the aviation sector to contribute to broader, economy-wide goals. To achieve ambitious climate goals, they will implement a series of policies designed to foster innovation and drive change across the U.S. aviation ecosystem. This plan builds on individual and sector-wide commitments announced by the U.S. aviation industry. Their vision is that emissions will be reduced through the introduction of new, more efficient aircraft; the development of energy-efficient technologies by manufacturers; improvements in aircraft operations throughout the National Airspace System (NAS); the production of Sustainable Aviation Fuels (SAF) by the energy sector; electrification and potentially hydrogen as solutions for short-haul aviation; advances in airport operations across the United States; international initiatives such as CORSIA; domestic policies and measures to help meet emissions targets; and support for climate science research related to aviation impacts.

The development and introduction of new aircraft and engines by Original Equipment Manufacturers (OEMs) represent critical advancements in the ongoing effort to mitigate future CO2 emissions. Substantial investments from both the aviation industry and the government are fueling the development of these next-generation aircraft, which are expected to bring significant improvements in fuel efficiency. Historically, new technologies typically take around seven years to transition from flight demonstration to commercial application.

Collaborative initiatives, such as the Sustainable Flight National Partnership (SFNP) are facilitating cooperation between the government and industry partners. This collaboration aims to showcase a suite of cutting-edge aircraft technologies by 2030. The ambitious target is a remarkable 30% improvement in fuel efficiency compared to today's most advanced aircraft.

This represents more than just technological innovation; it signifies a crucial step towards curbing the exponential growth of CO2 emissions and potentially achieving substantial reductions in the future.

Aircraft technology has been a game-changer in reducing aviation's environmental footprint, with a 70% improvement in fuel efficiency achieved over the past half a century. Continued progress is needed to address projected growth and maximize the use of sustainable aviation fuel. The collaborative effort between manufacturers and the government focuses on accelerating the development and demonstration of next-generation aircraft and engine technologies, aiming for a 25-30% reduction in fuel burn by 2030. The impact goes beyond US borders, with the government actively supporting international collaboration through the International Civil Aviation Organization (ICAO) to establish global environmental standards. This collaborative approach aims to drive the integration of cleaner technologies, reduce noise pollution around airports, and improve local air quality.

Governments worldwide, including the USA, are spearheading initiatives like the SAF Grand Challenge to accelerate the production and adoption of Sustainable Aviation Fuels (SAF). Integrating new aviation technologies presents a significant challenge. While innovations like hydrogen or electric aircraft hold promise, their widespread implementation requires extensive research and development, with designs taking decades to materialize.

Airport infrastructure facilitates fuel uplift by airlines, making them key partners in integrating SAF into existing fuel systems seamlessly. The high cost of SAF remains an obstacle. To overcome this barrier, airports can play a vital role in supporting investments in SAF production infrastructure. Fortunately, biomass resources offer a promising solution. Through rigorous assessments, various feedstocks from agriculture, forestry, and waste sectors have been identified, aiming to find sustainable sources that won't compete with food production. SAF derived from sustainable biomass presents an alternative for applications that are challenging to electrify. In the United States, the different regions offer a plethora of feedstocks, including fats, oils, greases, alcohols, wood crops, and municipal solid waste.

Incentives in the USA

The Inflation Reduction Act (IRA) of 2022 is a comprehensive legislation that addresses various aspects of the U.S. economy, including deficit reduction, energy security, climate change, and healthcare. For aviation, the IRA has significant implications. The IRA focuses on reducing emissions from the aviation sector by incentivizing SAF production. SAF is a liquid fuel that can be used in today's aircraft and achieves significant emissions reduction compared to fossil-based jet fuel. The act aims to reduce carbon emissions by 40% by 2030 and encourages companies across the aviation industry and fuel supply chain to transition toward a low-carbon future. The IRA provides tax incentives and grants to boost domestic manufacturing, create good-paying jobs, and build more resilient supply chains in the aviation sector. Specifically, it includes provisions for aviation. Section 40007 Grant Program is a competitive grant program that supports eligible entities in the United States that produce, transport, blend, or store sustainable aviation fuel, or develop, demonstrate, or apply low-emission aviation technologies. The IRA aligns with the SAF Grand Challenge.

The Sustainable Aviation Fuel (SAF) Grand Challenge is a collaborative effort across U.S. government agencies and industry partners. Its mission is to reduce costs, enhance sustainability, and expand production of sustainable aviation fuel (SAF). The goal is to achieve 3 billion gallons per year of domestic SAF production by 2030, with a minimum of 50% reduction in life cycle greenhouse gas emissions compared to conventional fuel. By 2050, the aim is to reach 100% of projected aviation jet fuel use, equivalent to 35 billion gallons of annual SAF production.

To achieve these ambitious objectives, the SAF Grand Challenge Roadmap outlines coordinated policies and actions by relevant U.S. government agencies. Here are the six key action areas covered in the roadmap:

- Focusing on developing innovative feedstocks for SAF production.
- Advancing technologies for converting feedstocks into SAF.
- Establishing robust supply chains to facilitate SAF production and distribution.
- Analyzing policies and valuations to support SAF adoption.
- Promoting SAF adoption in aviation.
- Engaging stakeholders and communicating progress toward SAF goals.

This comprehensive roadmap ensures alignment between government and industry efforts, fostering collaboration and driving progress toward a more sustainable aviation industry.

The European Union Aviation Safety Agency (EASA)

EASA stands for the European Union Aviation Safety Agency. It is an agency of the European Union (EU) responsible for civil aviation safety. EASA was established in 2002 and is headquartered in Cologne, Germany. The agency works to ensure the highest level of safety and environmental protection in civil aviation within the EU and its associated countries. EASA is responsible for regulating and overseeing various aspects of aviation safety, including aircraft design and manufacturing, maintenance, flight operations, licensing of pilots and aircrew, air traffic management, and the approval of aviation training organizations. It collaborates closely with national aviation authorities, industry stakeholders, and international organizations to develop and implement common safety standards and regulations across Europe's aviation sector.

The EASA Sustainable Aviation Program aims to make air travel greener and more sustainable. Like its counterparts in the United States and other parts of the world, it focuses on three key areas, promoting new technologies through certification, encouraging the use of Sustainable Aviation Fuels (SAF), and improving operational efficiency. EASA facilitates the use of SAF through initiatives like ReFuelEU Aviation and explores the potential of electric, hybrid, and hydrogen-powered aircraft. Additionally, they are developing an environmental labelling system to improve transparency and encourage sustainable choices and publish the European Aviation Environmental Report to track progress and inform decision-making.

The European Green Deal

Faced with the existential threat of climate change and environmental degradation, the European Union has crafted a bold vision for the future, the European Green Deal. This comprehensive plan outlines a roadmap for transforming the European economy into a sustainable powerhouse, achieving climate neutrality – net-zero greenhouse gas emissions – by 2050. At its core, the Green Deal aims to decouple economic growth from environmental damage. The European Commission has set forth an ambitious vision for sustainable and smart mobility, aiming to revolutionize the transport system while aligning with the goals of the European Green Deal. Within this framework, aviation plays a crucial role. The strategy emphasizes a 90% reduction in emissions by 2050 across all modes of transport. Concrete milestones include deploying zero-emission large aircraft by 2035 and ensuring that nearly all cars, vans, buses, and new heavy-duty vehicles are zero-emission by 2050. Additionally, the strategy promotes the expansion of high-speed rail traffic, making collective travel for journeys under 500 km carbon-neutral, and enhancing automated mobility. These measures collectively contribute to a greener and more resilient aviation sector. The strategy recognizes the pivotal role of digital technologies in shaping the future of mobility. The proposed EU Pact for Sustainable Aviation fosters cooperation between industry stakeholders and EU leaders. Through joint sustainability targets, effective regulatory mechanisms, and financial incentives, the aviation sector can transition toward a more environmentally friendly and economically viable future.

The Green Deal seeks to create a clean, circular economy where resources are used efficiently, products are designed to last and be recycled, and waste is minimized. This means significant investments in renewable energy sources like wind and solar power, energy-saving technologies in buildings and industries, and cleaner transportation options. It also recognizes the crucial role of innovation in this transition, so it fuels research and development for cutting-edge green technologies and materials. The Green Deal promotes practices that extend product lifespans, encourage responsible recycling, and minimize waste generation. It also encourages close collaboration with national governments, businesses, NGOs, and citizens to create a broad coalition for change.

ReFuelEU Aviation

As an important element of the European Green Deal's push for sustainable transportation, ReFuelEU Aviation was launched in 2023 to specifically address the environmental impact of aviation. Recognizing the limitations of completely replacing jet fuel by 2050, this initiative takes a two-pronged approach. First, it mandates a progressive increase in the use of Sustainable Aviation Fuels (SAF) by requiring fuel suppliers to blend an increasing percentage of SAF into their offerings at EU airports. This creates guaranteed demand, incentivizes SAF production and sets clear targets: a minimum of 1% blend by 2025, rising to 5.5% by 2030 (with an option for an additional 0.7% e-kerosene blend) and increasing thereafter. Second, ReFuelEU Aviation limits the amount of kerosene that airlines can take on board when departing from EU airports. This discourages unnecessary fuel transport and encourages strategic planning, ultimately reducing overall emissions. The environmental benefits are clear, lower CO_2 emissions contribute to the EU's climate neutrality goals, while cleaner air around airports and flight paths becomes a reality. The economic benefits are twofold: stimulating investment and innovation in European SAF production creates a new green sector and positions European airlines as leaders in sustainable aviation practices, enhancing their competitiveness. Cooperation is the key to success. Fuel suppliers need to ramp up SAF production, airlines need to adapt their operations and potentially invest in SAF-compatible technologies, and continued research and development is critical to advancing SAF technology and improving cost-effectiveness. ReFuelEU Aviation is an important step towards a greener future for European aviation, paving the way for further regulations and clean technology advances to minimize the environmental footprint of the aviation sector.

Here are the main provisions of the new regulation under the ReFuelEU Aviation initiative.

Minimum SAF Content

Aviation fuel suppliers are obligated to ensure that all fuel provided to aircraft operators at EU airports contains a minimum share of SAF. Starting from 2025, fuel suppliers must incorporate 2% SAF in the fuel. By 2030, this share increases to 6%, and by 2050, it reaches 70%. Additionally, from 2030, 1.2% of fuels must be synthetic fuels, rising to 35% by 2050.

To prevent additional emissions from extra weight due to tankering practices, aircraft operators must ensure that the yearly quantity of aviation fuel uplifted at an EU airport is at least 90% of the yearly aviation fuel required.

The scope of eligible sustainable aviation fuels includes.

- Certified biofuels
- Renewable fuels of non-biological origin (including renewable hydrogen)
- Recycled carbon aviation fuels complying with the Renewable Energy Directive (RED) sustainability and emissions saving criteria (up to a maximum of 70%)
- Low-carbon aviation fuels (including low-carbon hydrogen) that contribute to meeting the minimum share requirements.

Enforcement and Fines

Member states will designate competent authorities to enforce this regulation. The new law provides legal certainty to both aircraft operators and fuel suppliers in Europe, kick-starting large-scale production of sustainable aviation fuels and significantly greening the EU's aviation sector.

EU ETS

The European Union Emissions Trading System (EU ETS) is a carbon emission trading scheme, also known as a "cap and trade" system. Launched in 2005, it aims to lower greenhouse gas emissions across European Union countries.

The EU ETS operates through a carbon market. It sets a cap on the total amount of greenhouse gas emissions allowed within the system. This cap decreases over time, ensuring a gradual reduction in emissions. Companies participating in the EU ETS receive emission allowances. These allowances represent the right to emit a specific amount of CO_2. If a company exceeds its allocated allowances, it must either reduce emissions or purchase additional allowances from others. The default method for allocating emission allowances is auctioning, where companies bid for allowances. The "polluter pays" principle is put into practice. Transparency and accuracy are ensured through monitoring, reporting, and verification of emissions. The Union Registry keeps track of allowance ownership. To enhance resilience against shocks, the EU established the Market Stability Reserve. It adjusts the supply of allowances based on market conditions. The EU ETS allows the use of international credits, representing CO_2 removed or reduced elsewhere. These credits contribute to emission reduction efforts. Under the European Climate Law, EU Member States collectively strive to become climate neutral by 2050.

HUMAN SUSTAINABILITY IN AVIATION

The human dimension of Aviation Sustainability.

Aviation relies on the skill, dedication, and well-being of countless individuals – from pilots and air traffic controllers to cabin crew and maintenance personnel. Their performance directly impacts safety, efficiency, and the overall sustainability of the industry. This book delves into the concept of human sustainability in aviation, exploring the challenges and opportunities related to the well-being, performance, and social and economic conditions of the people who keep the world flying.

Human sustainability in aviation goes beyond just ensuring physical safety. It encompasses mental health, fatigue management, fair labor practices, and creating an inclusive and supportive work environment. It also involves recognizing the impact of technological advancements and ensuring that human-machine interactions are optimized for safety and efficiency.

The accomplishments of the aviation industry are undeniably remarkable, marked by exponential growth in passenger and cargo traffic globally and an impressive level of safety and reliability. While technological advancements have played a crucial role, it is ultimately the people behind the scenes who make it all possible. They are the ones who operate the technological wonders and drive the entire industry forward. When discussing sustainability in aviation, it's imperative not to overlook the human element.

With the rapid growth rates experienced in the industry, some aviation professionals have reported experiencing high levels of stress. If the aviation industry is projected to double in size by 2050, as estimated, it becomes increasingly crucial to address these human factors to avoid reaching a breaking point or compromising on quality and safety standards. Sustainability in aviation must encompass not only sustainable practices and cultures but also comprehensive training and support systems to ensure that aviation professionals are equipped to navigate the industry's future challenges.

Beyond just addressing the surface issues, it's essential get to the core of the human condition and provide aviation professionals with the tools they need to thrive and succeed. Recognizing this need, initiatives such as the Top Mind for Aviation Professionals course and book have been established to promote well-being and resilience within the industry.

In this section we aim to provide an overview of human sustainability in aviation, addressing key issues, highlighting innovative solutions, and outlining a path for a more sustainable future. It is intended for a diverse audience, including aviation professionals, policymakers, researchers, students, and anyone interested in the human dimension of this vital industry.

Defining Human Sustainability. People at the Heart of Aviation

Sustainability has become a crucial focus across industries, with the aviation sector facing increasing pressure to address its environmental impact. A truly sustainable future for aviation cannot be achieved without considering the human dimension. This section will examine the concept of human sustainability and its specific relevance to the aviation industry.

We begin by exploring the broader concept of sustainability, typically understood through its three pillars, environmental, social, and economic. Environmental sustainability focuses on minimizing ecological impact, social sustainability emphasizes fair and equitable treatment of people, and economic sustainability ensures financial viability and responsible resource management.

In the context of aviation, human sustainability primarily falls within the social pillar, focusing on the well-being, safety, and fair treatment of all individuals involved in the industry. This includes aviation personnel such as pilots, cabin crew, air traffic controllers, maintenance technicians, ground staff, and other professionals who ensure the safe and efficient operation of aircraft, airports, and the overall running of the businesses. Then we have the passengers, the individuals who rely on air travel for business, leisure, and connecting with loved ones as well as the communities served. Local populations impacted by airport operations and air traffic, including noise pollution and economic development opportunities.

Human sustainability in aviation entails addressing a range of issues, including:

Fatigue

Long working hours, irregular schedules, and time zone changes can lead to fatigue, impacting alertness, decision-making, and performance.

Mental health

The demanding nature of the job and associated pressures can contribute to mental health issues among aviation personnel.

Work-life balance.

Irregular schedules and extended periods away from home can make achieving a healthy work-life balance difficult for aviation professionals.

Diversity and inclusion

Ensuring equal opportunities and fair treatment for all individuals regardless of gender, race, ethnicity, or other factors is crucial for a sustainable and equitable industry.

Social and economic impact

Aviation activities can have both positive and negative impacts on communities, including job creation, economic development, and noise pollution. It's vital to address these challenges and prioritize the well-being of individuals, the aviation industry can achieve human sustainability, ensuring a safe, efficient, and equitable future for all stakeholders.

Mitigating Error and Optimizing Performance underscores the enduring significance of human performance amidst the backdrop of technological advancements in aviation. Despite the strides made in safety and efficiency, human involvement remains indispensable, encompassing tasks from piloting aircraft to managing air traffic and intricate systems. Recognizing the multifaceted nature of human performance is paramount for curbing errors and enhancing safety within the aviation sector.

Physiological factors such as fatigue, stress, illness, and medication can significantly impair alertness, cognitive function, and decision-making abilities. Psychological factors, including workload, pressure, distractions, and emotional states, further influence attention, memory, and situational awareness. Organizational factors, encompassing workplace culture, communication norms, teamwork dynamics, and leadership styles, also wield considerable influence over individual and collective performance. Additionally, environmental factors such as noise, lighting, temperature, and vibration can impact comfort, concentration, and overall performance.

To address these multifarious factors and optimize human performance in aviation, several key strategies are imperative. Rigorous and recurrent training programs equip aviation personnel with the requisite knowledge, skills, and strategies to navigate complex scenarios and respond adeptly to unforeseen circumstances. Implementing fatigue management systems, optimizing scheduling practices, and ensuring adequate rest periods are critical measures for mitigating fatigue-related errors and maintaining personnel well-being.

Fostering a culture of open communication, collaboration, and effective teamwork is essential for enhancing situational awareness and decision-making processes. Human-centered design principles, integrating considerations of human capabilities and limitations into aircraft, systems, and procedures, can minimize the likelihood of errors and bolster overall performance. While automation offers potential benefits in terms of efficiency and workload reduction, it is imperative to maintain human engagement and situational awareness to mitigate complacency and errors arising from overreliance on automated systems.

Fatigue Management

Combating the Silent Threat of fatigue addresses the pervasive challenge of fatigue within the aviation industry, recognizing its profound implications for safety and performance.

The causes of fatigue in aviation are diverse and encompass disruptions to circadian rhythms due to irregular work schedules and time zone changes, inadequate sleep resulting from long duty hours, demanding schedules, and high workload coupled with stress. Environmental factors such as cabin pressure, noise, and lighting can exacerbate fatigue levels.

Fatigue manifests in various consequences that compromise safety and performance, including reduced alertness, vigilance, and cognitive function. This impaired state increases the risk of errors and contributes to accidents and incidents within the aviation domain. Chronic fatigue can precipitate severe health issues, including sleep disorders, cardiovascular disease, and mental health disorders.

To effectively manage fatigue, several strategies are imperative. Fatigue Risk Management Systems (FRMS) play an important role in identifying, assessing, and mitigating fatigue risks comprehensively. Optimizing scheduling practices to prioritize adequate rest periods, limit extended duty hours, and align with circadian rhythm principles is essential. Clear regulations and guidelines regarding minimum rest requirements are crucial for ensuring compliance and safeguarding personnel's well-being.

Education and awareness initiatives are instrumental in raising consciousness among aviation personnel regarding fatigue risks and promoting healthy sleep habits. Furthermore, leveraging fatigue detection and mitigation tools such as biomathematical models and wearable devices facilitates proactive monitoring of fatigue levels and the implementation of timely interventions to mitigate risks.

Why Is Good Sleep Hygiene Important?

Sleep plays an important role in maintaining both physical and mental health, with poor sleep quality linked to a myriad of adverse outcomes. Insufficient sleep has been correlated with heightened stress levels, diminished cognitive functioning, and an elevated susceptibility to chronic ailments such as obesity, diabetes, cardiovascular diseases, and mental health disorders like depression and anxiety.

Good sleep hygiene holds paramount importance for multiple reasons. Primarily, it facilitates the attainment of adequate sleep duration. While adults typically require 7-9 hours of sleep per night, many individuals fall short of this target due to suboptimal sleep practices. Prioritizing good sleep hygiene enables individuals to meet their nightly sleep quota, which in turn yields manifold benefits for overall health and well-being.

Beyond promoting optimal sleep duration, good sleep hygiene is instrumental in bolstering sleep quality. Poor sleep hygiene habits can disrupt sleep continuity, precipitate frequent awakenings, and yield shallow sleep patterns. Consequently, individuals may experience daytime fatigue, cognitive sluggishness, and impaired physical performance. Embracing good sleep hygiene practices fosters deep, restorative sleep, fostering heightened alertness and vitality throughout the day.

Here are some tips for improving sleep hygiene:

- Maintain a Consistent Sleep Schedule. It's beneficial to aim for a regular sleep routine by going to bed and waking up at the same time every day, including weekends. This helps regulate the body's internal clock.
- Create a Relaxing Bedtime Routine. Engage in calming activities before bedtime, such as reading, meditation, or gentle stretching. These activities signal to the body that it's time to wind down and prepare for sleep.
- Optimize the Sleep Environment. Ensure the bedroom is conducive to rest by keeping it dark, quiet, and cool. Investing in a comfortable mattress and pillows can also promote comfort and better sleep quality.
- Limit Stimulants and Electronics. Minimize consumption of caffeine and alcohol, especially in the hours leading up to bedtime. Additionally, reduce exposure to screens emitting blue light, such as smartphones and computers, as they can interfere with the ability to fall asleep.
- Stay Active During the Day. Engage in regular physical activity, aiming for at least 30 minutes of moderate exercise most days of the week. However, avoid vigorous exercise close to bedtime, as it can be stimulating and interfere with sleep.
- Monitor the Diet. Avoid heavy meals, spicy foods, and excessive fluid intake before bedtime to prevent discomfort and sleep disturbances.
- Practice Stress-Reduction Techniques. Incorporate stress-reduction techniques into the bedtime routine, such as deep breathing exercises, mindfulness meditation, or progressive muscle relaxation. These techniques can help alleviate tension and promote relaxation before sleep.

Good sleep hygiene is paramount for maintaining optimal physical and mental health. By adhering to sound sleep practices, individuals can ensure they obtain sufficient high-quality sleep each night, leading to numerous benefits for their overall well-being.

In professions such as aviation and aerospace, where precision and performance are of utmost importance, prioritizing sleep becomes even more critical. The ramifications of errors in these industries can be severe. Therefore, it is imperative for individuals to prioritize rest and ensure they are adequately rested before undertaking any tasks related to their work.

Research underscores the significance of combating fatigue in aviation, as it is identified as a risk factor in aviation accidents. Recognizing this, regulatory bodies like the Federal Aviation Administration (FAA) have implemented measures to mitigate fatigue among pilots and aviation personnel. These regulations include restrictions on the number of flight hours permitted within a given day or week, as well as mandatory rest periods to safeguard against the adverse effects of fatigue on performance and safety. As you may know, flying an aircraft is a complex and demanding task that requires a high level of alertness and focus. That's why it's essential for flight crews to get enough rest and sleep to maintain their mental and physical health.

The aviation industry has recognized the importance of rest time, and there are specific regulations and guidelines that airlines must follow to ensure their flight crews have adequate rest periods. In the United States, the Federal Aviation Administration (FAA) mandates the minimum rest requirements for flight crews.

According to the FAA regulations, flight crews must have at least 10 hours of rest between duty periods. The rest period should include a continuous period of at least 8 hours of sleep opportunity at the crew member's designated sleep period, with an additional 2 hours of rest or sleep opportunity. Furthermore, the maximum flight duty period is generally limited to 14 hours.

These rest time requirements are essential to prevent fatigue, which can affect a pilot's ability to perform their duties safely. Fatigue can impair cognitive function, decision-making, and reaction times, which can lead to errors and accidents.

The FAA also requires airlines to develop and implement a Fatigue Risk Management System (FRMS) to identify and mitigate the risk of fatigue in flight crews. The FRMS includes measures such as scheduling policies, training programs, and fatigue monitoring tools to ensure that flight crews are adequately rested.

In addition to the FAA regulations, the International Civil Aviation Organization (ICAO) has developed guidelines for rest time requirements for flight crews. These guidelines recommend that flight crews should have at least 10 hours of rest between duty periods, with a maximum of 14 hours of flight duty time per day.

In Europe pilots' rosters must adhere to all FTL Flight Time Limitations as stipulated in the EASA regulations which can be even more restrictive as adopted by the European Parliament of the European Commission proposal to harmonize flight and duty time limitations (FTL) for cabin crew and pilots across the European Union. Other regions in Latin America and Asia and all around the globe have regulations regarding rest time.

All airlines recognize the importance of rest time for flight crews and have implemented their own policies to ensure their flight crews are adequately rested.

Rest time requirements for flight crews are pivotal in safeguarding the safety of airline operations. Regulatory frameworks and guidelines are in place to ensure that flight crews receive adequate rest periods to uphold their mental and physical well-being. As aviation professionals, it's imperative to prioritize rest time and ensure that we are sufficiently rested before executing our duties. Additionally, personal responsibility for one's own sleep hygiene is paramount. This entails ensuring adequate sleep, maintaining a consistent sleep schedule, and abstaining from activities that can disrupt sleep, such as consuming caffeine or using electronic devices before bedtime.

Sleep quality is as significant as quantity. Even if individuals obtain the recommended hours of sleep each night, frequent disruptions or poor-quality sleep can still lead to the effects of sleep deprivation. Creating an environment conducive to quality sleep is essential, which involves ensuring a quiet, cool, and dark sleep environment, and refraining from activities that can disturb sleep, such as working or watching TV in bed.

Acknowledging the impact of mental health and well-being on sleep hygiene is crucial. Conditions like anxiety, depression, and stress, whether stemming from work or personal life, can all influence one's ability to sleep. Therefore, attending to both mental and physical health is vital, which may entail seeking professional support if necessary, practicing relaxation techniques like meditation or deep breathing, or implementing stress-reducing strategies.

Mitigating Jetlag

Mitigating the effects of jetlag and solving the age-old problem of disrupted sleep due to travel. Here are some practical tips that can help you mitigate the effects of jetlag and sleep better while traveling and flying regularly.

Adjust sleep schedule before a trip if possible.

For travelers embarking on journeys across multiple time zones, adjusting their sleep schedule prior to departure can be a strategic tactic to combat the effects of jet lag. By gradually shifting their bedtime routine several days in advance to align with the time zone of their destination, individuals aim to ease the transition and minimize the abrupt disruption to their internal body clock. However, for professionals like long-haul pilots whose flight schedules often entail frequent shifts in time zones, fully adhering to this pre-travel adjustment may prove challenging. In such circumstances, pilots may opt for a modified approach, striving to optimize their sleep patterns within the constraints of their itinerary. While complete eradication of jet lag's effects may remain elusive, proactive measures can nonetheless mitigate its impact and enhance the overall travel experience.

Staying hydrated is crucial when dealing with jet lag. It's important to drink plenty of water before and during your flight and try to minimize alcohol and caffeine intake during layovers, as they can contribute to dehydration.

Exposure to sunlight can help regulate one's body's internal clock and aid in adjusting to the new time zone. Spending time outdoors and soaking up natural light can be beneficial.

Taking short naps, around 20-30 minutes in duration, can help one recharge and stay alert during the day. However, it's best to avoid napping too close to bedtime, as this can interfere with one's ability to fall asleep at night.

Another helpful tip is to limit screen time before bedtime. The blue light emitted by electronic devices such as smartphones, tablets, and laptops can disrupt one's body's natural sleep-wake cycle by suppressing the production of melatonin, the hormone that regulates sleep. One should try to avoid using these devices for at least an hour before bedtime to help fall asleep faster.

Lastly, incorporating some light exercise into one's routine can also be beneficial. Moving around and stretching during the flight can improve blood flow and prevent muscle stiffness. Once one arrives at their destination, they should try to get some exercise to help reset the body clock and alleviate jet lag symptoms.

It's crucial to be aware of regulations and policies regarding the use of sleep aids, especially in professions like aviation where safety is paramount. Before considering any sleep aid, whether it's melatonin supplements or prescription medication, it's important to review the regulations and policies outlined in manuals, regulatory guidelines, and company policies. Flight deck crews may have strict restrictions due to safety concerns. While policies may vary for ground personnel and other administrative roles, consulting with an aeromedical doctor is essential, especially if there are underlying health conditions or other medications involved.

Mitigating jet lag and improving sleep while traveling regularly requires planning and effort, but the benefits are significant. By following practical tips and strategies, such as staying hydrated, getting sunlight exposure, and limiting screen time before bedtime, individuals can optimize their sleep and maintain alertness during travels. However, it's essential to recognize that everyone's body is different, so listening to one's body and finding what works best for them is key.

Prioritizing rest is fundamental for safe and effective performance in the aviation industry. Whether on or off the job, ensuring adequate sleep is crucial for maintaining optimal cognitive function and decision-making abilities. By prioritizing sleep and taking necessary precautions regarding sleep aids, individuals can safeguard their well-being and contribute to overall safety in aviation operations.

Recognizing that well-being encompasses various aspects of our lives, including physical health, mental clarity, and social connections, is essential. It's not just about feeling happy or avoiding negative emotions; it's about achieving a holistic state of being.

To cultivate a sense of complete well-being, there are practices we can incorporate into our daily lives. Gratitude journaling, for example, involves writing down things we are thankful for each day, fostering a positive mindset and increasing feelings of happiness and fulfillment. Additionally, engaging in hobbies and passions that bring us joy can significantly contribute to our overall well-being.

It's important to understand that achieving complete well-being is a journey, not a destination. It requires consistent effort and the cultivation of healthy habits and practices. While it may take time, the rewards of prioritizing our well-being are immeasurable.

To begin fostering a sense of well-being, one might explore avenues for social connection through activities like music. The power of music in bringing people together and fostering social connections is profound. Attending live concerts and events hosted by favorite bands or artists can evoke a sense of magic and camaraderie. Creating group playlists and sharing favorite songs can also strengthen connections and generate positive emotions.

Similarly, creative expression through art can be a valuable tool for self-expression and well-being. Exploring different forms of art, such as painting, drawing, or sculpture, allows individuals to tap into their creativity and express themselves authentically. By experimenting with various mediums and discussing the benefits of artistic expression, individuals can discover the joy and fulfillment that comes from engaging in creative endeavors.

Exploring mindful movement practices like yoga or tai chi can greatly benefit both physical and mental health. These practices promote flexibility, strength, and relaxation while fostering mindfulness and stress reduction. Additionally, integrating a gratitude practice into daily routines can cultivate a positive mindset and enhance overall well-being. Keeping a gratitude journal or simply reflecting on one thing to be grateful for each day can shift focus towards appreciation and contentment.

Connecting with nature is another powerful way to nurture well-being. Spending time outdoors in parks or nature reserves allows individuals to immerse themselves in natural surroundings, which can promote relaxation and reduce stress. Engaging in outdoor activities such as hiking, cycling, or trekking through forests with friends not only provides physical exercise but also fosters a sense of connection with the natural world. Joining social walking clubs or similar groups can further enhance well-being by combining physical activity with social interaction.

When contemplating well-being, it's essential to recognize that it's not a one-size-fits-all concept. While exercise, a healthy diet, and meditation are vital components, individual needs and preferences vary. What works for one person may not work for another, highlighting the importance of personalized approaches to well-being. Embracing diversity in well-being practices allows individuals to tailor their routines to suit their unique needs, ultimately promoting holistic health and fulfillment.

How can we achieve complete wellbeing? It starts with understanding the three key components, which I recap here physical, mental, and social.

Physical wellbeing includes taking care of our bodies through exercise, nutrition, and sleep. It also means avoiding harmful habits such as smoking and excessive alcohol consumption. But physical wellbeing also means something else, listening to our bodies. Too often we push ourselves too hard and ignore our physical needs. If we feel tired, we need to rest. If we feel pain, we need to seek medical attention. By listening to our bodies, we can prevent injury and maintain optimal physical health.

Mental wellbeing includes taking care of our emotional and psychological health. This includes managing stress and anxiety, seeking help when needed, and engaging in activities that bring us joy and fulfillment. Mental wellbeing also means being mindful of our thoughts and self-talk. Negative self-talk can be harmful and lead to feelings of depression and anxiety. By practicing positive self-talk, we can improve our mental wellbeing.

Social wellbeing includes building and maintaining positive relationships with others. This means connecting with others on a deeper level, being a good listener, and supporting one another. Social wellbeing also means setting healthy boundaries and knowing when to say no. Meditation and mindfulness practices have proven to be very beneficial.

Coping Mechanisms

Coping is an essential aspect of emotional regulation and resilience, and it is vital for maintaining good mental health and wellbeing. Coping strategies are the actions and techniques we use to manage stress and emotional distress, and they can help us feel more in control and better equipped to deal with challenging situations.

There are many different types of coping strategies, and they can be broadly classified into two categories, problem-focused coping, and emotion-focused coping. Problem-focused coping involves taking active steps to address the root cause of the stressor, such as seeking information, planning, or taking action to solve the problem. Emotion-focused coping, on the other hand, involves managing the emotional impact of the stressor, such as seeking social support, engaging in self-care activities, or using relaxation techniques.

Both types of coping can be effective in different situations, and it is essential to have a range of coping strategies available to us. However, some coping strategies are more effective than others, depending on the situation and the individual. For example, problem-focused coping may be more effective when dealing with a specific and controllable stressor, such as a work deadline, while emotion-focused coping may be more effective when dealing with a more significant and uncontrollable stressor, such as a natural disaster or accident or incident.

Not all coping strategies are healthy or helpful. Some coping strategies, such as substance use or avoidance, can be harmful and may exacerbate the problem in the long run. It is essential to be aware of our coping strategies and to choose those that are healthy, effective, and appropriate for the situation.

Here are some examples of healthy and effective coping strategies that can help enhance emotional wellbeing and resilience:

Physical activity is an excellent way to reduce stress and boost mood. Exercise releases endorphins, which are natural mood-boosters, and can help reduce feelings of anxiety and depression.

Relaxation techniques. Mindfulness and relaxation techniques, such as deep breathing, meditation, and progressive muscle relaxation, can help reduce stress and promote relaxation.

Talking to friends, family, or a mental health professional can be an effective way to manage stress and cope with difficult emotions.

Cognitive restructuring. This involves changing the way we think about a stressor or problem and can help reduce negative emotions and increase feelings of control and optimism. We talked about this kind of reframing in detail in the section on it is what it is, and it's a part of life sections.

Engaging in activities that promote self-care, such as taking a bath, reading a book, or listening to music, can help reduce stress and promote emotional wellbeing.

Using a combination of these and other healthy coping strategies, individuals can enhance their emotional wellbeing and resilience, and better manage stress and difficult emotions and avoid a total burnout.

Coping with Incidents and Accidents

Coping with aviation accidents and trauma is a complex and challenging process, and it requires a range of psychological and emotional coping strategies. It is vital to engage with qualified experts with evidence-based approaches that are trained to assist industry professionals in these cases. An example of coping with aviation accidents and trauma is using peer support programs and CARE teams.

Peer support programs are designed to provide emotional and psychological support to those who have experienced traumatic events, such as aviation accidents. These programs involve trained peer supporters, who have themselves experienced similar traumas, and can provide a unique level of understanding and empathy to those who are struggling to cope.

After a fatal aviation accident, a peer support program could be established for the surviving family members and colleagues. The program would provide a safe space for participants to express their emotions, share their experiences, and receive emotional support and guidance from trained peers. This can help to promote feelings of connection, reduce isolation, and build resilience in the face of adversity.

In addition to peer support programs, other coping strategies include seeking professional help from trained mental health professionals, engaging in self-care activities such as exercise and relaxation techniques, and maintaining social connections with supportive friends and family members.

It is important to note that everyone copes with trauma and grief differently, and there is no one "right" way to cope. However, by engaging in a variety of coping strategies and seeking support when needed, individuals can build resilience and successfully navigate the challenging process of coping with aviation accidents and trauma.

Critical Incident Stress Management (CISM) teams are specialized groups of mental health professionals who are trained to respond to crises and provide support to individuals who have been affected by traumatic events, such as aviation accidents or other disasters. Some airlines set up Emergency Response Special Assistance Team (SAT), which can also be referred to as the CARE Team or Family Assistance Team, is the team that assists survivors and family members of injured survivors or fatalities in serious aircraft and aviation accidents and deploys a Go Team for set up of the Family Assistance Center. The purpose of these teams is to help individuals and communities to cope with the psychological impact of a crisis, reduce the risk of long-term mental health problems, and facilitate the process of recovery.

When responding to an aviation accident, a trained professional team may provide a range of services, including on-site support and debriefing for survivors, family members, and witnesses, as well as follow-up care and referrals to additional mental health services as needed. CARE team members may include mental health professionals, such as psychologists and social workers, as well as other trained volunteers, such as peer counselors, chaplains, and emergency response personnel.

CARE teams typically use a variety of techniques and interventions to help individuals and communities to cope with traumatic events. These may include:

Psychological first aid. This involves providing immediate support and assistance to individuals who have been affected by a crisis. Psychological first aid may include basic needs assessment, active listening, and practical support such as food, shelter, and transportation.

A critical incident stress debriefing is a structured group process that allows individuals to share their experiences, emotions, and reactions to a traumatic event in a supportive and safe environment. The goal of critical incident stress debriefing is to help individuals to process their feelings and experiences, reduce the risk of post-traumatic stress disorder (PTSD), and promote recovery.

Psychoeducation and coping strategies. CARE teams may provide information and education to individuals and communities about common reactions to trauma, coping strategies, and self-care techniques. This may include teaching relaxation techniques, providing resources for support groups or counseling services, and helping individuals to develop a personalized self-care plan.

Referrals and follow-up care, CARE teams may also provide referrals to additional mental health services as needed, such as counseling or medication. They may also follow up with individuals and communities to provide ongoing support and care.

Mental Health and Well-being. Supporting the Human Mind in Aviation

The demanding nature of the aviation industry, with its high-pressure environment and unique challenges, can take a toll on the mental health and well-being of personnel. We will explore the prevalence of mental health issues in aviation, the stigma surrounding them, and strategies for promoting mental well-being among aviation professionals.

The aviation industry's unique demands and the critical nature of its operations render aviation personnel susceptible to higher rates of mental health issues compared to the general population. Anxiety, depression, stress, and fatigue are prevalent concerns among those working in aviation, exacerbated by a myriad of factors including irregular schedules, long duty hours, frequent time zone changes, and the inherent stressors associated with the responsibility of ensuring passenger safety. Despite the prevalence of these mental health challenges, stigma remains a significant barrier to seeking help or disclosing struggles. Aviation personnel often fear repercussions such as jeopardizing their professional licenses, job security, or being perceived as unfit to fly. A lack of awareness and understanding of mental health issues perpetuates this stigma.

To address these challenges and promote mental well-being within the aviation industry, various strategies are necessary. Firstly, raising awareness and providing education about mental health issues is crucial in helping personnel recognize symptoms and seek appropriate support. Establishing peer support programs offers a confidential and empathetic platform for individuals to connect, share experiences, and receive encouragement from colleagues who understand their unique challenges. Employee assistance programs (EAPs) play a vital role by providing access to confidential counseling and support services tailored to the specific needs of aviation personnel. Moreover, implementing clear and supportive mental health policies and procedures ensures that individuals experiencing mental health issues receive the necessary assistance and accommodations without fear of negative repercussions.

Proactive measures are essential for promoting overall well-being. Encouraging healthy lifestyles through initiatives such as promoting adequate sleep hygiene, regular exercise, and stress management techniques can enhance resilience and mitigate the impact of stressors. By fostering a culture of openness, support, and understanding, the aviation industry can create an environment where mental health is prioritized, stigma is reduced, and individuals feel empowered to seek help when needed. Ultimately, these efforts contribute not only to the well-being of aviation personnel but also to the safety and efficiency of aviation operations.

Technological Advancements and Human-Machine Interaction.

The aviation industry is constantly evolving, with new technologies continuously emerging and shaping the way we fly. There is an impact of technological advancements on human roles and responsibilities in aviation. Let's look at the crucial interaction between humans and machines.

The introduction of automation in the aviation industry has revolutionized the cockpit environment, with sophisticated systems assuming many tasks previously handled by pilots. While automation undoubtedly offers benefits such as increased efficiency and reduced workload, concerns have been raised regarding potential drawbacks, including skill degradation and diminished situational awareness. It is imperative to strike a balance where automation complements human abilities without leading to overreliance or complacency.

Central to effective human-machine interaction is the design of interfaces and systems that are intuitive, user-friendly, and mindful of human cognitive limitations. Clear communication between humans and automated systems is essential for maintaining situational awareness and facilitating informed decision-making. Consequently, training programs must evolve to accommodate new technologies, ensuring that aviation personnel are adept at interacting with automated systems.

Emerging technologies like artificial intelligence (AI), virtual reality (VR), and augmented reality (AR) hold promise for various aviation applications, including pilot training, maintenance, and air traffic control. These innovations offer opportunities to enhance efficiency, improve training effectiveness, and provide valuable support to human operators. Careful consideration of ethical implications and risk mitigation is imperative to ensure responsible implementation.

Ultimately, the key to navigating the integration of automation lies in finding synergy between human capabilities and machine intelligence. While humans possess strengths in critical thinking, creativity, and complex decision-making, machines excel in tasks requiring efficient data processing, automation, and assistance.

Training and Education.

Incorporating human sustainability is not just an ethical imperative, but also a strategic decision that benefits the aviation industry, its workforce, passengers, and the communities it serves. A healthy and satisfied workforce is more productive, engaged, and less prone to errors, contributing to safer and more efficient operations. Training and education play a critical role in ensuring human sustainability in aviation. As technology advances and the industry evolves, it is crucial to equip aviation personnel with the knowledge, skills, and adaptability needed to perform their roles safely and effectively. This chapter will explore the importance of training and education in the context of human sustainability.

Aviation personnel rely heavily on comprehensive training programs to equip them with the necessary technical knowledge, operational proficiency, and understanding of human factors principles. These programs are tailored to individual roles and responsibilities, ensuring that each person is adequately prepared to execute their duties with safety and efficiency. Recurrent training is also vital for maintaining proficiency and staying abreast of advancements in technology and procedures.

Incorporating human factors into training is essential to enhance situational awareness, decision-making, and teamwork skills among aviation personnel. This entails recognizing the impact of factors like fatigue and stress on performance and implementing strategies to mitigate potential errors. Crew resource management (CRM) training plays a critical role in fostering effective communication and collaboration within the cockpit and across the aviation system.

As new technologies emerge, training programs must adapt to ensure that personnel can safely and effectively utilize them. This includes providing training on new aircraft systems, automation, and emerging technologies such as artificial intelligence (AI) and virtual reality (VR). Emphasis should be placed on maintaining situational awareness and avoiding over-reliance on automation.

Promoting mental health and well-being is another crucial aspect of training programs. Incorporating mental health awareness and providing resources for stress management and well-being can help personnel cope with the demands of their roles. This may involve training in stress management techniques, promoting healthy sleep habits, and fostering a supportive work environment. Investment in education and training is paramount for the aviation industry. Airlines, regulatory agencies, and training providers must allocate resources to develop and deliver high-quality training programs. This includes investing in qualified instructors, modern training facilities, and innovative technologies to ensure that aviation personnel are well-prepared to meet the challenges of their profession.

Collaboration and Partnerships. Working Together for a Shared Goal

Achieving human sustainability in aviation demands collaboration among various stakeholders. This collective effort involves airlines, regulatory bodies, unions, research institutions, and other relevant organizations. Through collaborative partnerships, stakeholders can leverage their collective expertise and resources to address challenges and advance initiatives aimed at promoting human sustainability in aviation.

One of the primary benefits of collaboration is the development of industry-wide standards. Through collective efforts, stakeholders can establish common standards for managing fatigue, supporting mental health, designing training programs, and other critical aspects of human sustainability. These standardized practices ensure consistency and effectiveness across the aviation industry, promoting safer and more sustainable operations. Collaboration enables stakeholders to pool resources and funding, facilitating research, development, and implementation of new initiatives. While sharing costs and expertise, all participants can achieve more significant outcomes than they could individually, driving progress in promoting human sustainability.

Successful collaborations in aviation serve as inspiring examples of the power of collective action. For instance, partnerships have led to the widespread implementation of Fatigue Risk Management Systems (FRMS), effectively managing fatigue-related risks across the industry. Similarly, collaborative efforts have resulted in the establishment of mental health initiatives, including peer support programs and improved access to mental health resources for aviation personnel. International organizations like the International Civil Aviation Organization (ICAO) and the International Air Transport Association (IATA) play vital roles in promoting collaboration and setting global standards for human sustainability in aviation, fostering cooperation among stakeholders worldwide.

Regulatory Framework and Policy Initiatives.

Effective regulations and policies play a crucial role in promoting human sustainability in aviation. Governments, regulatory agencies, and international organizations have a responsibility to establish and enforce regulations that protect the well-being, safety, and rights of aviation personnel, while also ensuring the economic viability of the industry. This chapter will explore the regulatory framework and policy initiatives that can shape a sustainable future for aviation.

Existing regulations and policies in aviation are primarily established and overseen by international organizations such as the International Civil Aviation Organization (ICAO), which sets global standards and recommended practices for safety, security, and environmental protection. These standards are then implemented and enforced by national and regional regulatory agencies within their respective jurisdictions. Current regulations cover various aspects of human sustainability, including flight time limitations, rest requirements, training standards, and health and safety regulations. However, there are challenges and limitations, such as regulations not adequately addressing emerging issues like mental health and the impact of new technologies, inconsistencies in regulations and enforcement across different regions, and the challenge of balancing economic considerations with the need to protect human well-being.

To address these challenges and advance human sustainability in aviation, several policy initiatives are recommended. Firstly, evidence-based policymaking is crucial, ensuring that regulations and policies are informed by scientific evidence and data, particularly concerning fatigue, mental health, and human factors. Additionally, regulatory frameworks should be adaptable and open to continuous improvement based on new evidence and emerging challenges. Collaboration with stakeholders is essential, involving airlines, unions, research institutions, and others in policy development to ensure effectiveness and relevance. Policymakers should also focus on addressing emerging issues such as the impact of automation, new technologies, and the increasing demand for air travel. Examples of policy initiatives include the implementation of Fatigue Risk Management Systems (FRMS), mental health support programs, and diversity and inclusion initiatives within the aviation workforce.

Passenger Experience and Health

While the environmental impact of aviation garners significant attention, passenger experience and health constitute a crucial yet often overlooked dimension of sustainable air travel. Long-haul flights, in particular, present unique challenges to passenger well-being. Extended periods of immobility increase the risk of deep vein thrombosis, while dehydration becomes a concern due to the dry cabin air. The disruption of circadian rhythms caused by crossing time zones can lead to fatigue, jet lag, and potentially long-term health consequences. Addressing these issues is a strategic move to enhance passenger satisfaction and loyalty, ensuring the industry's long-term sustainability.

Airlines can implement several measures to improve passenger experience and health. Promoting in-flight movement through exercises and regular walks can alleviate the risk of deep vein thrombosis. Providing passengers with information on staying hydrated and offering healthy food options can combat dehydration and promote overall well-being. Dimming cabin lights and adjusting temperature settings can facilitate better sleep and minimize jet lag.

In aviation and aerospace, professionals encounter myriad challenges demanding resilience. Each day presents hurdles necessitating adaptation and triumph. Resilience, however, transcends mere recovery from setbacks; it embodies an inner strength enabling individuals to persist through adversity and emerge fortified. The cultivation of resilience emerges as a cornerstone in personal and professional advancement. The book endeavors to introduce innovative methodologies, equipping individuals with tools to nurture mental health, pursue excellence, and navigate the dynamic landscape of the industry. Rooted in decades of industry expertise and a fusion of ancient wisdom and modern evidence-based practices, these approaches offer a unique pathway toward self-improvement. Central to this journey is the cultivation of innovative thinking, crucial in today's era dominated by digital distractions and algorithmic influences. Divergent thinking, a pivotal facet of innovative cognition, encourages the exploration of multiple perspectives and solutions. The text aims to instill a mindset of curiosity, challenging entrenched beliefs and fostering mental flexibility. Through disciplined mental training, individuals can break free from conventional thought patterns and unlock their creative potential. The book underscores the significance of awakening the human spirit, an intangible yet formidable force driving individuals to persevere amidst adversity. It advocates for harnessing the power of the mind to cultivate positivity, resilience, and unwavering belief in one's abilities. By nurturing a positive mindset and embracing continual growth, individuals can unleash the full potential of their inner strength, propelling them towards excellence in both personal and professional spheres.

In the domain of high-performance work scenarios, the cultivation of mental toughness and focus emerges as a pivotal aspect for achieving excellence. Mental toughness denotes the capacity to maintain composure, concentration, and resilience amidst adversity, enabling individuals to navigate challenges with fortitude. Reframing challenges as opportunities for growth is a cornerstone in fostering mental toughness. Individuals who relish challenging situations, viewing them as avenues to showcase their capabilities, epitomize this mindset. Discipline, as a habitual practice, underpins mental toughness, enabling individuals to persevere even in the face of daunting obstacles. Embracing a routine and adhering to it, coupled with a focus on controlling one's attitude and effort, forms the essence of this discipline. Physical fitness constitutes an integral facet of mental toughness development, as the exertion required in physical challenges translates to mental fortitude. The pursuit of physical exertion not only fosters resilience but also instills discipline and routine. Moreover, maintaining a focus on what one can control, rather than dwelling on external factors, bolsters mental toughness. The belief in one's capacity for improvement and the ability to learn from setbacks are fundamental tenets in this journey. The cultivation of a clear sense of purpose and direction in life serves as a guiding force, fostering commitment and motivation amidst adversity. The practice of discipline is indispensable in nurturing mental toughness, requiring individuals to challenge themselves and push beyond their comfort zones. Additionally, the cultivation of a positive mindset and demeanor, exemplified through confident posture and self-assuredness, reinforces mental resilience. Leveraging setbacks as opportunities for growth and improvement underscores the importance of resilience in the face of adversity. Physical well-being also plays a pivotal role, with regular exercise, a balanced diet, and sufficient sleep contributing to enhanced cognitive function and stress management. Focusing on cognitive flexibility, individuals can cultivate resilience by embracing uncertainty and adopting an open-minded approach to problem-solving. Role-playing exercises, creative problem-solving techniques, and cross-training initiatives are instrumental in honing cognitive flexibility and adaptability. Experiential learning, coupled with self-directed action and learning autonomy, fosters continuous growth and development. Innovative approaches, such as mind mapping and language learning, further enhance cognitive flexibility and broaden perspectives. Through these concerted efforts, individuals can cultivate mental toughness and focus, equipping themselves with the resilience and adaptability necessary to excel in high-performance work environments.

The Three Pillars of Wellbeing

A. Body. Biological Aspect of Wellbeing

Our physical health is a critical component of our overall wellbeing. The body pillar of wellbeing involves taking care of our physical needs, including exercise, healthy eating, getting enough sleep, and avoiding harmful substances. By maintaining a healthy body, we can reduce the risk of developing physical illnesses, improve our energy levels and mental clarity, and enhance our ability to cope with stress.

B. Mind. Psychological Aspect of Wellbeing

Our psychological wellbeing is just as important as our physical health. The mind pillar of wellbeing involves taking care of our mental health, including managing stress, cultivating positive emotions, developing healthy coping mechanisms, and addressing any mental health conditions. By prioritizing our mental wellbeing, we can improve our ability to manage challenges, enhance our relationships, and increase our overall life satisfaction.

C. Social. Social Aspect of Wellbeing

The social pillar of wellbeing involves our social connections and relationships. Our social networks are a critical aspect of our overall wellbeing, and studies have shown that individuals with strong social support systems tend to have better physical and mental health outcomes. By prioritizing our social connections, we can reduce feelings of loneliness and isolation, increase our sense of belonging and purpose, and improve our overall wellbeing.

Interdependence of the Three Pillars

The three pillars of wellbeing are interdependent. Neglecting one pillar can have a negative impact on the other two, and improving one pillar can positively impact the others. For example, engaging in regular exercise not only benefits our physical health but can also enhance our mood and reduce stress levels, positively impacting our mental and social wellbeing. Similarly, cultivating positive social connections can provide a sense of purpose and belonging, which can enhance our physical and mental wellbeing. To achieve optimal wellbeing, it is essential to prioritize all three pillars and take a holistic approach to health and wellness. This can involve developing healthy habits and routines that support each pillar, seeking support from healthcare professionals or mental health professionals when necessary, and building and maintaining positive social connections. By prioritizing our overall wellbeing, we can enhance our ability to cope with life's challenges, increase our resilience, and experience greater joy and fulfillment in our daily lives.

How the Three Pillars of Wellbeing can be Applied to Flight Crews.

A. Body. The biological aspect of wellbeing is crucial for flight crews as they need to maintain good physical health to perform their duties effectively. This includes getting adequate sleep, staying hydrated, and eating nutritious foods. They can make sure to prioritize rest during layovers, bring healthy snacks on flights, and stretch or do light exercise during breaks to keep their bodies feeling good.

B. Mind. The psychological aspect of wellbeing is also important for flight crews as they need to be able to handle stress and maintain focus during long flights. They can practice mindfulness or meditation techniques to help calm their minds, utilize stress-management tools like deep breathing exercises, and make sure to take breaks to rest and recharge as needed.

C. Social. The social aspect of wellbeing involves maintaining positive relationships and a sense of connection with others. Flight crews can foster a sense of community within their team by supporting and encouraging each other, as well as trying to connect with passengers in a positive and friendly way.

D. Interdependence. It's important to note that these three pillars are interconnected and influence each other. For example, if a flight crew member is feeling physically unwell, this can also affect their mental and emotional wellbeing. Similarly, if there is tension or conflict within the team, this can also impact their overall wellbeing and performance. Therefore, it's important for flight crews to prioritize all three pillars to achieve optimal wellbeing and performance.

Recommendations of how the Lessons on Improving Wellbeing can be Applied to the Flight Crews:

A. Self-awareness

- Take time to reflect on your own wellbeing regularly, using tools such as self-assessment questionnaires or journaling.
- Identify your own strengths and weaknesses related to wellbeing and set specific goals for improvement.
- Seek feedback from colleagues or supervisors to gain additional insight and perspective.

B. Identifying triggers and sources of stress:

- Keep a stress diary to track when and where stress occurs, as well as the associated symptoms.
- Identify common triggers of stress, such as long flights or difficult passengers, and develop strategies to minimize their impact.
- Seek support from colleagues or supervisors when dealing with particularly challenging situations.

C. Lifestyle factors that impact wellbeing:

- Focus on getting enough sleep, exercise, and a balanced diet to maintain physical wellbeing.
- Seek out opportunities for social connection and community involvement to promote social wellbeing.
- Prioritize time for hobbies, relaxation, and self-care activities to promote psychological wellbeing.

D. Coping strategies for stress and anxiety:

Practice relaxation techniques such as deep breathing or meditation.

Use cognitive-behavioral strategies to challenge negative thoughts and reframe situations in a more positive light. Cognitive-behavioral therapy (CBT) is a type of psychotherapy that can be helpful for the flight crews to manage their mental health and cope with the unique stressors associated with their profession. CBT is based on the idea that our thoughts, feelings, and behaviors are interconnected, and that by changing one of these components, we can change the others.

In the context of flight crews, CBT can be useful in addressing specific issues related to their job, such as anxiety related to training or flying with difficult colleagues or dealing with difficult passengers. CBT can also be used to address more general issues such as managing anxiety and improving self-esteem.

One technique used in CBT is cognitive restructuring, which involves identifying negative thoughts and replacing them with more positive and realistic ones. For example, if a flight crew member has a negative thought about their ability to handle an emergency, a CBT therapist might help them reframe that thought by asking for evidence that supports their negative thought and then challenging that evidence with more realistic thoughts.

Another method used in CBT is behavioral activation, which involves engaging in positive activities that can improve mood and reduce stress. For example, a flight crew member might be encouraged to engage in regular exercise or hobbies that they enjoy promoting physical and mental wellbeing.

Cognitive-behavioral therapy (CBT) can also be helpful for pilots who are experiencing stress related to the potential of failing a line check or exam and losing their license and livelihood. CBT is a form of therapy that focuses on changing negative thought patterns and behaviors that may be contributing to stress, anxiety, or other mental health issues.

In the context of a pilot facing the fear of failure, a CBT therapist would help the pilot identify negative thought patterns related to the fear of failure, such as "If I fail, I'll never be able to fly again" or "If I fail, everyone will think I'm a bad pilot". These thoughts can be challenged and replaced with more realistic and positive thoughts, such as "Failing doesn't mean I can never fly again. It just means I need to work on improving my skills" or "Everyone makes mistakes. Failing doesn't make me a bad pilot".

The therapist may also work with the pilot on relaxation techniques to help reduce physical symptoms of stress, such as deep breathing exercises, progressive muscle relaxation, or meditation. Additionally, the therapist may work with the pilot to develop coping strategies for stress, such as breaking down tasks into smaller, manageable steps, or focusing on the present moment rather than worrying about the future. This can help pilots facing the fear of failure to reframe their negative thought patterns, reduce physical symptoms of stress, and develop coping strategies to improve their resilience. In such cases seek support from trusted colleagues or mental health professionals if needed and develop a plan for accessing resources and support when necessary.

By applying these strategies, flight crews can better cope with the demands of the profession.

A. Understanding resilience and its impact on wellbeing. Resilience refers to the ability to bounce back from challenges and adversity. Maintaining resilience is crucial to maintaining overall wellbeing, as it allows individuals to effectively manage stress and overcome obstacles. The impact of resilience on wellbeing can be seen in improved physical health, increased positive emotions, and reduced stress and anxiety.

B. Building physical and mental resilience. There are several ways that flight crews can build physical and mental resilience. Physical resilience can be built through regular exercise, proper nutrition, and adequate rest and recovery. Mental resilience can be built through practices such as meditation, positive thinking, and the methods and techniques outlined in this Top Mind system of mental training.

C. The role of positive thinking and meditation. Positive thinking and meditation are powerful tools for building resilience and maintaining wellbeing.

Examples of how flight crews can apply these lessons.

A. Self-awareness. Flight crews can cultivate self-awareness by regularly checking in with themselves and taking note of their emotional and physical states. This can involve practices such as journaling or meditation, or simply taking a few minutes each day to reflect on how you are feeling.

B. Identifying triggers and sources of stress. You can identify triggers and sources of stress by paying attention to the situations and circumstances that tend to cause you to feel overwhelmed or anxious. This can involve keeping a journal of stressful situations or taking note of patterns in your mood or behavior.

C. Lifestyle factors that impact wellbeing/ You can improve your wellbeing by focusing on lifestyle factors such as nutrition, exercise, and sleep. This might involve setting aside time each day for physical activity, making healthy food choices while on the job, or establishing a regular sleep schedule.

D. Coping strategies for stress and anxiety. Develop coping strategies for stress and anxiety by practicing meditation, engaging in relaxation techniques such as deep breathing or progressive muscle relaxation, or seeking support from colleagues, family, or mental health professionals.

Relationship Management Skills Contribute to Wellbeing.

Relationship management is one of the key components of emotional intelligence, and it refers to the ability to build and maintain positive relationships with others. In the context of aviation, pilots and crew with strong relationship management skills are better able to collaborate with colleagues, communicate effectively with air traffic controllers, and manage interactions with passengers. The same skills are vital for astronauts who must work in isolated confined spaces for long periods of time.

Here are some examples of relationship management skills that are particularly valuable for pilots and astronauts,

Effective communication. Pilots with strong relationship management skills can communicate clearly and effectively with others. They listen actively to others, express their own ideas and feelings clearly, and seek to find common ground with others. Astronauts must be able to communicate effectively with each other, mission control, and scientists on the ground. They must be able to convey complex information clearly and concisely, and they must be able to listen actively to others to ensure that they understand their needs and concerns.

Conflict resolution. Pilots and astronauts with strong relationship management skills manage conflicts effectively when they arise. They listen to the perspectives of others, seek to find common ground, and work collaboratively to find solutions that meet everyone's needs.

Collaboration. Pilots and astronauts with strong relationship management skills can work effectively with others to achieve common goals. They build and maintain positive relationships with colleagues, air traffic controllers, and passengers, and they can work collaboratively to find creative solutions to complex problems.

Empathy. Pilots with strong relationship management skills can understand and relate to the emotions of others. They see situations from multiple perspectives and respond in a way that is compassionate and understanding.

Influence. Pilots with strong relationship management skills influence others in a positive way. They can inspire and motivate others, and they are able to use their interpersonal skills to achieve positive outcomes.

The unique environment of space can create additional challenges for relationship management. Astronauts are in a confined space for long periods of time, and they may experience isolation, homesickness, and other emotional stresses. This can make effective communication and collaboration even more important.

Relationship management skills can also be important for maintaining positive relationships with loved ones back on Earth. Astronauts may experience long periods of separation from their families and friends, and effective communication and empathy can help to maintain these relationships and provide support during the mission.

Here are some tips and hacks for developing relationship management skills as an astronaut,

Practice active listening. Active listening is an essential component of effective communication and conflict resolution. To practice active listening, make a conscious effort to focus on what the other person is saying, ask clarifying questions, and summarize what they've said to ensure that you understand their perspective.

Learn about other cultures. When working with international colleagues, take the time to learn about their culture and communication style. This can help you to build positive relationships and avoid misunderstandings.

Develop emotional intelligence. Emotional intelligence is the foundation of relationship management skills. Practice self-awareness, self-regulation, empathy, and social skills to develop your emotional intelligence and improve your ability to manage relationships.

Use nonverbal communication. Nonverbal communication can be just as important as verbal communication, especially in a confined space. Use body language, facial expressions, and other nonverbal cues to convey your thoughts and feelings and to build rapport with others.

Take breaks. Spending long periods of time in a confined space can be emotionally challenging. Take breaks when you need to and find ways to recharge and take care of yourself.

Use technology to stay connected. Technology can be a valuable tool for maintaining relationships with loved ones back on Earth. Use video calls, messaging apps, and other tools to stay connected with family and friends.

Practice conflict resolution. Conflict is inevitable in any group setting, especially when spending long periods of time in a confined space. Practice conflict resolution techniques such as active listening, seeking common ground, and finding creative solutions to problems.

Zen

Zen is a philosophy and practice that can help you find inner peace and alleviate stress and anxiety. One of the core teachings of Zen is being fully present in the moment. In your line of work, being present and focused is crucial for safety. When you are flying, try to let go of any distractions or worries and focus completely on the task at hand. Pay attention to your breath and your surroundings, and let your mind be still.

A principle in Zen is the idea of letting go of attachments and expectations. In your job, you may experience a lot of pressure to perform perfectly. This can create unnecessary tension and anxiety. Instead of clinging to expectations and outcomes, try to let go of them and focus on the process. Trust in your training and your abilities and stay present in the moment.

In Zen, meditation is a key practice for cultivating inner peace. You can incorporate meditation into your daily routine by taking a few moments to sit quietly and focus on your breath. Even just a few minutes of daily meditation can help reduce stress.

Zen also focusses on the qualities of compassion and empathy. As flight crew, you can serve and help others. Cultivating compassion and empathy will help you connect with your passengers and create a more positive and peaceful atmosphere on board. Zen is not just a practice, but a way of life. Incorporating Zen principles into your daily routines, thoughts, and actions can help you find greater peace and fulfillment in all aspects of your life, both on and off the plane.

In the case of aerospace professionals and astronauts, as space explorers, you experience unique challenges. Isolation, confinement, and uncertainty can take a toll on your physical and mental wellbeing. Zen can offer a valuable approach to help you navigate these challenges and cultivate a sense of inner peace and calm. An aspect of Zen that may also benefit you is the principle of non-attachment. This involves recognizing that everything is impermanent and letting go of our attachment to specific outcomes or experiences. In the context of space exploration, this may mean accepting the inherent risks and uncertainties and focusing on the present moment rather than worrying about the risks. As astronauts, you are part of a larger community working towards a common goal. Practicing Zen philosophy and compassion towards yourself and others can help you navigate the challenges of space exploration and cultivate a sense of connection and support. Incorporating Zen into your life may take time and practice, but with dedication, it can offer valuable tools for navigating the challenges of space exploration and cultivating resilience and excellence. The practice of Zen involves emphasizes rigorous self-control, meditation and other contemplative techniques aimed at cultivating inner peace, insight, and wisdom, and ultimately leading to the experience of enlightenment or realization of one's true nature. Zen is also characterized by a direct and intuitive approach to spiritual practice, emphasizing the experience of the present moment and the importance of letting go of conceptual thinking and intellectual analysis.

Zazen Exercise

As mentioned earlier in the section on Samurai, one fundamental practice in Zen that you as professionals can apply is zazen or sitting meditation. Zazen involves sitting still and focusing on the breath, in some practices you may mentally repeat a phrase or mantra, bringing awareness to the present moment and letting go of distracting thoughts.

Here are some examples of how you can incorporate zazen into your life:

- Before a flight. Taking a few minutes to sit in zazen can help you clear your mind and reduce any pre-flight jitters or anxiety.
- During a break. When you have some downtime, they can take a few minutes to sit in zazen, helping them to recharge and stay focused.
- In moments of stress. If a stressful situation arises during a flight or mission, you can take a few deep breaths and practice zazen to help you regain focus and composure.
- When dealing with jet lag. Zazen can also help the flight crew adjust to time zone changes and overcome the effects of jet lag by promoting relaxation and reducing stress.
- Through regular practice of zazen, you can develop a greater sense of mental clarity, focus, and inner peace, which can improve your overall performance.

Brain Performance and Enhancement.

Our brain is one of the most complex organs in our body, and it's responsible for everything we think, feel, and do. Just like other muscles in our body, it can be trained and enhanced through the right kind of practices and activities.

Physical exercise increases the blood flow to the brain, which helps to nourish and maintain healthy brain cells. Aerobic exercise is particularly beneficial, as it helps to increase the production of growth factors that support the growth and survival of new neurons in the brain. Our brains thrive on new experiences and challenges, and it's essential to provide it with the right kind of mental stimulation to keep it active and healthy. Engaging in activities that require problem-solving, critical thinking, and creativity can help to enhance our brain's performance and increase our cognitive abilities.

Our brain needs adequate rest and sleep to function at its best. Sleep is essential for memory consolidation, learning, and overall brain health. Getting enough sleep can help to improve our cognitive abilities, including our attention span, memory, and problem-solving skills. Nutrition is also a critical factor in brain performance and enhancement. Our brain needs the right kind of nutrients to function at its best. A diet rich in omega-3 fatty acids, antioxidants, and other brain-boosting nutrients can help to improve our cognitive abilities and overall brain health. All these health and performance enhancing insights will help you to not only improve your medical exam results but also contribute to your wellbeing and quality of life.

Did you know that some astronauts have reported experiencing a phenomenon called the "overview effect" while in space? This is a cognitive shift in awareness that occurs when seeing the Earth from the perspective of outer space. Astronauts have described feeling a sense of unity with humanity and a heightened awareness of the fragility of our planet.

This experience can be linked to the Power of Mental Force because it highlights the incredible ability of the human brain to perceive the world in new and transformative ways. By challenging our preconceptions and opening ourselves up to new experiences, we can unlock more of the potential of our minds.

Aviators can take several steps to avoid brain fog, including:

- Getting enough sleep. Lack of sleep can lead to cognitive impairment, memory problems, and difficulty focusing, which can contribute to brain fog. Aviators should prioritize getting adequate sleep and establishing a regular sleep schedule to avoid sleep deprivation.
- Staying hydrated. Dehydration can also contribute to brain fog, as it can affect cognitive function and impair concentration. Aviators should make sure to drink enough water and other fluids throughout the day, especially during long flights.
- Eating a balanced diet. Proper nutrition is essential for brain function, and a diet that is high in processed or sugary foods can lead to brain fog. Aviators should aim to eat a

- balanced diet that includes whole grains, fruits and vegetables, lean protein, and healthy fats.
- Taking breaks. Extended periods of concentration or mental exertion can lead to fatigue and brain fog. Aviators should take regular breaks during flights, especially on long flights, to give their brains a chance to rest and recharge.
- Practicing stress management techniques. Stress can also contribute to brain fog, so aviators should practice stress management techniques such as meditation, deep breathing exercises, or yoga to help reduce stress levels.

By taking these steps, aviators can help reduce their risk of experiencing brain fog and maintain their cognitive function and focus during flights.

Those in the industry can take several steps to avoid confusion and maintain clear thinking when disoriented or overwhelmed by stimuli or workload. Please bear in mind that these are ideas, however crew members should follow all regulatory and company policies and standard operating procedures in relation to these issues. Here are some tips as to possible approaches,

Communicate with your crew. Seeking assistance from the captain or co-pilot is vital when an aviator is experiencing confusion or cognitive overload. The captain and co-pilot are trained to work as a team and can help each other manage workload and maintain situational awareness. In fact, it is common practice for pilots to communicate with each other and cross-check each other's actions and decisions to ensure that they are both on the same page and that the flight is proceeding safely. During multiple alarms or malfunctions and a lot of confusing information, the crew member may refer to the other crew member for clarification example "Have you any better ideas?" "Do you have any suggestions on how to solve this issue?"

In such situations where an aviator is experiencing cognitive overload, it can be helpful to ask for assistance from the other pilot, who may be better able to maintain situational awareness and help manage the workload. This can also help to prevent errors or accidents that could result from the aviator's reduced ability to process information and make decisions.

It is important for aviators to maintain open communication with their fellow crew members and to work together as a team to ensure that the flight proceeds safely and efficiently.

- Prioritize and focus on the most critical tasks. When under pressure, it's easy to get overwhelmed by the sheer volume of tasks and information. By prioritizing and focusing on the most critical tasks, aviators can stay on track and avoid getting bogged down in unimportant details. We will discuss the priority list of aviate, navigate, and communicate in just a moment.
- Use checklists. Checklists are an essential tool for ensuring that nothing is overlooked, and all necessary steps are taken. They can help aviators stay organized and reduce the cognitive load associated with complex tasks.

- Regularly practice stress management techniques. High levels of stress can impair cognitive function and lead to confusion and poor decision-making. Aviators can reduce stress by practicing relaxation techniques such as deep breathing, meditation, or yoga.
- Practice situational awareness. Situational awareness involves being aware of one's surroundings and the context in which tasks are being performed. This can help aviators anticipate potential problems and respond proactively.
- Use visual aids and quick reference guides. Visual aids such as quick reference guides, maps, diagrams, manuals, and charts can help aviators process information more efficiently and reduce cognitive overload.
- Take short breaks when possible. Taking short breaks can help aviators recharge and maintain focus. Even a brief rest can help alleviate stress and improve cognitive function.

Communication is key in these situations and it's important for your team to know if you are unclear about anything. You should be very clear about instructions and what you need to do, and when unsure follow your standard operating procedures and regulations in those instances.

Optimum spatial awareness is critical for aviators to safely navigate through the airspace. Here are some key factors that can help enhance spatial awareness:

Visual scanning. Aviators should develop the habit of scanning their environment and checking their instruments frequently to maintain situational awareness. They should use the "Scan and Interpret" method, which involves scanning the horizon for reference points, interpreting their position relative to those points, and adjusting accordingly.

Mental mapping. Pilots should develop a mental map of their surroundings and the airspace in which they are flying. This involves creating a mental picture of the terrain, landmarks, airports, and airspace structures in their area.

Instrument proficiency. Aviators should be proficient in using their aircraft's instruments and navigation systems to enhance their spatial awareness. They should be able to interpret their instruments and use that information to make informed decisions quickly and accurately.

Training. Regular training and practice can help aviators improve their spatial awareness skills. This can include simulators, flight training, and ground school instruction.

Attention to detail. Aviators should pay close attention to details in their environment, such as changes in the weather, terrain, or other aircraft. They should also be aware of their own physical and mental state, such as fatigue or stress, which can impact their spatial awareness.

Teamwork. In multi-crew aircraft, effective communication and teamwork can help enhance spatial awareness. Pilots should work together to cross-check each other's instruments and maintain situational awareness.

Optimum spatial awareness requires a combination of visual scanning, mental mapping, instrument proficiency, training, attention to detail, and teamwork. By developing these skills and habits, aviators can enhance their situational awareness and safely navigate through the airspace.

Brain Hemisphere Synchronization

Brain hemisphere synchronization can lead to improved cognitive abilities such as increased creativity, problem-solving skills, and overall mental clarity. This is because when the two hemispheres of the brain are working together in harmony, they can access and process information more efficiently.

One way to achieve brain hemisphere synchronization is through activities that require the use of both hemispheres, such as playing musical instruments, engaging in physical exercise, or practicing meditation. Additionally, certain types of music, such as binaural beats, have been shown to promote brain synchronization when listened to with headphones. By training the brain to work in harmony, pilots and other aviation professionals can better manage stress and make more effective decisions in complex and uncertain operational scenarios. By training the brain to function more cohesively and efficiently, pilots can increase the odds to enhance their situational awareness and response time in emergency situations. For creative teams such as the aerospace and aircraft design engineers Another potential benefit of brain hemisphere synchronization is increased creativity and innovation. By tapping into both the logical and intuitive aspects of the brain, individuals may be able to approach problems in new and unique ways, leading to breakthroughs and advancements in the aviation and aerospace industries. Achieving brain hemisphere synchronization is easier said than done. It requires consistent practice and dedication. The potential benefits are worth the effort for anyone looking to enhance their mental performance and well-being.

Habits

Habits are the building blocks of our lives, and if we can design them to work for us instead of against us, we can achieve incredible success. A habit is a behavior that has been repeated enough times to become automatic. We all have habits, both good and bad, that we perform every day without even thinking about them. But the good news is that we can change our habits by understanding how they work and using that knowledge to our advantage. One of the key principles to designing successful habits is to make them small and specific. Instead of trying to change everything at once, focus on one small habit that will move you towards your goal. For example, if your goal is to improve your physical fitness, start by doing five push-ups every morning. It may seem small, but over time, those five push-ups will lead to more and more until you've built a habit of daily exercise.

Another principle is to make your habits visible. If you can see your habits, you're more likely to stick to them. For example, if you want to drink more water throughout the day, place a water bottle on your desk where you can see it. Seeing the bottle will remind you to drink more water and make it easier to create the habit.

Create a supportive environment for your habits. Surround yourself with people who support your goals and avoid those who might hinder your progress. For example, if your goal is to reduce your caffeine intake, try to avoid spending time in coffee shops or with friends who drink a lot of coffee.

Track your progress. Keep a record of your habits and the progress you've made. This will help you stay motivated and provide a sense of accomplishment as you see how far you've come.

Let's say you start a new habit of exercising every morning before work. First, you need to identify a cue or trigger for this habit. In this case, it might simply be putting on workout clothes as soon as you wake up or leaving them ready beside the bed. This will act as a signal to your brain that it's time to exercise.

Next, you need to create a small, manageable action that follows this cue. It could be something as simple as doing 5 push-ups or going for a 10-minute walk. The key is to make the action so easy that it's hard to say no.

Once you've completed the action, reward yourself with something that reinforces the habit. This could be as simple as a few minutes of relaxation or listening to your favorite music. By consistently following this process of cue-action-reward, you'll begin to form a new habit that will eventually become automatic. Once you've formed a habit, it becomes much easier to stick to your goals and make progress towards achieving them.

Emotional Intelligence

Psychologists Peter Salovey and John D. Mayer first introduced the concept of emotional intelligence back in 1990. Emotional intelligence refers to the ability to perceive, understand, and regulate emotions in oneself and others. It is composed of four dimensions: self-awareness, self-regulation, social awareness, and relationship management.

Emotional intelligence is essential for effective communication, decision-making, and teamwork. Pilots and crew members for example, must be able to work together cohesively, manage stress effectively, and make quick decisions in intense workload situations. I recommend training programs incorporate elements of the four dimensions of emotional intelligence. Training programs can teach individuals to recognize and understand their own emotions and the emotions of others, manage their emotions in stressful situations, and communicate effectively with others.

Organizations can promote a culture that supports emotional intelligence by fostering open communication, encouraging feedback, and creating a sense of teamwork and collaboration. This culture can help to create a positive work environment, enhance safety, and improve performance.

Salovey and Mayer's work on emotional intelligence has made significant contributions to our understanding of how to develop and apply emotional intelligence in various fields, including aviation and aerospace. By focusing on emotional intelligence, the aviation and aerospace industry can create a more effective and efficient workforce while also promoting safety and reducing errors.

Here are some ways in which emotional intelligence can be leveraged to achieve these goals.

Communication is a vital component of the aviation and aerospace industry, and effective communication is essential for safety and efficiency. By developing emotional intelligence, pilots and crew members can better understand their own emotions and the emotions of others, allowing them to communicate more effectively and resolve conflicts more efficiently. This can help to reduce misunderstandings and promote a culture of open communication. Especially in the cockpit, and cabin environments. The effective use of CRM Crew Resource Management principles and emotional intelligence all contribute to a safer and more effective and harmonious operational environment.

Decision-making. Emotional intelligence can help individuals to manage their emotions and make rational decisions, even in challenging circumstances. By developing emotional intelligence, pilots and crew members can make more informed decisions, reducing errors and promoting safety.

Effective teamwork is essential, and emotional intelligence can help to create a more cohesive and collaborative team. By developing emotional intelligence, pilots and crew members can better understand the emotions and perspectives of others, leading to more effective teamwork and improved performance.

Safety is the top priority, and emotional intelligence can help to promote a culture of safety. By developing emotional intelligence, pilots and crew members can better manage stress, communicate more effectively, make better decisions, and work together more efficiently, all of which can lead to a safer and more efficient operation. In most of the effective teams I have observed, Emotional Intelligence ranked high and was an important element in their success.

Organizations such as airlines, airports, Air Traffic Control, Group and Flight Ops as well as Space Centers can play a significant role in helping their crews develop emotional intelligence. Here are some strategies that can be employed,

Offer Training and Development Programs. Organizations can provide training and development programs that focus on emotional intelligence, including workshops, courses, and coaching. These programs can help individuals to understand and manage their emotions, communicate more effectively, and work together more efficiently. They can also help to promote a culture that values emotional intelligence and encourages individuals to develop these skills.

Create a Supportive Work Environment. Organizations can create a work environment that supports emotional intelligence development. This can be done by encouraging open communication, providing feedback, recognizing, and rewarding positive behavior, and fostering a culture of teamwork and collaboration. When individuals feel supported and valued, they are more likely to develop emotional intelligence skills.

Encourage Self-Reflection and Self-Awareness. Organizations can encourage their crews to engage in self-reflection and self-awareness activities. This can include practices such as journaling, mindfulness, and regular check-ins with a mentor or coach. By promoting self-awareness, individuals can better understand their emotions, motivations, and behaviors, leading to better emotional regulation and management.

Organizations can lead by example and model emotional intelligence themselves. Leaders who demonstrate emotional intelligence skills, such as active listening, empathy, and effective communication, can inspire and motivate their crews to develop these skills themselves. Organizations can create a culture that values these skills and encourages their development.

Regular feedback is essential to emotional intelligence development. Organizations can provide their crews with constructive feedback, both positive and negative, to help them improve their emotional intelligence skills. Feedback should be specific, actionable, and focused on behaviors, rather than personal traits. It should also be delivered in a timely manner, so individuals have a chance to reflect on their actions and make improvements.

Emotional intelligence is a lifelong learning process, and organizations can support their crews continued learning and development by providing access to resources and opportunities to practice their skills. This can include online resources, books, peer support groups, and mentoring programs. By encouraging continued learning and growth, organizations can create a culture of continuous improvement and development.

Organizations can incorporate emotional intelligence into their performance metrics, emphasizing the importance of these skills and encouraging individuals to develop them. This can be done by including emotional intelligence-related behaviors and competencies in performance evaluations and setting goals related to emotional intelligence development. By making emotional intelligence a priority in performance evaluations, organizations can ensure that individuals are held accountable for their development in this area.

How Crew and Team Members Develop Emotional Intelligence

There are several ways that pilots can develop their emotional intelligence (EI) skills:

- Self-awareness. The first step in developing EI is to become more aware of one's own emotions. Pilots can practice mindfulness techniques, such as meditation, to help them become more attuned to their own thoughts and feelings.

- Self-regulation. Once pilots are more aware of their emotions, they can practice regulating them in healthy ways. This might involve techniques such as deep breathing, progressive muscle relaxation, or cognitive restructuring.
- Social awareness. Pilots can also develop their social awareness by practicing active listening, observing the emotions of others, and trying to see situations from others' perspectives.
- Relationship management. Pilots can work on their relationship management skills by practicing effective communication, conflict resolution, and collaboration with colleagues and passengers.
- Seek feedback. It can also be helpful for pilots to seek feedback from others about their emotional intelligence skills. This feedback can help them to identify areas where they need to improve and to develop a plan for doing so.
- Training and coaching. Finally, pilots can benefit from formal training and coaching programs that are designed to help them develop their emotional intelligence skills. These programs might include workshops, online courses, or one-on-one coaching sessions with a certified coach.

By practicing these techniques and seeking out opportunities for formal training and coaching, pilots, cabin crew and industry professionals can develop their emotional intelligence skills and become more effective and resilient aviators.

Emotional intelligence (EI) can be particularly helpful in conflict resolution, as it can help pilots to navigate challenging situations with colleagues, air traffic controllers, and passengers in a way that promotes safety and positive outcomes. Here's an example of how EI can help in conflict resolution:

Imagine a situation where the captain and first officer are experiencing a miscommunication. The captain is issuing instructions to the co-pilot, but the pilot is struggling to understand them due to high workload and stress. As a result, the captain becomes frustrated and begins to argue with the colleague.

In this situation, the captain's emotional intelligence skills could come into play. Specifically, the captain could use his or her social awareness skills to recognize the emotions of the co-pilot, who is likely feeling stressed and overwhelmed too. The captain could then use his or her relationship management skills to de-escalate the conflict by acknowledging the pilot's feelings and taking steps to resolve the miscommunication.

For example, the captain might say something like, "I'm sorry for getting frustrated earlier. I can tell that you're under a lot of pressure, and I want to make sure we're on the same page. Can you please repeat the information so that I can confirm that I understand correctly?" This approach demonstrates empathy and understanding towards the co-pilot's feelings, while also promoting safety and effective communication.

By applying emotional intelligence skills in conflict resolution, pilots can help to reduce the risk of misunderstandings and promote positive outcomes for everyone involved. It is important that communication be respectful and professional.

Emotional intelligence can help cabin crew to manage their own emotions during conflicts, which can prevent them from becoming overly aggressive or defensive. For example, if a passenger becomes upset about a flight delay, an experienced crew member with high emotional intelligence might take a few deep breaths and try to understand the passenger's perspective before responding. This can help the pilot to always remain calm and professional, even in the face of a difficult situation.

The Spiral Training concept from Simple to Approaching Complex Tasks.

Aerial display teams train elite aviators use a method that allows for the mastery of complex maneuvers through a graduated process of learning in degrees. This approach is critical in the aviation industry, particularly for display teams who perform complex high-speed formation flying and aerial acrobatics near one another.

The method of training involves starting with simple maneuvers and mastering each one in sequence before moving on to the next training element. This approach is akin to starting the training in the center of a swirling seashell, where the inner points are mastered before moving out to the outer training.

For instance, aviation display teams have their new trainees master the simple fly past in proximity before they attempt the next phases of angled or inverted aircraft fly past in opposite directions. By layering on the levels of complexity in a safe manner, the pilot becomes extraordinarily competent and builds confidence as the course progresses. The clearly marked stages of training provide a shared understanding of the training objectives and allow team members to work together in a cohesive manner. During this process the student learns about the actions and reactions of the other crew members of the team, which is critical for achieving synchronized maneuvers safely.

The key to training elite aviators is to start with simple maneuvers and progressively layer on complexity in a graduated manner. As we all know, aviation is an industry where safety and excellence are paramount, and this approach ensures that we achieve both.

Identify the core skills and knowledge required for the job, break them down into manageable chunks, and then build on each skill or task in sequence. By doing so, you can create a strong foundation of skills and knowledge that can be built upon over time, leading to greater competency, confidence, and success in your work.

Precision can Beat Power, and Timing can Beat Speed.

While power and speed are certainly important factors in aerial combat, they are not always the key to victory. A skilled pilot who can execute precise maneuvers and time their attacks correctly can often outmaneuver and outsmart a more powerful opponent. Consider the example of a bird of prey, such as a peregrine falcon. Despite being one of the fastest birds in the world, it is their precision and timing that make them such effective hunters. They can execute precise dives at high speeds, and time their attacks perfectly to strike their prey with deadly accuracy. The same principles can be applied to aerial combat. A skilled pilot who can execute precise maneuvers and time their attacks correctly can often outmaneuver and outsmart a more powerful opponent. It's not just about raw power or speed, but rather about being able to use your skills and knowledge to gain the upper hand. Develop your skills and knowledge and learn to anticipate your opponent's moves. By doing so, you will be able to outmaneuver and outsmart your opponents, even if they have more raw power or speed than you do. Although all those elements are important, do work on developing your precision and timing skills through practicing at optimum levels of intensity and focus. While learning to perfect the rhythm, of an oscillating pattern between intensity of focus and relaxation you will be able to navigate your mental states to ever greater degrees of effectiveness.

Psychological Safety in Workplace and Its High Importance in Company and Cultures.

Having worked in many diverse work cultures in different parts of the world, I've come to realize the value of a work culture that allows you to be comfortable and feel natural about being yourself. What I refer to here is the importance of psychological safety in the workplace and its impact on effective collaboration, problem-solving, and safe operations. For example, I have observed that when individuals feel safe to speak their minds without fear of judgment or retribution, they are more likely to contribute their unique perspectives and ideas, which can lead to better outcomes for the team and the organization.

I recommend that the leadership and stakeholders of aviation and aerospace companies work to consistently create cultures of psychological safety in their workplaces. I believe this can be achieved by,

Encouraging open communication. Leaders should actively encourage team members to speak up and share their opinions, ideas, and concerns. This can be achieved through regular team meetings, one-on-one sessions, and other communication channels.

Valuing diversity of thought. Teams should value and celebrate diversity of thought, recognizing that different perspectives and ideas can lead to more creative and effective solutions.

Listening actively. Leaders and team members should listen actively and empathetically to each other, seeking to understand each other's perspectives and concerns.

Creating a blame-free culture. Teams should strive to create a culture where individuals feel safe making mistakes and learn from them, without fear of blame or punishment. Creating a culture of psychological safety is essential for effective collaboration. By valuing and encouraging open communication and active listening, aviation and aerospace leaders and their teams can create a work environment where everyone feels safe to contribute their best ideas and work towards shared goals and best serve the needs of the industry. Psychological safety enables effective implementation of processes like the voluntary self-disclosure mechanisms between the airlines and the regulatory authorities that are vital for safe operations around the world. It allows for early detection of potential issues or hazards, enabling teams to identify and mitigate them before they turn into significant problems and safety concerns. These are integral elements in any organization's Safety Management System. It considers that human error will invariably occur and provides feedback and a mechanism for addressing issues before they become a pattern of deteriorating standards and safety concerns.

In addition, it creates an environment where individuals are comfortable admitting mistakes or errors, which is essential for continuous improvement and learning. When team members feel psychologically safe, they are more likely to be open and honest about what went wrong and how to improve.

To ensure psychological safety in your team or organization, it's essential to create an environment of trust and respect. Companies and authorities alike should encourage open communication, actively listen to employees' ideas and concerns, and avoid punishing mistakes or failures. This creates a culture where team members feel valued and respected, and it fosters a sense of shared responsibility for achieving the organizational goals.

Training elite level teams for top performance starts with a clear focus on the mission and a commitment to excellence in every aspect of our work.

It's important to build teams that are composed of individuals who are passionate about their work and committed to achieving the mission. Look for people who are not only skilled but also have the right attitude, work ethic, and team-oriented mindset. We believe that the whole is greater than the sum of its parts, and we strive to create a culture of mutual respect, trust, and collaboration.

Successful teams place a high value on structured training that builds skills in a progressive and systematic way, starting with the basics and gradually increasing the level of difficulty. Ensure that each team member has a solid foundation of knowledge and skill before moving on to more advanced techniques and maneuvers. This approach not only helps to develop individual competence but also fosters team cohesion and trust. Effective communication is essential to high performance. Display teams, for example, practice clear and concise communication in all aspects of their work, from mission planning to executing maneuvers in the air. They use standardized procedures and terminology to ensure everyone is on the same page and encourage open and honest feedback so that they can continuously improve performance.

Professionalism and Airmanship

As pilots, you already have many skills that are essential for success - technical knowledge, attention to detail, and a dedication to safety, to name a few. But when it comes to performing during intense workload situations, such as during an emergency or a challenging flight, it's important to develop additional skills that will help you stay calm, focused, and engaged with your passengers and crew. One of the most important performance skills for aviators is confidence. When you're in the cockpit, your passengers are looking to you for reassurance that everything is under control. This means projecting an air of calm and competence, even if you're feeling anxious or uncertain. Practice deep breathing and visualization techniques to help calm your nerves and stay focused on the task at hand. Maintain postures of assurance, not arrogance or showiness but a classy professionalism that instills confidence in all who are along with you for the operation. Try to stay engaged with your passengers and crew at key moments throughout the flight. This means making eye contact, asking questions, and taking the time to listen to their concerns and feedback. By creating a sense of personal connection, you can help build trust and confidence among your team. Belief is a powerful force that can shape our thoughts, actions, and outcomes. When we believe in ourselves and our abilities, we are more likely to perform at our best and achieve our goals. On the other hand, when we doubt ourselves or our abilities, we may struggle to perform at our full potential.

As aviators, it's important to cultivate a strong sense of belief in ourselves and our abilities. This means having confidence in our training and experience, and trusting in our ability to handle any situation that may arise during a flight.

One way to build belief is through positive self-talk. This means consciously replacing negative or self-doubting thoughts with positive, affirming statements. For example, if you find yourself thinking, "I'm not sure if I can handle this," try reframing that thought into something like, "I am trained and prepared to handle this."

Another way to build belief is through visualization. This means mentally rehearsing a successful outcome in your mind before it happens. For example, before a flight, you might visualize yourself completing the flight safely and confidently, and handling any challenges that may arise.

It's important to note that building belief takes time and effort. It's not something that happens overnight, but rather a process of consistent practice and reinforcement. With patience and dedication, you can cultivate a strong sense of belief in yourself and your abilities as an aviator. By repeating positive affirmations and adding in "I feel it" you add an emotional component that will help it stick in your mind.

Autosuggestion

Autosuggestion is a useful technique that can help you to achieve your goals and improve your performance as an aviator. Autosuggestion is the process of repeating positive affirmations to yourself to reinforce positive beliefs and attitudes.

The key to effective autosuggestion is to use positive, affirming statements that are specific to your goals and desires. For example, if your goal is to improve your performance during takeoff, you might repeat to yourself something like, 'I am confident and skilled during takeoff, and I am able to handle any challenges that may arise.

When practicing autosuggestion, it's important to use visualization techniques to reinforce the positive statements. This means visualizing yourself performing the desired behavior or achieving the desired outcome. For example, you might visualize yourself taking off smoothly and confidently, and handling any issues that arise with ease and competence. The key to effective autosuggestion is repetition. You should repeat your positive affirmations and visualizations to yourself daily, ideally multiple times per day. Your positive statements should be in the present tense indicating that the desired outcome is already manifest. The more you repeat the positive statements and visualize the desired outcomes, the more deeply ingrained they will become in your subconscious mind.

It's important to note that while autosuggestion can be a powerful tool for achieving your goals, it is not a magic solution. It requires consistent practice and effort, and it may take time to see results. By proceeding with patience and dedication, you can use autosuggestion to reinforce positive beliefs and attitudes and improve your performance as an aviator. Your thinking stream is always flowing so you might as well make it a positive stream. The alternative is not so good, and it's important to understand how negative thought forms, such as fear or anxiety, can impact their mental and physical states during operations. Negative thought forms can trigger a stress response in the body, which can result in physiological changes such as increased heart rate and respiration, decreased cognitive performance, and decreased ability to make effective decisions. Negative thought forms such as pessimism and self-doubt can have a detrimental effect on mental and physical health, as well as overall performance and success. Negative thought forms can lead to a cycle of negative self-talk and self-sabotage, which can limit aviators' potential and create unnecessary barriers to success.

Aviators can learn to recognize and challenge negative thought forms and develop a more positive and adaptive mindset that allows them to perform at their best even under stressful conditions. This can involve techniques such as cognitive reframing, positive self-talk, and visualization exercises, which can help to rewire the brain to respond more effectively to stressors. Professionals can develop a more resilient and adaptive mindset that enables them to perform their duties safely and effectively, even under challenging conditions.

Visualization

To become good at visualization takes time and practice, but there are several techniques that can be helpful in developing this skill. Here are some strategies that you can try:

Practice visualization regularly. One of the most important things you can do to become a master visualizer is to practice visualization regularly. Set aside time each day to visualize a specific image or scenario, and focus on building vivid, detailed mental images.

Use all your senses. To create a truly immersive visualization experience, engage all your senses. Try to imagine the sights, sounds, smells, tastes, and textures associated with your mental image or scenario.

Focus on details. Pay close attention to the details of your mental images. Visualize the texture of objects, the colors of the scene, and the shapes of the objects. The more specific and detailed you can make your mental images, the more immersive and engaging they will be.

Use guided visualizations. Guided visualizations can be helpful in developing your visualization skills. Listen to a guided visualization recording and follow along with the instructions to build your visualization skills.

Create a vision board. A vision board is a physical representation of your goals and aspirations. Create a board with pictures and words that represent the things you want to achieve or experience. Spend time looking at your vision board each day and use it to help you visualize your goals.

Exercise

Here's an exercise that can help you develop their visualization skills,

1. Find a quiet, comfortable space where you won't be disturbed for a few minutes.

2. Close your eyes and take a few deep breaths to relax your body and clear your mind.

3. Choose a simple image or scene to visualize. For example, you could imagine a beach, a forest, or a waterfall. Start with something simple and easy to visualize.

4. Begin to build the image in your mind, using all your senses to create a vivid and immersive mental picture. Imagine the colors, textures, and shapes of the scene, as well as any sounds, smells, or sensations associated with it.

5. Hold the image in your mind for a few minutes, focusing on the details and allowing yourself to fully immerse yourself in the scene.

6. When you're ready, slowly open your eyes and take a few more deep breaths.

7. Take a few moments to reflect on your experience. How vivid was your mental image? Did you notice any areas where you struggled to create a clear mental picture? What could you do differently next time to improve your visualization skills?

Mental images are the visual representations that we create in our minds. These mental images can be based on real-life experiences or completely imagined scenarios, and they are created through the process of visualization. By practicing visualization exercises, such as the one I just provided, aviators and astronauts and flight crews can develop their ability to create and hold clear mental images in their minds. Thought forms refer to the energy patterns that are created by our thoughts and emotions. When we think a thought or feel an emotion, we are creating a vibrational energy that can affect our mental, emotional, and physical states. By becoming more aware of our thought forms, we can begin to consciously direct our thoughts and emotions towards positive outcomes, such as improved performance and well-being.

Thought patterns are the recurring mental habits and tendencies that shape our thinking and behavior. For example, if we tend to dwell on negative thoughts, this can create a negative thought pattern that can impact our overall mindset and outlook on life. By becoming more aware of our thought patterns, we can begin to identify and challenge negative thinking habits and replace them with more positive and productive thought patterns. By understanding and developing these mental skills, you can become more effective at managing your thoughts and emotions and creating positive mental states that support optimal performance and well-being.

These mental skills are critical for aviation professionals because they directly impact their ability to perform their jobs safely, effectively, and efficiently. Here are some examples of how these mental skills are important in aviation.

Pilots need to be able to focus their attention on multiple tasks at once, such as monitoring instruments, communicating with air traffic control, and scanning for other aircraft. They also need to be able to sustain their attention over long periods of time, such as during long flights or during critical phases of flight. Pilots need to be able to remember and recall vast amounts of information, such as procedures, checklists, and regulations. They also need to be able to recall information quickly and accurately in emergency situations. They need to be able to analyze complex situations and make informed decisions quickly and accurately. For example, if an instrument malfunctions, the pilot needs to be able to assess the situation, determine the appropriate course of action, and execute that action safely and efficiently. Flight Deck Crew need to be able to think creatively and adapt to changing circumstances. For example, if weather conditions change unexpectedly, the pilot needs to be able to adjust their flight plan and make decisions quickly to ensure the safety of the flight. Emotional regulation, pilots need to be able to manage their emotions and remain calm under pressure. For example, if an emergency occurs, the pilot needs to be able to stay focused and make clear decisions, even in a stressful and chaotic environment.

Pilots need to be able to bounce back from setbacks and adapt to changing circumstances. For example, if a flight is delayed or cancelled, the pilot needs to be able to adjust their plans and stay motivated and focused. All these are important mental skills to learn and develop through training, practice, and application.

Metacognition

Metacognition is the process of thinking about thinking. It involves being aware of your own thoughts and thought processes, monitoring them, and adjusting as needed. Essentially, it's thinking about how you think. It can help you become more aware of your own thinking patterns and identify when you might be making errors or overlooking important details. It can also help you regulate your emotions.

So, how can you apply metacognition in your work? First, start by becoming more aware of your own thought processes. Take a moment to reflect on how you approach tasks and problem-solving. Are there patterns or tendencies that you notice? Once you're aware of these patterns, you can start to adjust them.

After completing a task or solving a problem, take some time to reflect on what went well and what could be improved. This can help you identify areas where you need to focus your attention in the future. This refers to our approach to the feedback loop of continuous improvement. What went well? What did not go so well? And what I do better next time? Metacognition can help you become more effective at learning and skill-building. By being aware of your own thinking processes and identifying areas for improvement, you can develop more targeted and efficient strategies for learning and practicing new skills. Being aware of your own thinking patterns and adjusting as needed makes you a more effective problem-solver and better equipped to handle your work.

Here are some strategies for Metacognition,

Planning. Setting clear goals, defining the steps required to achieve them, and monitoring progress towards these goals.

Monitoring. Being aware of your own thinking and learning process, recognizing when you are making mistakes or encountering difficulties, and adjusting your approach accordingly.

Evaluation. Reflecting on your learning experience, identifying what worked well and what did not, and using this information to improve your approach in the future.

Regulation. Regulating your own learning process by managing your attention, selecting appropriate learning strategies, and adapting your approach as needed.

Feedback. Seeking feedback from others, evaluating the feedback you receive, and using it to make improvements in your learning and thinking process.

Self-Regulated Learning (SRL)

I want to go a bit further and discuss self-regulated learning, which is the process of taking control of your own learning by setting goals, monitoring your progress, and adjusting your learning strategies as needed. Since when it comes to wellbeing and mental training, many of the airlines, and aviation organizations around the world do not have structured courses in place that are adequate to address the needs of professionals. When it comes to learning, we often rely on external factors such as teachers, textbooks, and lectures to guide us. However, self-regulated learning is about taking responsibility for your own learning and using internal resources to improve your skills and knowledge. One of the key components of self-regulated learning is goal setting. This means setting specific and achievable goals for yourself, and identifying the steps you need to take to achieve those goals. By setting goals, you give yourself direction and purpose, and can measure your progress along the way.

Let's look at the aspect of self-regulated learning known as monitoring. This means keeping track of your progress, and reflecting on your learning to identify areas where you need to improve. In the process of monitoring your progress, you identify what's working well and what needs to change and adjust your learning strategies accordingly. In short, self-regulated learning is about using effective learning strategies. This means identifying the strategies that work best for you and using them consistently to achieve your goals. Effective learning strategies can include things like active reading, note-taking, and practice testing.

How can you start practicing self-regulated learning? One technique is to start with small, achievable goals, and gradually work your way up to more challenging ones. Set a goal for yourself, and then break it down into smaller steps that you can tackle one at a time. By doing this, you can build your confidence and motivation, and develop the skills you need to take control of your own learning.

Self-regulated learning is a process, not a destination. It's about developing the skills and habits that will help you become a lifelong learner. By setting goals, monitoring your progress, and using effective learning strategies, you can take control of your own learning.

Cognitive Restructuring

Cognitive restructuring can be used to change negative thought patterns into positive ones. This technique can be especially useful for individuals who struggle with anxiety, stress, or self-doubt.

The basic idea behind cognitive restructuring is to identify negative or unhelpful thoughts that are contributing to a negative emotional state or negative behavior. Once these negative thoughts have been identified, the individual can work to challenge and change them by looking for evidence that contradicts them, re-framing the thought in a more positive or neutral way, or coming up with more balanced and realistic thoughts that consider the full picture.

For example, a passenger who experiences anxiety about flying may have a negative thought like "I'm going to crash and die." This thought can be challenged by looking for evidence to the contrary, such as statistics on the safety of air travel, or by re-framing the thought in a more positive or neutral way, such as "I'm going to take all the necessary precautions and trust in the expertise of the pilots and crew."

Cognitive restructuring can also be helpful for changing negative self-talk that contributes to low self-esteem or self-doubt. For example, an airman who is struggling with self-doubt may have a negative thought like "I'm not good enough to handle this situation." This thought can be challenged by looking for evidence to the contrary, such as past successes or positive feedback from colleagues, or by re-framing the thought in a more positive or neutral way, such as "I have the skills and experience necessary to handle this situation."

One example of a structured cognitive restructuring technique is the ABCDE model developed by Dr. Albert Ellis, the founder of Rational Emotive Behavioral Therapy (REBT). The ABCDE model is a simple framework for identifying and challenging irrational beliefs that can lead to negative emotions and behaviors.

A stands for Activating event, which refers to a specific situation or event that triggers negative thoughts and emotions.

B stands for Belief, which is the negative thought or belief that arises from the activating event. This belief can be irrational or unrealistic.

C stands for Consequence, which refers to the negative emotional and behavioral responses that result from the negative belief.

D stands for Dispute, which involves questioning and challenging the negative belief using rational and evidence-based thinking.

E stands for Effective new belief, which involves replacing the negative belief with a more rational and positive belief.

For example, let's say a trainee pilot has made a mistake during a flight and starts to think, "I am a terrible pilot and I'm going to get fired." In this case, the activating event is the mistake made during the flight, the negative belief is "I am a terrible pilot and I'm going to get fired," and the consequence is feelings of anxiety and self-doubt. Using the ABCDE model, the pilot can challenge the negative belief by disputing it with evidence-based thinking. They can ask themselves, "Is this belief based on fact or is it an overgeneralization? Have I made mistakes before and not gotten fired? What evidence is there that I am a competent pilot?" By disputing the negative belief, the student pilot can replace it with a more rational and positive belief, such as "I made a mistake, but I am still a competent pilot, and I can learn from this experience." This can lead to a more positive emotional and behavioral response.

Exposure Therapy

Exposure therapy is a type of cognitive-behavioral therapy that involves gradually exposing a person to the feared situation or object in a controlled and safe environment. It is often used to help individuals overcome anxiety disorders, phobias, and post-traumatic stress disorder (PTSD). In the context of military pilots who have survived a near-fatal incident or close call-in combat, exposure therapy can be a highly effective treatment option.

When a military pilot experiences a traumatic event, such as surviving a near-fatal incident while flying or near-death experience in combat, it can lead to feelings of fear, anxiety, and apprehension that can significantly impact their ability to perform their job. Exposure therapy helps to reduce the intensity of these feelings by gradually exposing the pilot to the situation or object that triggers the fear response.

The therapy can be conducted in various ways, including in live exposure, which involves real-life exposure to the feared situation or object, or imaginal exposure, which involves exposure to the feared situation or object in the person's imagination. The goal is to help the airman learn to cope with the anxiety and fear associated with the traumatic event and to develop effective coping strategies.

For example, a military pilot who has survived a near-fatal crash may experience intense fear and apprehension when flying again. Through exposure therapy, the pilot would be gradually exposed to the elements of flying that trigger their fear, such as turbulence or steep high G turns, in a safe and controlled environment. Over time, the pilot would learn to tolerate these experiences and develop effective coping strategies, such as deep breathing or positive self-talk, to manage their anxiety.

Exposure therapy has been shown to be highly effective in treating PTSD and anxiety disorders in military populations. It is a structured and evidence-based technique that can help military pilots overcome the fear and apprehension associated with a traumatic event and get back to performing their job with confidence and resilience.

Let's look at an example, if an airman has developed a fear of flying after experiencing a close call during a combat mission, the exposure therapy may involve starting with simulators or virtual reality training, which simulate the cockpit environment and the experience of flying.

As the pilot becomes more comfortable with the simulator or virtual reality training, they can progress to actual flights in a safe and controlled environment, such as with an experienced flight instructor or in a dual-control aircraft. The pilot can then gradually increase their exposure to more challenging flights or maneuvers until they are able to fly with confidence and without experiencing the same level of fear or apprehension. Through this gradual process of exposure and desensitization, the pilot's brain can learn to associate the once-fearful stimuli with a sense of safety and control, ultimately leading to a reduction in fear and anxiety.

Rest and Recovery

One of the most important aspects of achieving elite level performance and maintaining it is recovery. It is not just about pushing yourself to the limit during training or operations, but also taking the time to rest, recover, and recharge.

Aviators and astronauts are exposed to unique stressors that can take a toll on both their physical and mental health. The high altitude, exposure to cabin pressures, zero gravity, long hours, and intense workload can lead to exhaustion and burnout if proper recovery measures are not taken.

Some effective recovery techniques include getting adequate sleep, maintaining a healthy diet, engaging in relaxation techniques like yoga or meditation, taking time off for vacations or hobbies, and seeking support from peers, friends, and family.

Sleep is a critical component of recovery. It allows the body to repair and restore itself and supports cognitive functioning and memory consolidation. Aim for 7-9 hours of sleep each night and prioritize a consistent sleep schedule even during periods of travel or shift work where possible. Nutrition is also an important factor in recovery. Eating a balanced diet rich in whole foods can provide the necessary nutrients for optimal recovery and performance. Proper hydration is also key, as dehydration can cause fatigue and impair cognitive functioning. Relaxation techniques like yoga, meditation, and deep breathing exercises can also be effective in reducing stress and promoting relaxation. These techniques have been shown to lower cortisol levels, decrease blood pressure, and improve mood and cognitive functioning.

Taking time off for vacations, spending time with family and hobbies is also important for recovery. This allows for a mental break from work, which can help to reduce stress and promote overall well-being. Engaging in activities you enjoy can also promote feelings of happiness and fulfillment, which can contribute to better overall mental health. Seeking support from peers, friends, and family is essential for maintaining mental health and promoting recovery. Having a strong support system can help individuals cope with stress and feel less isolated. Additionally, seeking professional help from a therapist or counselor can be beneficial for those experiencing significant stress or mental health challenges.

Recovery is a crucial aspect of achieving elite level performance for aviation and aerospace professionals. Prioritizing rest, relaxation, and support can help individuals to maintain optimal physical and mental health and achieve their professional goals. Do not suffer in silence, talk with someone. To maintain a top level, high intensity performance it is essential to rest and recover well at correct intervals. Light exercise, such as walking or cycling, increases blood flow to the muscles and can help to flush out metabolic waste products that can build up during periods of intense activity. This can help to reduce muscle soreness and stiffness and improve overall mobility. Foam rolling, or self-myofascial release, involves using a foam roller or similar tool to apply pressure to specific muscles and soft tissues to release tension and promote relaxation. This can help to improve circulation and reduce muscle tightness and soreness.

Stretching is another important active recovery technique that can help to improve flexibility and mobility, reduce muscle soreness, and prevent injury. Stretching can be done in a variety of ways, including static stretching, dynamic stretching, and PNF stretching. Static stretching involves holding a stretch for a period, while dynamic stretching involves moving through a range of motion in a controlled manner. PNF stretching is about contracting and relaxing muscles while stretching to improve range of motion. Active recovery techniques should be used in conjunction with other recovery strategies, such as rest, hydration, and nutrition, to achieve optimal results. By incorporating these techniques into your recovery routine, you can help to reduce muscle soreness and fatigue, improve flexibility and mobility, and ultimately optimize your performance. Massage can also help to increase blood flow and oxygenation, reduce inflammation, and muscle tension, and promote relaxation and stress reduction. It can also help to improve range of motion and flexibility, which can be particularly beneficial for aviation and aerospace professionals who spend long periods of time in cramped and confined spaces. Massage is the manipulation of soft tissues to reduce muscle tension, increase blood flow, and promote relaxation. Massage therapy can help alleviate soreness, stiffness, and inflammation, which are common after intense physical activity. There are different types of massage techniques that can be used, including Swedish massage, deep tissue massage, and sports massage. Each type of massage targets different muscle groups and tissues and has specific benefits for the body. Swedish massage is a gentle form of massage that uses long strokes, kneading, and circular movements to promote relaxation and improve circulation. Deep tissue massage, on the other hand, uses slow, deep pressure to target the deeper layers of muscle and connective tissue, which can help alleviate chronic muscle pain and stiffness. Sports massage is a type of massage that is specifically designed for athletes and can help improve flexibility, prevent injuries, and enhance performance.

Massage therapy can be a beneficial recovery strategy, particularly after long flights or intense training sessions. It can help reduce muscle soreness, improve circulation, and promote relaxation and stress relief.

Qualities of Excellence

One of the most important qualities that any person can possess is courage. The courage to stand up for what you believe in, to face your fears head-on, and to persist in the face of adversity. I know you have faced challenges and obstacles in your life. You may have faced financial difficulties, health problems, or personal setbacks. These are a part of life. I'm here to tell you that it is not the adversity that defines you, but rather how you respond to it. As I mentioned earlier, true courage is not the lack of fear, but rather the willingness to face it and to act despite it. It is the ability to push through your doubts and uncertainties, and to persist in the pursuit of your goals and dreams.

Persistence is key. Success is not something that happens overnight. It is the result of hard work, determination, and the willingness to keep pushing forward even when the going gets tough.

During my many years in the industry, I saw firsthand the power of courage and persistence in the face of adversity. Our teams faced incredible challenges over the years, from emergency situations, incidents, accidents, terrorist attacks, and even personal and touching family circumstances. I've seen emergency response teams rise to the occasion and deal with very impactful and some traumatic things. I've lost colleagues in the field and seen the impact of tragedy. However, despite these obstacles, the resilient folks never gave up. They never lost sight of their mission or their commitment to their mission and goals. That same spirit of courage and persistence is just as relevant in our personal lives as it is in our professional lives. Whether you're striving to achieve a personal goal, overcome a difficult challenge, or make a positive difference in the world, the key is to keep moving forward, one step at a time. Let me be clear here, persistence does not mean stubbornness. It's important to be willing to adapt and adjust your approach as needed, to learn from your mistakes, and to seek help and guidance when necessary. However, at the same time, you must never lose sight of your goal, and you must always be willing to put in the hard work and effort required to achieve it. Action is required.

As you face the many challenges and obstacles that come your way cultivate the spirit of courage and persistence within yourselves. Embrace your fears and use them as a source of motivation rather than a source of paralysis. Convert that energy into excitement and readiness rather than a hindrance. Keep pushing forward, even when it feels like the odds are against you. Personal excellence comes not from avoiding adversity, but from facing it head-on and emerging stronger on the other side. Courage and persistence are about living a meaningful and purposeful life and making a positive difference in the world. Cultivate these qualities within yourselves and keep your focus on the bigger picture, and to use your courage and persistence to create positive change in your own life and in the lives of those around you.

Developing Courage

Courage is essential in your line of work. It takes great courage to venture into the unknown, to take on difficult challenges, and to risk your lives for the sake of exploration and discovery. Courage is not just about facing danger; it's also about facing uncertainty, doubt, and fear. It takes courage to persevere in the face of adversity and to stay true to your values and principles. You can foster courage by facing your fears and embracing uncertainty. True courage is not the absence of fear but the ability to act despite it.

Fear is a natural response to new and challenging situations, and it is not something to be ashamed of. We all pass through different states of mind each day, and some are resourceful and others limiting and doubtful.

To develop courage, it is important to practice facing your fears head-on. Think of specific situations that make you feel anxious or scared and actively seek them out. For example, practicing emergency procedures or simulating difficult scenarios during training can help you become more confident in your abilities and reduce the impact of fear on your performance. Many professionals become very competent in the flight simulators and benefit from the training in realistic flight-like conditions.

Courage is not just important for your missions in space, in the air or facing heavy stressful days at ATC but also for your personal lives. Take this opportunity to reflect on areas where you may be holding back due to fear and commit to taking small steps towards facing those fears. With practice and perseverance, you will find that you can achieve more than you ever thought possible.

When it comes to courage, there are three things that I want to emphasize.

You need to know your 'why.' What is your purpose? Why are you doing what you're doing? When you have a strong sense of purpose, it gives you the courage to face any obstacle. Take a few minutes to think about your 'why.' Write it down and always keep it with you.

Just like you condition your body at the gym, you need to condition your mind for courage. This means exposing yourself to challenging situations, facing your fears, and pushing through discomfort. When you do this consistently, you'll find that courage becomes a habit.

Surround yourself with people who inspire you. As the saying goes, you are the average of the five people you spend the most time with. Make sure you're spending time with people who encourage and motivate you. If you can't find those people in your immediate circle, seek out mentors, coaches, and communities that align with your values and goals. Be in the company of supportive individuals who can encourage you and remind you of your strengths. Foster cultures of positive encouragement in your line of work develop the trust that your fellow crew members are there to support you, and that you support them.

Optimum Performance Focus.

I have come across many aviation professionals who have faced adversity and triumphed through the power of purpose, conditioning, and community. Whether you're a pilot navigating through turbulent weather, an astronaut exploring the unknown depths of space, or a ground crew member dealing with a high-pressure situation, courage is what drives you forward. You must learn to embrace fear and use it as a catalyst to propel you forward. Numerous aviation professionals I've worked with have developed the ability to transform nervous energy into excitement within their mindset, utilizing it as fuel to propel them forward and enhance their performance to an elite level. This reframing technique enables them to maintain a heightened state of alertness and sharpness, allowing them to stay focused and adaptable in the face of high-pressure situations. By channeling their nervous energy in a positive direction, they can utilize it as a catalyst for courage and a means for achieving their goals. This powerful shift in mindset can be a game changer for aviation professionals, enabling them to achieve their objectives with a sense of confidence, determination, and purpose.

A mindset shift that can make all the difference in your performance and success in the aviation industry. It's the idea of approaching a task or challenge with the mindset of reducing it to a more manageable level, rather than "bigging it up."

When we perceive a task as too significant or insurmountable, it can be overwhelming and paralyzing, leading to anxiety and stress. It can even cause us to procrastinate or avoid the task altogether, which only adds to our stress levels and creates a negative cycle of inaction or inhibited performance.

The aviation industry is one of the most demanding fields out there, with critical safety concerns and tight deadlines. It's easy to feel the weight of these responsibilities, but it's essential to remember that our perception of these tasks can be a significant determinant of our ability to handle them.

One of the keys to success in any field is to approach tasks with a growth mindset. This means believing that our abilities are not fixed and that we can continually improve and grow in our skills and knowledge. When we approach a task with a growth mindset, we are more likely to view it as an opportunity to learn and develop, rather than a test of our fixed abilities.

When we "big up" a task or challenge, we are essentially telling ourselves that we are not up to the task, that we don't have the skills or knowledge required to succeed. This kind of self-talk can be incredibly limiting and self-defeating. Instead, we need to focus on the progress we've made so far, the skills and knowledge we've acquired, and the support we have around us to help us tackle the task at hand. It's an old adage that whether you think you can or think you can't your right.

Another essential technique is to reframe our perception of nervousness or anxiety as excitement. Many top performers in the aviation industry have learned to use the energy of nervousness to fuel their performance, rather than allowing it to undermine their confidence and focus. By reframing this feeling as excitement, we can tap into the positive energy and focus it towards achieving our goals and grow sustainably.

When we approach a task with a sense of gratitude and appreciation, we are more likely to approach it with a positive and motivated mindset, rather than a negative and defeated one.

Approaching tasks in the aviation industry with a growth mindset, breaking them down into smaller, manageable steps, reframing nervousness as excitement, and cultivating a sense of gratitude can make all the difference in your performance and success. Practice these techniques and focus on the progress you're making, rather than the challenges you're facing. With the right mindset and approach, there's no limit to what you can achieve in this exciting and critical field.

These issues affect all kinds of pilots who operate in different arenas. For example, a research study (Bauer, H., Herbig, B., 2019) investigated work stressors and resources and their association with work engagement, subjective well-being, and energy levels in European Helicopter emergency medical services (HEMS) pilots. HEM pilots' work is highly demanding and safety critical, and much more data is needed to be gathered on occupational stress and strain symptoms.

The Discipline of Professional Excellence

Discipline is another crucial quality that you must possess as astronauts and flight crews. Discipline is the ability to stay focused on your goals and to maintain a high level of performance even in the face of distractions and temptations. Discipline requires self-control, determination, and the willingness to do what needs to be done, even when it's difficult or unpleasant. I encourage you to cultivate your discipline by setting clear goals, developing good habits, and maintaining a strong sense of purpose. Discipline is the foundation upon which all success is built. It's the ability to do what needs to be done, even when you don't feel like doing it.

To truly excel in your field, you must be disciplined in every aspect of your work. This means having the discipline to show up on time, to stay focused and engaged throughout the day, to constantly strive to improve your skills and knowledge, and to push yourself beyond your comfort zone. In the aviation and aerospace industry, discipline is not just a nice-to-have attribute, it's an absolute necessity. The slightest lapse in discipline can have consequences for safety. That's why it's so important to develop and maintain a high level of professional discipline.

How do you cultivate discipline? One of the keys is to establish a routine and stick to it. Plan your flight and fly your plan. This means setting clear goals, creating a plan of action, and following through on that plan, day in and day out. Developing habits of following through in the best way you can.

Another important aspect of discipline is accountability. Hold yourself accountable for your actions and take responsibility for your mistakes. Learn from your failures and use them as an opportunity to grow and improve.

Always keep in mind the bigger picture. Remember why you got into this field in the first place and keep that vision at the forefront of your mind. Stay focused on your goals, and let your discipline guide you towards achieving them.

Discipline is an essential ingredient for success in any profession, but particularly so in the aviation and aerospace industry. By establishing a routine, holding yourself accountable, and keeping your eye on the bigger picture, you can cultivate the discipline you need to excel in your field.

Commitment

When it comes to achieving personal excellence, there are few qualities more important than discipline and commitment. These are the qualities that allow us to stay focused on our goals, to push through our fears and doubts, and to stay on track even when the going gets tough. I know that discipline and commitment are not always easy. They require hard work, sacrifice, and a willingness to put in the time and effort required to achieve your goals. However, the rewards of discipline and commitment are well worth the effort.

In many of the world-class teams I have worked with, discipline and commitment were essential to our success. We had to be disciplined in our training, our strategies and tactics, and our execution of the mission. We had to be committed to our fellow colleagues and to the values that we held in common. Whether you're striving to achieve a personal goal, to improve your health and fitness, or to make a positive difference in the world, the key is to stay disciplined and committed to your vision.

What does discipline and commitment really mean, and how can you cultivate these qualities within yourself? Let me share a few thoughts on this.

Discipline means setting clear boundaries for yourself and sticking to them. It means creating a routine or a plan of action, and committing to it, even when it's not easy or convenient. This might mean getting up early every morning to exercise or committing to a regular schedule of work, study, or practice.

Commitment, on the other hand, means staying focused on your goals, even when there are distractions or obstacles in your way. It means making a promise to yourself to see things through, no matter what challenges you may encounter.

To cultivate these qualities within yourself, it's important to start small. Set small, achievable goals for yourself, and commit to them. Once you've achieved these goals, set larger ones, and continue to push yourself outside of your comfort zone.

Never give up on your dreams. Remember that true personal excellence comes not from talent or intelligence, but from the willingness to work hard, to stay focused, and to stay committed to your vision. Always remember that you have the power within you to achieve greatness, if only you have the discipline and commitment to see things through.

Values and Principles

Few things are more important than our values and principles. These are the guiding lights that keep us on track, even in the face of adversity or temptation. For me, my values and principles were instilled in me from a young age, and they have been the cornerstone of my personal and professional life ever since. There are few things as powerful as having a clear sense of your values and principles and living your life in accordance with them. Values are the fundamental beliefs and attitudes that guide our behavior and decision-making. They are the things that we hold dear, and that give our lives purpose and meaning. Principles, on the other hand, are the rules and standards that we live by the code of conduct that governs our actions and interactions with others. In many ways your values and principles are entirely personal to you. They are shaped by your experiences, your beliefs, and your unique perspective on the world and that's why it's so important to take the time to identify your values and principles, and to live your life in accordance with them.

When you live your life in alignment with your values and principles, you will find that everything falls into place. You will have a clear sense of purpose and direction, and you will be able to make decisions with confidence and conviction. And even when faced with difficult choices or challenging situations, you will have a rock-solid foundation to fall back on. How can you identify your values and principles? Start by reflecting on what is most important to you.

What are the things that you care deeply about, that give your life meaning and purpose? What are the principles that you hold dear, and that guide your interactions with others?

Once you've identified your values and principles, it's important to live your life in accordance with them. This means making conscious choices that reflect your values and holding yourself accountable for the principles that you've set for yourself. Values and principles are not set in stone. As you grow and evolve as a person, your values and principles may shift and change. The important thing is to always stay true to yourself, and to continue to live your life in alignment with your own personal code of conduct. I also want to emphasize that your values and principles should not just be theoretical concepts, but they should be reflected in your actions and behaviors. It's not enough to simply state that you believe in certain values or principles, you must demonstrate them through your actions. This is especially important in times of adversity or challenge. When things get tough, it's easy to abandon our values and principles in the pursuit of a quick fix or an easy way out. In fact, it is during these trying times that our values and principles are most important. They serve as a compass, guiding us towards the right course of action, even when the path is difficult or uncertain.

Courage, persistence, discipline, and commitment, which we have discussed before, all play a role in living a life in accordance with your values and principles and contribute to human sustainability in aviation. It takes courage to stand up for what you believe in, even when it's unpopular or difficult. We have all seen the consequences of compromising on quality and integrity at major aircraft manufacturers and the devastating price it invariably brings in terms of economics and public safety. It takes persistence to keep going, even when you encounter setbacks or obstacles. It takes discipline to stay true to your values and principles, even when you are tempted to compromise. It takes commitment to maintain your values and principles over the long haul, even in the face of adversity or temptation. Personal excellence is not just about achieving success, but about living a life of integrity and authenticity, in accordance with your own personal values and principles.

Additional Resources

This section provides a list of additional resources for readers who wish to explore the topic of human sustainability in aviation further.

Organizations

International Civil Aviation Organization (ICAO): https://www.icao.int/

International Air Transport Association (IATA): https://www.iata.org/en/

Federal Aviation Administration (FAA): https://www.faa.gov/

European Union Aviation Safety Agency (EASA): https://www.easa.europa.eu/en

International Federation of Air Line Pilots' Associations (IFALPA): https://www.ifalpa.org/

International Cabin Crew Association (ICCA): https://www.icca-cabincrew.org/

Research Institutions:

NASA Ames Research Center: https://www.nasa.gov/centers/ames/

EUROCONTROL: https://www.eurocontrol.int/

University of California, Berkeley, Human Factors in Transportation Safety Laboratory: https://hf.berkeley.edu/

Websites and Online Resources

Aviation Human Factors Association: https://www.ahfa.org/

Human Factors and Ergonomics Society: https://www.hfes.org/

SKYbrary Aviation Safety: https://skybrary.aero/

Avcox: https://www.avcox.com/

ATAG: https://aviationbenefits.org/

This list is not exhaustive, and many other valuable resources are available on the topic of human sustainability in aviation. Readers are encouraged to explore these resources and stay informed about the latest developments in this important field.

Printed in Great Britain
by Amazon